A Story of Conquest and Adventure

IRANIAN STUDIES SERIES

The *Iranian Studies Series* publishes high-quality scholarship on various aspects of Iranian civilisation, covering both contemporary and classical cultures of the Persian cultural area. The contemporary Persian-speaking area includes Iran, Afghanistan, Tajikistan, and Central Asia, while classical societies using Persian as a literary and cultural language were located in Anatolia, Caucasus, Central Asia and the Indo-Pakistani subcontinent. The objective of the series is to foster studies of the literary, historical, religious and linguistic products in Iranian languages. In addition to research monographs and reference works, the series publishes English-Persian critical text-editions of important texts. The series intends to publish resources and original research and make them accessible to a wide audience.

CHIEF EDITOR

A.A. Seyed-Gohrab (Leiden University)

ADVISORY BOARD OF ISS

F. Abdullaeva (University of Cambridge)
B. Behrooz Mahmoodi-Bakhtiari (University of Tehran)
F. de Blois (University of London, SOAS)
J.T.P. de Bruijn (Leiden University)
D.P. Brookshaw (Stanford University)
N. Chalisova (Russian State University of Moscow)
J.T.L. Cheung (Institut national des langues et civilisations orientales)
A. Adib-Moghaddam (SOAS)
D. Davis (Ohio State University)
M.M. Khorrami (New York University)
A.R. Korangy Isfahani (Societas Philologica Persica)
J. Landau (Harvard University)
F.D. Lewis (University of Chicago)
L. Lewisohn (University of Exeter)
S. McGlinn (unaffiliated)
Ch. Melville (University of Cambridge)
D. Meneghini (University of Venice)
N. Pourjavady (University of Tehran)
Ch. van Ruymbeke (University of Cambridge)
A. Sedighi (Portland State University)
S. Sharma (Boston University)
K. Talattof (University of Arizona)
Z. Vesel (CNRS, Paris)
M.J. Yahaghi (Ferdowsi University of Mashhad)
R. Zipoli (University of Venice)

A STORY OF CONQUEST AND ADVENTURE

THE LARGE FARĀMARZNĀME

translated and with an introduction by

Marjolijn van Zutphen

Leiden University Press

Cover design: Tarek Atrissi Design
Cover illustration: 'Farāmarz kills Ṭoworg'. New York Public Library, Spencer Coll., Pers. ms. 3 (Ferdowsī, *Shāhnāme*), fol. 166r. (https://digitalcollections.nypl.org/items/5e66b3e8-8d2c-d471-e040-e00a180654d7)
Lay-out: TAT Zetwerk, Utrecht

ISBN 978 90 8728 272 1
e-ISBN 978 94 0060 277 9 (ePDF)
e-ISBN 978 94 0060 278 6 (ePub)
NUR 635

© Marjolijn van Zutphen / Leiden University Press, 2017

All rights reserved. Without limiting the rights under copyright reserved above, no part of this book may be reproduced, stored in or introduced into a retrieval system, or transmitted, in any form or by any means (electronic, mechanical, photocopying, recording or otherwise) without the written permission of both the copyright owner and the author of the book.

This book is distributed in North America by the University of Chicago Press (www.press.uchicago.edu)

Contents

Preface

The present translation of the *Large Farāmarznāme* (*Farāmarznāme-ye bozorg*) is based on the critical edition of the text, which was published in March 2016 (Tehran: Sokhan). This edition resulted from a cooperation between myself and Dr Abolfazl Khatibi. Whilst I took the first steps by transcribing and collating the three texts upon which the edition is based, Dr Khatibi made the painstaking efforts of re-editing my rough first version, correcting all my mistakes and making the necessary emendations to the text, translating my notes to the text from English into Persian and checking and re-checking the final version before its publication.

The plan to compile the critical edition, and subsequently its translation, sprang from my doctoral research, which was part of a larger project, funded by NWO (the Netherlands Organisation for Scientific Research), led by Dr Gabrielle van den Berg and dealing with 'the Persian epic cycle' or 'the later epics', a collective term for poems that were written in emulation of Ferdowsī's *Shāhnāme* between the eleventh and fourteenth centuries. The project's main aim was to pay attention to this, until then largely neglected, corpus of literary works and to shed light on the circulation and reception of the later epics, both as separate entities and in connection with the *Shāhnāme*. My own research focused on the traditions surrounding a son of the famous hero Rostam, Farāmarz. This warrior is the protagonist of two later epics that are entitled *Farāmarznāme*, the longer one – of the present translation – exceeding the shorter one by some 3.5 times in length, as well as differing completely in content. Farāmarz in addition appears in six other later epics, which means that he plays an important role in the narrative traditions that derived from the *Shāhnāme*.

Whilst the later epics, with regard to subject matter and use of language, clearly have their roots in the *Shāhnāme*, they at the same time represent a new narrative genre: the poems each centre on one main hero and they tend to include many romantic elements such as love stories, distant voyages, fantastic creatures and other marvels. Both the appeal of this genre to contemporary audiences and its close connection to Ferdowsī's epic caused the *Shāhnāme* tradition, in terms of its contents and context, to change with the times and as a consequence retain its popularity, in oral and written form, throughout the centuries. Testimony to the appeal of the later epics is the occurrence of many of these poems as interpolations in a large number of *Shāhnāme* manuscripts. Therefore, for research on the textual traditions and the reception of the *Shāhnāme* it is important that the later epics are taken into account. In order for this to be possible, these poems need to be widely accessible. For this reason, as no printed text of the *Large Farāmarznāme* existed at that time, I felt it was necessary for a critical edition of the poem to be compiled, as well as for an English translation of the text to be published, in order for this later epic to gain a wider audience.

I would like to thank Dr Asghar Seyed-Gohrab for his time and effort in reading my text and helping me solve certain translation problems, as well as for his valuable additional suggestions. Any errors that remain in the translation or in the footnotes are all mine.

A Note on the Transcription of Persian Names

The transcription of Persian words follows a basic system. Short vowels are represented as *a*, *e* and *o*, long ones as *ā*, *ī* and *ū* and diphthongs as *ey* and *ow*, whilst a final *hā-ye hawwaz* appears as *–e*. Consonants are rendered with a minimal use of diacritical signs, which thus gives *j* (ج), *ch* (چ), *kh* (خ), *zh* (ژ), *sh* (ش), *gh* (غ) and *q* (ق). The usual distinction has been made between *h* (ه) and *ḥ* (ح), or *t* (ت) and *ṭ* (ط), whilst the various *s*'s and *z*'s are transcribed as: *ṡ* (ث), *s* (س), *ṣ* (ص), *ż* (ذ), *z* (ز), *ẓ* (ض) and *z̲* (ظ).

A Note on the Translation

Firstly, it should be noted that the Persian text of the *Large Farāmarznāme* as it appears in the critical edition is not ideal, since it has been compiled on the basis of three texts which each have their faults (see the Introduction: The Text of the *Large Farāmarznāme*). As a result of this, several verses in the edition contain uncertain readings or are difficult to interpret correctly, so that the translation in places remains open for reinterpretation. Secondly, the present translation takes account of a number of alterations – fourteen in all – that ought to be made to the published Persian text, in order for the verses in question to make more sense. These emendations were proposed to me by Abolfazl Khatibi on the basis of a longer list of suggestions drawn up by Sajjād Āydenlū in his meticulous review of the edition of the *Farāmarznāme-ye bozorg*. The proposed alterations to the critical edition in the main consist of changing the reading from the one that was originally chosen by the editors to one of the texts cited in the footnotes, whilst in a few other cases a certain word or phrase should be reinterpreted, because the reading in all three texts that were used for the compilation of the edition seems incorrect. These alterations concern the following verses: 111, 734, 822, 1566, 2248, 2560, 2876, 2905, 2906, 3124, 4001, 4480, 4525 and 4560. Reference to these changes to the text is made in the Notes to the Translation.

Introduction

The Later Epics

One of the best known works of Persian literature is Abū'l-Qāsem Ferdowsī's *Shāhnāme*. This epic 'Book of the Kings' in verse, completed in AD 1010, gives a half mythical-legendary and half historical account of the events surrounding the kings and warriors of pre-Islamic Iran. Far less-known are the poems that were written in the course of the following four centuries in emulation of Ferdowsī's magnum opus, collectively termed 'the later epics' or 'the epic cycle'. Set against the background of legendary Iran as known from the *Shāhnāme* and often including figures familiar from this work, each poem narrates the adventures of one specific figure. The protagonists of the greater majority of these later epics are warriors from the family of the most famous *Shāhnāme* hero, Rostam. In this manner, later epics exist that, besides Rostam himself, his grandfather Sām or his ancestor Garshāsp, surround characters not known from the *Shāhnāme*, such as Rostam's son Jahāngīr, his daughter Bānū Goshasp or his grandson Barzū.[1] Another later epic protagonist, who does appear in the *Shāhnāme*, albeit in a considerably smaller role than Rostam, is his son Farāmarz. Two eponymous poems celebrating this hero are known to exist, one considerably shorter than the other. The present translation deals with the longer of the two, the *Large Farāmarznāme*.[2]

The later epics can be seen as supplements to the *Shāhnāme*'s legendary section. They are all *maśnawī*s that, like the *Shāhnāme*, have the internal rhyme scheme *aa bb cc* etc. and the *motāqareb* metre (o – – / o – – / o – – / o –) and that to a large extent follow Ferdowsī's use of vocabulary and style of writing. Their stories are all set during the reign of one or more Iranian kings from Jamshīd down to Bahman, and they often feature several of these kings' warriors. Many of the poems also see the appearance of Rostam and his father Zāl, as well as his brother Zawāre and his son Farāmarz. In addition, several later epics hark back to certain *Shāhnāme* episodes, by narrating a sequel to a specific story, or they may repeat themes from this poem, such as two family members fighting without knowing each other's identity, as in the story of Rostam and Sohrāb, or one of the heroes performing seven trials (*haft khān*), as is done in the *Shāhnāme* by both Rostam and Prince Esfandīyār. A number of poems came to be linked even more closely to the *Shāhnāme* in a physical sense: since they agreed so much in form and content with Ferdowsī's work, the later epics lent themselves well to interpolation. Especially from the fifteenth century onwards,[3] various later epics were included in many *Shāhnāme* manuscripts, at points where they best fitted in with the storyline. By inserting one or more later epics into the manuscript he was copying, a scribe responded to his audience's increase in demand for adventures surrounding individual heroes.

The longer poems, such as the *Sāmnāme*, the *Jahāngīrnāme* and the *Barzūnāme*, which are made up of many thousands of verses, tell how their main heroes travel abroad and experience a series of adventures, which generally include one or more love affairs, but for the larger part consist of battles or individual fights, against man, demon, or beast. Some later epics are considerably shorter and, rather than having their hero go on a lengthy voyage, concentrate on just one or a few adventures. The *Bānū Goshaspnāme*, for example, the only later epic to feature a female warrior, numbers barely 1,000 verses and sees its heroine displaying her prowess in four separate stories. And there are several poems starring Rostam that each narrate just one adventure, set during the hero's younger years. To name just two, the story in which he fights a tiger in India, *Dāstān-e Babr-e Bayān*, comprises somewhat more than 400 verses, whilst the one in which he deals with a brigand closer to home, *Dāstān-e Kok-e Kūhzād*, has about 700 verses.[4]

Many of the later epics see the appearance of demons, sorcerers, fairies, dragons and other kinds of fierce animals or peoples with certain fantastic features. Whilst some adventures take place in countries neighbouring Iran, such as Tūrān (Turkestan), Rūm (the Roman Empire or Byzantium), Chīn and Māchīn (China and the adjoining lands to the south-west) or Hendūstān (India), others may be set in faraway fictional lands. By including fantastic creatures or peoples and distant countries, these poems did not just meet the contemporary taste for romance, but also tied in with another popular genre of the time, which had branched off from regular geographical works and consisted of accounts of the world's marvels (*'ajāyeb*).[5] On the whole, these epics are better appreciated as entertaining stories than as pieces of a high literary standard. Scholarship of the last two centuries has judged them to be of lesser quality than Ferdowsī's *Shāhnāme* in terms of subject matter and literary form,[6] which seems to have been the main cause of the epic cycle's long-term general neglect by researchers.

The first, most famous and generally most appreciated, of the later epic poems, written in 1066, was Asadī Ṭūsī's *Garshāspnāme*.[7] Consisting of close to 10,000 verses, it narrates a series of adventures experienced, partly in Iran but mainly abroad, by its eponymous hero in the service of Kings Ẓaḥḥāk and Fereydūn. Garshāsp travels to both the East and the West, to a large number of different countries, including several fictitious ones, and during his voyage fights several battles, slays ferocious creatures and sees many marvels. At the beginning of the poem, it is told how Garshāsp descends from the Iranian king Jamshīd. Halfway through the story, Garshāsp's son Narīmān is born, who later joins his father on his travels, and towards the end we are told of the birth of Narīmān's son Sām. The later epic tradition of Sām descending from Garshāsp deviates from the one told in the *Shāhnāme* – where Rostam's family is not given any royal ancestry – but Garshāsp's genealogy is repeated in a number of later epics starring Sām's descendants, and as such is referred to specifically in the *Large Farāmarznāme*.

Another later epic worth mentioning is the *Bahmannāme*. Named after the Iranian king Bahman, this poem assigns major roles to both Farāmarz and Zāl, as well as a few later epic characters, such as Farāmarz's sisters Bānū Goshasp and Zarbānū and his sons Sām and Āżar-borzīn (also known as Ādar-borzīn). This is another lengthy poem, of more than 10,500 verses, but instead of telling of its protagonist's lengthy voyages, it for the largest part focuses on Bahman's battles against Zāl and his offspring, to avenge Rostam's killing of his father Esfandīyār, which latter story is famously told in the *Shāhnāme*. Bahman especially cracks down hard on Farāmarz, who at a certain point in the poem is captured and killed, and then wages war against Āżar-borzīn. This narrative of Bahman's battles against Rostam's family clearly derives from, whilst at the same time greatly expanding on, the short *Shāhnāme* episode in which this Iranian king invades their province of Sīstān, captures Zāl and fights Farāmarz.[8] The *Bahmannāme* joins the *Garshāspnāme* in being one of the few later epics that can both be dated, to around 1102–1107, and attributed to a specific author, in this case Īrānshāh b. Abī'l-Kheyr.[9] The same author – whose name is alternatively believed to be Īrānshān – also composed another later epic, the *Kūshnāme*, which in more than 10,000 verses tells the adventures of the Chinese ruler Kūsh, a cousin of King Ẓaḥḥāk, and his son Kūsh Jr.[10]

Of most of the other later epics, the authors are unknown and the dates of composition have to be guessed from the texts themselves, such as their vocabulary or subject matter. The more Arabic words and Islamic references a poem contains, the later the date to which it tends to be ascribed. Sometimes, a text contains certain clues from which a possible author or dedicatee might be deduced, and subsequently the period in which the poem might have been composed. Nevertheless, since such deductions are the result of conjecture and remain unsupported by more concrete evidence, one can never be completely sure, and at times certain attributions later have had to be refuted.[11] What is more, just like the *Shāhnāme*, these later epics have passed through a copying tradition of many centuries, and, as their oldest known manuscripts most often do not date from before the sixteenth or seventeenth century, their original texts will have undergone a great many changes and additions before coming down to us in their few extant versions. This makes it very difficult on the one hand to date any of the anonymous epics with any near certainty, and on the other to know how the text may have read in its original form.

Farāmarz and the *Farāmarznāme*s

In the later epic traditions Farāmarz is a considerably popular character. This is testified to by his having been given more or less substantial roles, in addition to both *Farāmarznāme*s, in six other later epics: he thus appears in the aforementioned ones surrounding Bānū Goshasp, Jahāngīr, Barzū and Bahman, as well as in the poem named after Barzū's son, the *Shahrīyārnāme*, and in the one about the son of the White Demon that in the *Shāhnāme* was defeated by Rostam, the *Shabrangnāme*.[12] But well before any of these later epics were written down, a number of stories about Farāmarz were already in circulation.

Most famously of course, he appears in several *Shāhnāme* episodes. Farāmarz on a few occasions functions as a warrior in Rostam's army, but on the whole remains largely in the background. He most prominently comes to the fore after Rostam's death, in the aforementioned episode of Bahman, where the king's war against the province of Sīstān ends in Farāmarz's execution. He makes two other notable contributions to the story. The first one occurs directly after his introduction into the *Shāhnāme* during the reign of Keykāwos, when Farāmarz leads a contingent against Warāzād, the king of Sepenjāb and an ally of Tūrān, and kills that king in the name of vengeance for Sīyāwakhsh.[13] The second one is part of the episode of the fight between Rostam and Esfandīyār, during which Farāmarz and his uncle

Zawāre are provoked into a skirmish against the prince royal's troops and end up killing Esfandīyār's sons, the latter dealing with Nūshāżar and the former with Mehrnūsh.[14]

Besides these and a few other, more fleeting, mentions in the *Shāhnāme*, other stories about Farāmarz seem to have been known to the general public of the late tenth and early eleventh centuries. The Ghaznawid poet Farrokhī Sīstānī (*c.* 995–*c.* 1037), for instance, not only refers in one *qaṣīde* to Farāmarz as possessing great courage and skill, but also in another one mentions that he killed a dragon in Sind.[15] This heroic feat does not appear in the *Shāhnāme*, which means that Farrokhī must have learned about it from another source.

Both the mid-eleventh century anonymous 'History of Sīstān' and Shahmardān b. Abī'l-Kheyr's *Nozhatnāme-ye 'alā'ī*, an encyclopaedic work composed around 1100, mention a lengthy prose book about Farāmarz.[16] Regrettably, this prose book has long since been lost and its contents are unknown, so that it cannot be said to what extent its stories are represented in either one of the versified *Farāmarznāmes*. The only clue can be found in the *Nozhatnāme-ye 'alā'ī* itself, which retells two stories about Farāmarz during his campaign against the Raja of India: both stories to a certain extent reappear in the *Large Farāmarznāme*.[17] The first one recounts how a warrior named Ḥajjāw, who appears as Tajānū in the *Farāmarznāme*, tears the trunk off one of Farāmarz's elephants, but is subsequently captured, and when he breaks loose from his fetters he is defeated and killed by Farāmarz. The second story tells how the Raja ambushes Farāmarz, but the latter is rescued by Rostam, who was dispatched by Zāl when he was supernaturally warned of his grandson's situation.

How far back in time any of the stories featuring Farāmarz were first told is anyone's guess. It seems quite likely that such stories were part of the repertoires of storytellers and were developed into written poems on the basis of the oral narrative traditions of the early Islamic period, or maybe of the preceding centuries. During the Parthian period (*c.* 171 BC–AD 226), travelling minstrels (*gōsāns*) would have sung stories about various figures both from a distant past and the Parthian age itself, of which a number of stories in one form or another survived throughout the Sasanian period (226–651) and subsequently found their way into Ferdowsī's *Shāhnāme*,[18] so it is not unlikely that other stories, which were not incorporated in the Book of Kings, equally continued being transmitted down to the early Islamic period, including the heroic adventures of Farāmarz. Whereas it is impossible to do anything more than speculate on past oral traditions, the very fact that narrations involving Farāmarz, including those in Ferdowsī's *Shāhnāme*, were in circulation by the eleventh century and subsequently put down in writing and that this hero plays a reasonably prominent role in the later epic traditions testifies to his fame.

Farāmarz's popularity as an epic character is all the more underscored by his starring in two separate eponymous poems. Since these epics are set in two distinct periods, the shorter one during Keykāwos' reign and the longer one during Keykhosrow's, it seems likely that they were originally composed as separate entities, by two different poets. It appears that the younger of the two poems may be the shorter *Farāmarznāme*. Going by references at a certain point in the text by the poet himself to his penname, his age and his place of origin, Akbar Naḥawī has deduced that the epic was composed by the poet Rafīʿ al-Dīn Marzbān Fārsī, probably soon after 555/1161, whilst it would have been dedicated to Moḥammad Jahān-Pahlawān, brother and right-hand man of the Seljuk ruler of western Iran, Moʿezz al-Dīn Arslān (r. 555–571/1161–1176).[19] The gist of the story of the shorter *Farāmarznāme*, which consists of about 1,500 verses, is that Farāmarz leads his army to India to go to the assistance of a vassal of Keykāwos, King Nowshād, whose country is terrorised by a demon and several different fierce animals and who is oppressed by his neighbour King Keyd demanding tribute. Farāmarz slays the demon and the animals, defeats King Keyd and in addition holds two discussions with two different Brahmans, the latter of which leads to the conversion of the Indian king and his people.[20] The poem ends abruptly and contains some clues indicating that its story ought to continue. This means that either the poem was never completed or its end was cut off at a certain point during its copying tradition, maybe so that the epic could be interpolated in a *Shāhnāme* manuscript. An example of such an interpolation of the shorter *Farāmarznāme* can be found in, London, British Library, MS Or. 2926 (Shiraz, 1246/1830; *Shāhnāme*, first half), fols 167–180.[21]

The *Large Farāmarznāme*, which in its critical edition runs to 5,442 verses, completely lacks any mention of a date or author but, going by the appearance of two names in the text, Abolfazl Khatibi proposes a candidate for the poem's dedicatee, or rather one of possibly two dedicatees, and subsequently suggests its period of composition. The poem includes a short panegyric passage, which makes reference to a vizier and includes both the names Abū Bakr and Neẕām al-Dowal (vss 3025–3026). Khatibi believes that this dedicatee was one of the sons of the famous Seljuk vizier Neẕām al-Molk; this Abū Bakr, one of whose surnames was Neẕām al-Dowal, lived from 444/1052 to 494/1101 and like his father served as a vizier, for three brief periods between

476/1084 and 494/1101, to three different Seljuk sultans. Rather confusingly, the rubric heading this passage reads 'In praise of Sultan Neẕām al-Dowle and his vizier', which has led Khatibi to believe that the section in praise of the sultan himself has been lost from the poem and that the Neẕām al-Dowle of the rubric actually is the vizier.[22]

Whether or not this really is the case will be difficult, if not impossible, to ascertain, but Khatibi's dating of the poem to the last quarter of the 5th/11th century, and more precisely to the period between 487/1095 and 494/1101, does tie in with a reference made in the anonymous compendium of histories *Mojmal al-tawārīkh.* Written around 1126, this work mentions a – further unspecified – *Farāmarznāme* as one of four works that branched off Ferdowsi's *Shāhnāme.*[23] The other three works are the aforementioned *Garshāspnāme*, *Bahmannāme* and *Kūshnāme*, and since these have all been dated with near-certainty to the period between 1066 and 1107, the inclusion of the *Farāmarznāme* amongst these works seems to underscore Khatibi's assumption of its date of composition.

The Text of the *Large Farāmarznāme*

Even more than many other later epics, the *Large Farāmarznāme* was in the past greatly neglected by researchers. This is mainly due to the fact that this poem was not known to scholars such as Mohl and Ṣafā,[24] because for a long time no texts of the epic were known to exist in either Europe or Iran. As far as has been recorded, the only known manuscripts are either currently kept in India or were once part of the India Office collections, which in 1982 were incorporated in the British Library, where now two manuscripts of the *Large Farāmarznāme* can be found. Only one of these texts (MS RSPA 176; Nawsari, 1166/1752)[25] is complete and therefore has been used as the basis for the critical edition. Nevertheless, the text is relatively sloppily executed, at times includes incorrect readings and even seems to be missing certain verses, which makes it far from ideal. In this manuscript, in the first rubric of the poem, mention is made of the *Farāmarznāme* being 'large' (*bozorg*). The second text (MS IO Islamic 3263; Isfahan?, late 17th C.)[26] has been more carefully executed and includes often more reliable readings, but this manuscript, too, has its defects, first and foremost because it lacks more than 1,000 verses. In addition to these two manuscripts, there is a lithographed book entitled *Farāmarznāme* (ed. Rostam pūr-e Bahrām-e Sorūsh-e Taftī; Bombay, 1324/1907),[27] which joins together several later epics featuring Farāmarz, including both *Farāmarznāmes*, but its text contains a large number of orthographical mistakes and often contains doubtful readings. This lithographed version of the poem was the single one known to Khaleghi-Motlagh, who in addition only, and just briefly, had access to the book after he had completed his research on the shorter *Farāmarznāme*, so that his observations on the longer poem by necessity were limited, as well as hampered by the text's inferior quality.[28] Together with the two manuscripts, the lithographed text has been used to compile the critical edition of the *Large Farāmarznāme*.[29]

From the contents of the poem as it appears in the critical edition one can easily deduce that it is incomplete. Whilst the text in places seems to miss a few verses and has a rather abrupt ending, the poem's defectiveness most notably becomes clear from its beginning. Firstly, the introduction clearly is makeshift, as it lacks an original exordium that might have included any mention of the circumstances of the poem's composition, but instead consists of a praise of God followed by a praise of wisdom (vss 1–37), which factually is a copy of the opening of Ferdowsī's *Shāhnāme*.[30] Secondly, the following introductory section to the actual story of the *Farāmarznāme* (vss 38–195) borrows heavily from another section of the *Shāhnāme*, in which Keykhosrow, soon after he has ascended to the throne of Iran, launches his campaign against Tūrān to avenge the murder of his father Sīyāwakhsh.[31] The *Farāmarznāme* paraphrases parts of this *Shāhnāme* episode, with a focus on Farāmarz's role in the story, and at times even more or less literally copies one or more verses at a time.

This introduction tells how the newly ascended Keykhosrow calls on his nobles to assist him in his war of vengeance. Next, he distributes his treasures and appoints several army leaders to go to war against different allies of Tūrān.[32] Then Rostam presents himself before the king and suggests they launch an expedition to reconquer a province that borders to the east on Rostam's homeland, Zābolestān (i.e. Sīstān), but has been lost to Tūrān. This fictional province is called Khargāh. Keykhosrow applauds this idea and says that an excellent candidate to lead this expedition would be Rostam's son Farāmarz. So, Keykhosrow sends for Farāmarz and gives him counsel. Rostam also gives his son advice and then accompanies him on the first part of his journey. After they have said their goodbyes, Farāmarz travels onwards to Khargāh, at which point the main text of the *Large Farāmarznāme* begins. Whilst the *Farāmarznāme* continues with Farāmarz's adventures, which no longer at all resemble the storyline of the *Shāhnāme*, the episode of Keykhosrow's review in Ferdowsī's epic concludes by telling how Rostam turns back to join the king and they muse on the vicissitudes of life. The *Shāhnāme* includes no further reference to Farāmarz's expedition in Khargāh.

The close resemblance of this introduction to a section of the *Shāhnāme* points at it not having originally been part of the *Large Farāmarznāme*, but having been added at a later date, probably written by a scribe who was copying the later epic and found its introduction missing. It seems highly unlikely that the poem originally did not have a proper introduction, which probably would have included a praise of God that was written in the poet's own words, as well as an indication of a time of composition or a mention of a dedicatee. The current absence of such an introduction, in turn, seems to indicate that at a certain point it had been cut off from the *Large Farāmarznāme*, so that the later epic could be interpolated in the *Shāhnāme* – most likely in the aforementioned episode of Keykhosrow's war of vengeance. Since its introductory section had no place in the middle of Ferdowsī's poem, the poem was inserted in the *Shāhnāme* from the point at which Farāmarz departs for Khargāh. In all likelihood, a later scribe wanted to present the later epic once again as a separate poem and, in order to do so, had to compose a new introduction: his most obvious option would have been to borrow heavily from the *Shāhnāme* episode into which the poem had been interpolated.

The introduction of the lithographed text of the *Large Farāmarznāme* is not the same as in the manuscript version, but it does also go back to the *Shāhnāme*, and to an even more literal degree. This version of the later epic has no preamble at all, since it occurs in the book without any break after the shorter *Farāmarznāme*, but begins with a copy of 159 verses from a version that closely resembles Macan's edition.[33] Most likely this passage was derived from a lithographed *Shāhnāme*, of which a dozen or so editions were produced in Bombay from 1846 onwards and for which Macan's edition had served as the main, if not only, exemplar.[34] The extract from the *Shāhnāme* presented in the lithographed version tells of Rostam suggesting the reconquest of Khargāh and Farāmarz being dispatched to lead this expedition. The next day, in a passage that is not represented in the manuscript introduction to the *Farāmarznāme*, the king musters his army and Farāmarz is the last of the commanders to bring forward his troops. In this version, too, Keykhosrow gives him some counsel, after which Farāmarz departs and Rostam accompanies his son for the first part of the way, although here he speaks his words of advice when they say their goodbyes, after which Farāmarz continues his journey to Khargāh. Although this lithographed introduction has not been included in the critical edition of the *Large Farāmarznāme*,[35] it is worthwhile taking note of, because it supports the theory that the original introduction at one point became separated from the poem and had to be newly written by a later scribe – in this case either Sorūsh-e Taftī, the lithographed book's editor, or the copyist of the manuscript that the editor used as his exemplar but of which the provenance to date remains unknown.

Another clue to the shortening, and thus possible former interpolation, of the *Large Farāmarznāme* can be found in its ending. The final verse in the critical edition tells us how Farāmarz, after his return to India, ruled that country for sixty years. This ending is not only abrupt, but also does not fully reflect the manner in which it appears in two of the texts that were consulted for the edition. Whilst in MS IO Islamic 3263 the page that would have contained the poem's final verses is missing altogether, both MS RSPA 176 and the lithographed version of the *Farāmarznāme* lack a proper ending. The latter, after telling us how Farāmarz ruled India for sixty years, continues the book with an extensive extract (799 vss) from the *Bahmannāme*, in which Farāmarz battles against King Bahman and is eventually killed. The manuscript instead ends with six lines that first inform us that Ardashīr (i.e. Bahman) killed Farāmarz to avenge the blood of his father Esfandīyār, then announce that the narrator will return to the story of Ṭūs and Pīrān, before concluding with a single verse containing salutations to Zoroaster.[36] Not only this makeshift ending, clearly composed by a later copyist, but also the mention of a return to the main story, which quite likely is a reference to the *Shāhnāme* episode of Keykhosrow's war of vengeance, can be taken as another indication that the *Large Farāmarznāme* once existed as an interpolation. As in the case of the introduction, the original ending of the poem – which probably consisted of more than one verse of salutation, and most likely of an Islamic rather than a Zoroastrian nature – had no place amidst Ferdowsī's text and consequently upon its interpolation would have been removed.

The hypothesis that the *Large Farāmarznāme* at some time during its copying tradition may have been interpolated in the *Shāhnāme* is not very far-fetched. Because not only, as mentioned above, was this a practice that was applied to a number of lengthy later epics, such as the *Garshāspnāme* and the *Bahmannāme*,[37] but also there are five manuscripts from the early seventeenth century that present an interpolated version of the *Large Farāmarznāme* – albeit of merely its first part. Telling only of Farāmarz's expedition against three different commanders on the Indian mainland (*Large Farāmarznāme*, vss 196–1958), but leaving out a large number of individual verses dispersed throughout the text, as well as complete sections of the story, the first part of the later epic in this interpolated version has been contracted, in its longest version, to just 843 verses.[38] Whilst it is unclear why the poem was shortened before it came to be included in Ferdowsī's epic, it is quite possible that one or more other *Shāhnāme* manuscripts, which are either now lost or to date have not been properly examined or documented, included the *Large Farāmarznāme* in its full length.

There is even a possibility that the poem's original introduction and ending have not been completely lost, but are still present in another extant manuscript. Because, in addition to the three texts that were used for the critical edition, at least three other manuscripts of the *Large Farāmarznāme* supposedly exist in India. Three catalogue entries point to this poem being housed in three different libraries, namely the Cama Oriental Institute and the Mulla Firuz Library, both in Mumbai, and the First Dastur Meherji Rana Library in Nawsari.[39] The second Mumbai manuscript dates from the late nineteenth century and could possibly be a copy of the first one, which was produced in Udaipur, but is undated. The text housed in Nawsari dates from 1586–1587 and is believed to have been copied in India. Going by their catalogue descriptions, all three texts appear to be of a substantial length, of at least 5,000 verses, but it is unclear to what extent each one is complete or includes additional material, or even whether it agrees with the *Large Farāmarznāme* as presented in the critical edition and consequently the present translation. Regrettably, due to difficulties of access, in the compilation of the edition these manuscripts had to be left out of consideration. Quite possibly they include a number of interesting variants, which would form a valuable addition to the three other texts or might even provide some useful information about the circumstances of the poem's composition. It is hoped that the Indian manuscripts will be included in future research of the text of the *Large Farāmarznāme* and perhaps consulted for an updated version of its critical edition.

The Story of the *Large Farāmarznāme*

The storyline of the *Large Farāmarznāme* consists of two distinct parts. In the first one, following the introductory section and covering 1,832 verses (vss 196–2027), Farāmarz leads a military campaign on the Indian mainland against three different rulers. The first of these rulers is Ṭoworg, an ally of the Iranian archenemy Tūrān and the governor of Khargāh. After dealing with Ṭoworg, Farāmarz continues his campaign by subduing the Raja of India.

And when he and the Raja return from their visit to the Iranian court, where the Indian king has pledged his allegiance to Keykhosrow, they learn that during their absence the Raja's throne has been usurped by the governor of Kashmir, Mahārak. After Farāmarz has defeated this rebel, his receipt of a charter from the Iranian king granting him the kingship of Khargāh, Kashmir and India brings his Indian campaign to a conclusion.

This first part of the poem in the main consists of a report of the battles fought by Farāmarz's army against its enemies and of a number of bouts of single combat between the hero from Sīstān and different Indian warriors. In addition, it tells of Farāmarz's cunning: he devises a ruse to take the fortress in which Ṭoworg has ensconced himself and he disguises himself as his own messenger in order to investigate the Raja's forces and to try to dissuade the Indian from going to war. When the Raja nevertheless plots to ambush Farāmarz and his company when they leave his court, the Sīstāni hero has the foresight to suspect the Raja's deceitfulness and secretly send for reinforcements. Despite the cleverness he shows in defeating his enemies, the focus of the story lies with Farāmarz displaying his prowess in battle.

One section of the episode with the Raja is somewhat out of tune with the rest of the story, as it includes a supernatural phenomenon: Zāl is warned in a dream that his grandson is in danger and he sends Rostam to India to rescue Farāmarz from the Raja's ambush. The gist of this story is also told in Shahmardān b. Abī'l-Kheyr's *Nozhatnāme-ye 'alā'ī*, discussed above. However, unlike in the *Nozhatnāme*, in the *Farāmarznāme* Rostam and his men arrive at the scene of the battle when Farāmarz and his reinforcement troops have just defeated the Raja, which means that Rostam's role in the story is superfluous and Zāl's dream has no actual function for the development of the story. The original plot either passed through different narrative stages before it reached Shahmardān and the poet of the *Large Farāmarznāme*, respectively, or was deliberately changed by the poet in order to place Farāmarz in a more favourable light. Either way, in the *Farāmarznāme* Rostam's role has lost its significance. As the story reads now, Farāmarz and his men need neither outside help nor supernatural interference to defeat their enemies, and they obtain their victories in a straightforward, down-to-earth manner, by doing combat, and on their own strength.

The second part, the remainder, of the *Farāmarznāme*, which is almost twice as long as the first part, contains some more otherworldly phenomena. Farāmarz embarks on a voyage of discovery which takes him to a number of islands and distant countries inhabited by various kinds of peoples, often of a fantastic nature. This section is briefly introduced by several lines (vss 2028–2040), which refer to an unidentified narrator and tell how he wanted to write a story about famous heroes from the past that was not part of Ferdowsī of Ṭūsī's book, i.e. the *Shāhnāme*. The narrator could only find stories about Farāmarz, who had traversed the whole world and experienced different kinds of adventures. This introduction, brief as it may be, implies that the second part of the poem originally was a separate narration. It is linked to the first part by just a couple of verses, which recapitulate that Farāmarz had finished his business in Khargāh, India and Kashmir and received the crown and the seal of these regions from Keykhosrow (vss 2041–2042), before saying that he wished to explore the world and led his men across sea and land. This verbal separation may indicate that the poet of the *Large Farāmarznāme* joined together stories taken from different sources, or possibly that the second part of his epic derived solely from his own pen.

As part of his lengthy travels, Farāmarz reaches both ends of the earth. The first part of his journey takes him to the lands of the West (*khāwar*). He first sails past a number of islands, which are in turn inhabited by King Farāsang, King Kahīlā, the Dawāl-pāyān, the Pīl-gūshān, the Brahmans, a giant bird, a dragon and the Zangīs, after which Farāmarz and his men reach the mainland and at the end of a six-month march arrive in Qīrwān. This name is known to be synonymous with the end of the earth,[40] and in the poem this country is indeed said to lie next to the mountain range that surrounds the world. From Qīrwān, the Iranians head in the opposite direction, towards the lands of the East (*bākhtar*). They sail across a vast ocean towards Chīn and Māchīn and reach several more fictional places, such as the island inhabited by horse-headed people (Asp-sarān), an island on which lies a mountain with a fortress containing king Hūshang's tomb and the country of king Farghān, which adjoins the land that leads to the mythical Mount Qāf. As this mountain is well known to lie on the edge of the world,[41] although this is not noted in the poem, one may conclude that it should be part of the aforementioned world-surrounding – unnamed – mountain range next to Qīrwān. Next, Farāmarz embarks for the final time and heads in the direction of China. Having again reached the mainland, he first fights against the demons of Kalān-kūh and then marches for another six months to reach the vast country ruled by the king of the fairies, Farṭūrtūsh. After an absence of over fifteen years,[42] Farāmarz briefly returns to Iran, travelling via the borderlands of China and through India, to pay a visit to Keykhosrow's court and spend some time with his family in Zābolestān before settling in his Indian capital Qannowj, where his sons Sām and Ādar-

Borzīn (or Borzīn-ādar) are born. As noted above, the text as represented in the critical edition ends with a mention that Farāmarz ruled the Indians for sixty years.

During his voyages overseas, mention is made of Farāmarz and his men marvelling at a number of unfamiliar phenomena, but the passages describing them are short (vss 2051–2056, 2975–2976, 3780–3784 and 3979–3992),[43] so that the focus of the poem's second part, like that of the first, clearly lies much less on the wonders of the world than on Farāmarz's actions. As in India, he engages in a number of battles, only this time not just against regular armies of men, like the one commanded by King Farghān, but also against pugnacious peoples of different kinds, such as the cannibalistic warriors of the king of Farāsang, tall black men whose only weapons are bones (the Zangīs), peoples with limber legs or with giant ears (the Dawāl-pāyān and the Pīl-gūshān) and ferocious demons living in a fortress on top of a tall mountain, Kalān-kūh. He also fights a number of fierce creatures, namely lions, wolves, dragons, a rhinoceros and a giant bird. In addition, Farāmarz has some experiences of a more peaceful nature. He for instance holds a conversation with an ascetic, wise Brahman and visits the tomb of the ancient Iranian king Hūshang, where he reads that monarch's counsel regarding the transience of life. The *Large Farāmarznāme* includes another figure known from the *Shāhnāme*, the benevolent giant bird Sīmorgh: when Farāmarz is shipwrecked and has lost his men at sea, he calls for Sīmorgh's help by burning a piece of feather he received from Zāl. In the course of the poem, Farāmarz twice falls in love and marries, the first time with King Kahīlā's daughter, whom he has rescued from a savage demon, and the second time with a fairy princess. In order to reach the country of her father Farṭūrtūsh, Farāmarz has to pass through seven trials (*haft khān*), a feat that again harks back to the *Shāhnāme*.

Farāmarz's seven trials consist of fights against several supernormal fierce animals and a ghoul, as well as of the otherworldly phenomenon of an extreme heat followed by a sudden freeze and heavy snowfall, which can only be warded off through prayer. As King Farṭūrtūsh notes, Farāmarz's successfully passing through these trials is not only due to his superhuman strength and courage, but also to his standing under the protection of God. Farāmarz himself also points this out, when he at the end of several, successful, fights against ferocious creatures washes himself and then prays to God, to give thanks to his Creator for providing him with the power to defeat his opponents. Farāmarz's reliance on God also becomes clear from a number of his speeches at different points in the poem, when either he himself or his army find themselves in dire straits or opposed by a formidable enemy, and he reminds his men that they should strive to fight for what they are worth and thus obtain a good name, since they cannot avoid their deaths, as everyone's appointed time has been divinely ordained. As becomes a true epic hero, Farāmarz thus combines the qualities of a warrior and an insightful leader with those of a pious man.

In Imitation of Other Epic Heroes, Garshāsp and Eskandar

By travelling around the world, seeing marvellous things, visiting various kinds of places and fighting a number of different peoples and creatures along the way, Farāmarz's adventures, albeit in nature rather than in detail, resemble those of his ancestor Garshāsp. Whereas in the *Shāhnāme* Garshāsp appears during the reign of king Fereydūn as a peer of Farāmarz's great-grandfather Sām, in the later epic traditions he is presented as Sām's grandfather. Asadī's *Garshāspnāme* tells of its eponymous hero's peregrinations, during the reigns of Ẓaḥḥāk and Fereydūn, both to the East and the West. Although Garshāsp's travels take him to many other places than Farāmarz visits, including regions that actually exist, such as Rūm, Shām (Syria) and the Maghreb (Northern Africa), he also reaches Qīrwān.[44] That Garshāsp stopped here is referred to in the *Large Farāmarznāme* by means of a book in the king of Qīrwān's possession. It was written by Garshāsp, who predicted that in 1,500 years' time a descendant of his by five generations would come to this country and free it from five terrorising creatures, namely a dragon, two lions and two wolves. As a reward, Garshāsp has buried a treasure, joined with a tablet containing counsel, for his descendant to retrieve.

A less direct reference to Garshāsp's travels is made when Farāmarz arrives at Kalān-kūh and the poet tells us that no one has come here since Garshāsp (vs. 4018). Although the name Kalān-kūh does not appear in the *Garshāspnāme* and it is not directly clear to which stage of the hero's voyage this remark refers, its implication is obvious: being the first in centuries to travel this far around the world, Farāmarz in his feats equals a great hero like his famous ancestor. A similar kind of reference is made later in the poem, when Zāl tells his grandson that the troubles he has experienced are unlike those anyone else has gone through since the times of Sām and Garshāsp (vs. 5332).

There is another resemblance between Farāmarz's and Garshāsp's adventures, which consists of both heroes visiting a land inhabited by Brahmans.

They both spend some time with one of these wise men, pose him a few questions and receive some wise lessons. Whereas Farāmarz in the *Large Farāmarznāme* holds just one conversation with a Brahman, Garshāsp has two separate meetings at two different stages of his journey.[45] The theme of the protagonists receiving counsel is extended by them reading admonitions that were written on a tablet in a distant past by an ancient ruler or, additionally in Farāmarz's case, his ancestor. Besides receiving Garshāsp's counsel in Qīrwān, Farāmarz reads both an inscription on the fortress containing the tomb of Hūshang and, inside, that king's writing on a tablet. Garshāsp himself visits the tomb of Sīyāmak, the son of the very first ruler Gāyūmart and father of Hūshang, where he reads an inscription about the transience of the mortal world.[46]

By including counsel (*andarz*), both later epics imitate the *Shāhnāme*, where pieces of wisdom are imparted by various kings in their throne addresses or testaments, as well as by the poet himself, who concludes a number of stories with some musings on the vicissitudes of fate. Similar musings also appear at different points in the *Large Farāmarznāme*. In this manner, both Ferdowsī and the poets of the *Garshāspnāme* and the *Farāmarznāme* placed their epics within the rather broad genre of wisdom literature, which covers a range of works presenting *andarz*, varying from maxims or short passages to whole books of counsel.[47] In addition, the poet of the *Farāmarznāme* was clearly well versed in the contents of the *Garshāspnāme*, and it appears that he, in his presentation both of Farāmarz's travels and of the hero's encounters with wise lessons, in addition to imitating Ferdowsi, also wanted to follow the example of the first of the later epic poets, Asadī.

Besides Garshāsp, Farāmarz resembles another and internationally more famous hero, Alexander the Great, in Persian known as Eskandar. In historical reality, this Macedonian king (356–323 BC) conquered Asia Minor, the Near East, Egypt and the Iranian empire of the Achaemenids, and then marched onwards through Bactria and Sogdiana to the Indus valley, before returning westwards and dying in Babylon. But in the many legendary accounts that have been told about Alexander, in a large number of different languages, his travels cover a much larger geographical scope and take him to all kinds of marvellous places and peoples. In the main, these accounts originate in the Greek *Alexander Romance* mistakenly attributed to Alexander's contemporary and official historian Callisthenes. The main gist of pseudo-Callisthenes' narrative can be recognised, albeit with a number of variations and additions, in the section dealing with Eskandar, or Sekandar, in Ferdowsī's *Shāhnāme*.[48] Several Persian literary works were subsequently composed about this conqueror, probably most famously Neẕāmī Ganjawī's versified *Eskandarnāme* (made up of two parts, *Sharafnāme* and *Eqbālnāme*) from around 1200.[49] More relevant to the present discussion are the prose romances in which Eskandar stars, firstly the anonymous *Eskandarnāme*, which was written and reworked at uncertain dates anywhere between the eleventh and fourteenth centuries,[50] and secondly Abū Ṭāher Ṭarsūsī's *Dārābnāme*, which probably dates from the twelfth century.[51]

The most general resemblance between Farāmarz's and Eskandar's adventures, the latter in all four aforementioned Persian versions of his life story, is that both heroes travel to the earth's extremities. Also, the Eskandar of the *Shāhnāme*, like Farāmarz, visits Brahmans and obtains some pieces of wisdom by posing them a number of questions,[52] although such an encounter is missing from any of the other three versions. Further, both Farāmarz and Eskandar at different points in their respective stories battle against different peoples that are described as black and of a demonic appearance, sometimes in addition having cannibalistic tendencies. Such descriptions are however of a rather general nature and such encounters also apply to a number of other later epic heroes.

More remarkable similarities can be found in two specific peoples, whom Farāmarz fights on two separate islands during the first part of his voyage by sea. Firstly, in both the prose *Eskandarnāme* and the *Dārābnāme*, Eskandar, like Farāmarz, encounters the Dawāl-pāyān ('strap-legged'), whilst the *Shāhnāme* mentions a people called *narm-pāyān* ('soft-legged'). In all three narratives, Eskandar fights and defeats these people. Secondly, Pīl-gūshān or Fīl-gūshān ('elephant-ears') is the name of a pugnacious people with giant ears that battle the protagonist of the *Eskandarnāme*, albeit not on a separate island as in the *Farāmarznāme* but as part of Eskandar's lengthy battles against the infidel Turks in the East. In the *Dārābnāme*, Eskandar on two separate occasions comes across large-eared people, which are called Gelīm-gūshān ('Carpet-ears'). In the first case, these people inhabit an island in the ocean and they fight Eskandar, but thereafter make peace; the second Gelīm-gūshān live close to the Dawāl-pāyān, at the end of the world, whilst they submit to the conqueror without fighting. The *Shāhnāme* sees the appearance of just one giant-eared man, with peaceful intentions, who identifies himself as *gūsh-bestar* ('pillow-eared').[53] Even if the context of the main hero's encounters with these strangely-featured peoples varies from one narration to the next and from one protagonist, Eskandar, to the next, Farāmarz, it cannot be coincidental that peoples with certain remarkable appearances and corresponding names, either identically or somewhat transformed, reappear in the adventures of both heroes. It points to the narratives surrounding the two conquerors either going back on similar origins or to a certain extent having borrowed from one another.

In a similar manner, there is the theme of the hero displaying his cunning by going as his own messenger to the court of a ruler he wants to subdue, as Farāmarz does with the Raja of India. This theme reappears in two of the aforementioned literary works that surround Eskandar. In the *Shāhnāme*, the world-conqueror goes undercover, not just once, but three times: to the Persian king Dārā, the queen of Andalusia, Qeydāfe, and the Chinese emperor, or Faghfūr. In the *Eskandarnāme*, he visits the same latter two rulers – albeit in different circumstances than in the *Shāhnāme* – and although he does not go to Dārā as his own messenger, Eskandar instead comes to Fūr, who like the Raja in the *Farāmarznāme* is king of India.[54] Again, even though the storylines surrounding Eskandar's and Farāmarz's respective experiences as a messenger differ, the recurrence of such a specific theme in the *Large Farāmarznāme* seems to derive from a deliberate plan by its author.

By including the episodes of Farāmarz pretending to be his own messenger and of the islands of the Dawāl-pāyān and the Pīl-gūshān, in addition to having him travel to both ends of the earth, the poet of the *Large Farāmarznāme* seems to have wanted to place his hero within the traditions surrounding Eskandar. In this, he went beyond composing his poem in imitation of the *Shāhnāme*, a modus operandi that the authors of the later epics had in common and that becomes clear from the *Farāmarznāme* including names, themes, a vocabulary and a style of writing known from Ferdowsī's epic. The poet in addition borrowed some elements of his story from narratives that specifically feature Eskandar. With the dates when both the prose *Eskandarnāme* and the *Dārābnāme* were first written down being uncertain, it cannot be said whether the poet of the *Large Farāmarznāme* would have known, and subsequently borrowed from, either of those two prose romances, but he most likely would have been familiar with stories about Eskandar, besides the relevant *Shāhnāme* episode, which would have circulated in his days. These stories could have been transmitted orally or been part of written works that served as sources for books such as the *Eskandarnāme* and the *Dārābnāme* or even the Eskandar episode in the *Shāhnāme*, but now no longer exist. The audience of the *Large Farāmarznāme* probably would equally have been familiar with such narratives about Eskandar, so that by including both themes and peoples that were linked to this famous conqueror, the poet implied, just as in the case of Garshāsp, that

Farāmarz equalled a great man like Eskandar in prowess. In this manner, Farāmarz as a hero and conqueror would fill the poem's audience with even greater awe and admiration.

Notes to the Introduction

1 Żabīḥollah Ṣafā, *Ḥamāse-sarā'ī dar īrān* (Tehran, 1333/1954–1955), 283–340, gives an overview of the later epics, discussing sixteen different titles. Depending on the criteria defining a later epic, one could both add several titles to Ṣafā's list and remove a few. François de Blois, 'Epics', *Encyclopaedia Iranica*, vol. X (2001), 474–477, includes story outlines of several later epics. See also Abou'lkasim Firdousi, *Livre des rois*, ed. and trans. Jules Mohl, vol. I (Paris, 1838), liv and lxx, and William L. Hanaway, Jr., 'The Iranian Epics', in: *Heroic Epic and Saga: An Introduction to the World's Great Folk Epics*, ed. Felix J. Oinas (Bloomington, 1978), 76–98, at 89–93. Marjolijn van Zutphen, *Farāmarz, the Sistāni Hero: Texts and Traditions of the* Farāmarznāme *and the Persian Epic Cycle* (Leiden/Boston, 2014), deals with the later epics, incorporating and updating Ṣafā's survey, with a focus on the narrative traditions surrounding Farāmarz, discussing the Persian epics in which he appears, especially the two *Farāmarznāmes*.

2 This translation is based on the critical edition of the poem, *Farāmarznāme-ye bozorg* (*The Large Farāmarznāme*), eds Marjolijn van Zutphen and Abolfazl Khatibi (Tehran, 2016). The translation takes account of certain changes to the published Persian text which have been suggested by Abolfazl Khatibi (e-mail message to myself, 8 October 2016) in reaction to Āydenlū's review of the critical edition. Sajjād Āydenlū, 'Manẓūme'ī pahlawānī az sedde-ye panjom-e hejrī', *Jahān-e ketāb* 21:7–8 (1395/2016), 18–23, refers to a total of 61 different verses, of which he either questions whether the reading is correct or proposes a specific change to one or more words; Khatibi agrees with 16 of these propositions, of which just two (vss 311 and 2460) consist of a change of orthography, which makes no difference to the translation and therefore are ignored here. All other 14 changes to the Persian text are noted in the footnotes to the present translation.

3 Karin Rührdanz, 'About a Group of Truncated *Shāhnāmas*: A Case Study in the Commercial Production of Illustrated Manuscripts in the Second Part of the Sixteenth Century', *Muqarnas* 14 (1997), 118–134, at 118.

4 To date, only a few of the later epics have been published, let alone in critical editions. With regards to the six mentioned in this paragraph, they have all been brought out in lithographed books. The *Dāstān-e Babr-e Bayān* and the *Bānū Goshaspnāme* are the first two poems of the lithographed book entitled *Farāmarznāme* (ed. Sorūsh-e Taftī, 1907), which further includes both *Farāmarznāmes* (joined together) and a section of the *Bahmannāme* (see below). Only the *Bānū Goshaspnāme* has been produced in a critical edition, by Roohangiz Karachi, whilst a shorter version of the *Barzūnāme* joined to the *Dāstān-e Kok-e Kūhzād* has appeared in print, as part of the appendix to Macan's *Shāhnāme* edition of 1829, which was reproduced by Dabīr Sīyāqī in 1956–1957, although in the latter series of books the *Barzūnāme* is erroneously attributed to 'Aṭā' b. Ya'qūb 'Aṭā'ī Rāzī. For more extended references to these editions, including the lithographed *Jahāngīrnāme* and *Sāmnāme*, see the list of Works Cited in the Introduction.

5 C.E. Bosworth and I. Afshar, "'Ajā'eb al-makẖlūqāt', *Encyclopaedia Iranica*, vol. I (1985), 696–698.

6 Firdousi, *Livre des rois*, ed. and trans. Mohl, vol. I, liv and lxx. Mohl calls the later epics *Shāhnāme* imitations of a lesser quality and content, which tell their stories for their own sakes, to fill up the lacunae in the *Shāhnāme*. Later scholars on the whole have differed little in their opinions on the later epics.

7 'Alī b. Aḥmad Asadī Ṭūsī, *Garshāspnāme*, ed. Ḥabīb Yaghmā'ī (Tehran, 1317/1938). See also Asadī Junior de Toūs, *Le livre de Gerchāsp*, vol. I, ed. and trans. Clément Huart (Paris, 1926), and vol. II, trans. Henri Massé (Paris, 1951).

8 Abū'l-Qāsem Ferdowsī, *Shāhnāme*, ed. Djalal Khaleghi-Motlagh, vol. V (New York, 1997), 471–484.

9 Īrānshāh b. Abī'l-Kheyr, *Bahmannāme*, ed. Rahīm 'Afīfī (Tehran, 1370/1991).

10 Īrānshān b. Abī'l-Kheyr, *Kūshnāme* (*Kūsh-nāmeh*), ed. Jalāl Matīnī (Tehran, 1337/1998).

11 Thus, the *Barzūnāme* was once attributed to Abū'l-'Alā 'Aṭā' b. Ya'qūb al-Kāteb (see also above, at note 4), who was in addition given the mistaken patronymic 'Aṭā'ī Rāzī, as the result of a misinterpretation of the word *'aṭā* ('gift') in the text, but this attribution has long since been refuted. Also, it was once believed that different versions of the *Shahrīyārnāme* were composed by famous poets like Farrokhī Sīstāni and 'Osmān Mokhtārī, but these attributions, too, are strongly doubted. See François de Blois, *Persian Literature*, vol. V, pt 2 (London, 1994), 433–434 (*Shahrīyārnāme*) and 569 (*Barzūnāme*).

12 To date, neither of the latter two poems has been published in full and both are only known from a few manuscripts, although a small section of the *Shahrīyārnāme* is included in 'Osmān Mokhtārī, *Dīwān*, ed. Jalāl al-Dīn Homā'ī (Tehran, 1341/1962), as one version of this later epic is believed to have been written by this early-twelfth-century poet (see previous note). A critical edition of the *Shabrangnāme*, by Gabrielle van den Berg and Abolfazl Khatibi, is currently in preparation. Rostam's fight against the White Demon is the last of his seven trials, told in the story of 'the war in Māzandarān', Ferdowsī, *Shāhnāme*, ed. Khaleghi-Motlagh, vol. II (1990), 3–65.

13 Ferdowsī, *Shāhnāme*, ed. Khaleghi-Motlagh, vol. II, 385–387.

14 Ferdowsī, *Shāhnāme*, ed. Khaleghi-Motlagh, vol. V, 386.

15 Abū'l-Ḥasan 'Alī b. Jūglūgh Farrokhī Sīstānī, *Dīwān*, ed. Moḥammad Dabīr Sīyāqī, 4th edn (Tehran, 1371/ 1992–1993), 377–378, *qaṣīde* 198 ('In praise of Amīr Abū Aḥmad Moḥammad b. Maḥmūd-e Ghaznawī'), vss 7653–7655, and 51–53, *qaṣīde* 30 ('On the return of Solṭān Maḥmūd from Hendūstān and his second victory'), vss 1027–1029.

16 *Tārīkh-e Sīstān*, ed. Moḥammad Taqī Bahār (Tehran, 1314/1925–1926), 7, mentions a prose book of twelve volumes. Shahmardān b. Abī'l-Kheyr, *Nozhatnāme-ye 'alā'ī*, ed. Farhang Jahānpūr (Tehran, 1362/1983), 342, discusses an author called Pīrūzān, who around the first half of the eleventh century AD would have made translations from Pahlawi (Middle Persian) of stories from the *Shāhnāme* traditions, including some about Farāmarz.

17 Shahmardān, *Nozhatnāme-ye 'alā'ī*, 329–333. See *Large Farāmarznāme*, eds Van Zutphen and Khatibi, vss 874–941 and 1253–1461: the latter episode rather differs from the one told in the *Nozhatnāme* (see also below).

18 Mary Boyce, 'Gōsān', *Encyclopaedia Iranica*, vol. IX (2003), 166–170.

19 Akbar Naḥawī, 'Molāḥeẕātī dar bare-ye farāmarznāme wa sorāyande-ye ān', in: *Majle-ye dāneshkāde-ye adabīyāt wa 'olūm-e ensānī-ye dāneshgāh-e tehrān* 164 (1381/2002–2003), 119–136. Naḥawī's dating is somewhat later than had previously been assumed: Firdousi, *Livre des rois*, ed. and trans. Mohl, vol. I, lxiii, dates the poem to the eleventh century, whilst Jalāl Khāleghī-Motlagh, 'Farāmarznāme', *Irānnāme* 1 (1361/1982), 22–45, at 31, as well as Khaleghi-Motlagh, 'Farāmarz-nāma', *Encyclopaedia Iranica*, vol. IX (1999), 240–241, at 240, believes it was composed between the second half of the eleventh and the early twelfth centuries.

20 *Farāmarznāme*, ed. Majīd Sarmadī (Tehran, 1382/2004), is a critical edition of the poem. The text consists of 1,595 verses and is based on two

manuscripts and the lithographed version (as part of the book entitled *Farāmarznāme*, discussed below), although at least seven more manuscripts of the poem should exist in Europe, Iran and India (see Van Zutphen, *Farāmarz, the Sistāni Hero*, 280–297).

21 Charles Rieu, *Supplement to the Catalogue of the Persian Manuscripts in the British Museum* (London, 1895), 129–131 (no. 196), discusses this manuscript and its many interpolated later epics.

22 *Farāmarznāme-ye bozorg*, eds Van Zutphen and Khatibi, xxxii–xxxviii. The introduction to the edition was written by Abolfazl Khatibi, and whereas it is for a large part based on information given in Van Zutphen, *Farāmarz, the Sistāni Hero*, certain sections were added by Khatibi himself, including his conclusions on the supposed dedicatee or a more precise dating of the *Large Farāmarznāme*, which was not covered by my research.

23 *Mojmal al-tawārīkh wa'l-qeṣaṣ*, eds Seyf ad-Dīn Nadjmābādī and Siegfried Weber (Edingen-Neckarhausen, 2000), 2.

24 See note 1 (Ṣafā's book on Persian epics and Mohl's introduction to his *Shāhnāme* edition-cum-translation).

25 E. Denison Ross and E.G. Browne, *Catalogue of Two Collections of Persian and Arabic Manuscripts Preserved in the India Office Library* (London, 1902), 107–108 (no. CLXXVI). The *Large Farāmarznāme* makes up the whole of this manuscript.

26 Hermann Ethé, *Catalogue of Persian Manuscripts in the Library of the India Office*, vol. I (Oxford, 1903), 551 (no. 870). The *Large Farāmarznāme* appears in this manuscript as an appendix to a truncated *Shāhnāme* – which ends abruptly at a point early in the reign of Queen Homāy, daughter of Bahman – and covers fols 368^{v}–456^{r}, but the text is made up of three, mixed-up, parts, whilst fols 397^{r}–405^{v} and 414^{r}–449^{v} consist of two other later epics (the shorter *Farāmarznāme* and the *Shabrangnāme*).

27 The book is for instance catalogued in A.J. Arberry, *Catalogue of the Library of the India Office*, vol. II, pt 6, *Persian Books* (London, 1937), 135 (shelf mark Per. D. 11), as well as Edward Edwards, *A Catalogue of Persian Printed Books in the British Museum* (London, 1922), 205 (shelf mark 14797 e. 47). The *Large Farāmarznāme* can be found on pp. 159–408; for the other epics making up the book, see note 4.

28 Jalāl Khāleghī-Motlagh, 'Moṭāle'āt-e ḥamāsī 2. Farāmarznāme', *Nashrīyye-ye dāneshkāde-ye adābīyāt wa 'olūm-e ensānī* 31 (1362/1983), 85–121, at 107–112. Idem, 'Farāmarznāme', *Irānnāme* 1, 22–45, is practically the same in content, but incorporates the information on the *Large Farāmarznāme*, at 23–24 and 33–36.

29 *Farāmarznāme-ye bozorg*, eds Van Zutphen and Khatibi, lxvii–lxxvi. Van Zutphen, *Farāmarz, the Sistāni Hero*, 303–323, discusses the three texts and their physical appearance at length.

30 Ferdowsī, *Shāhnāme*, ed. Khaleghi-Motlagh, vol. I (1988), 3–5 (vss 1–34).

31 Ferdowsī, *Shāhnāme*, ed. Khaleghi-Motlagh, vol. III (1992), 3–24, entitled *dāstān-e ʿarẓ kardan-e keykhosrow*, 'the story of Keykhosrow's review'. See Van Zutphen, *Farāmarz, the Sistāni Hero*, 417–425, for a comparison between these sections of the *Shāhnāme* and the manuscript versions of the *Large Farāmarznāme*.

32 This section, in which Keykhosrow dispatches his commanders to deal with the enemy in different regions, harks back to a different *Shāhnāme* episode, Ferdowsī, *Shāhnāme*, ed. Khaleghi-Motlagh, vol. IV (1994), 3–166 (*dāstān-e razm-e yāzdah rokh*, 'the story of the battle of the eleven knights'), at 10–11, vss 105–122; the remainder of the introduction goes back to 'the story of Keykhosrow's review'.

33 Abool Kasim Firdousee, *The Shah Nameh*, ed. Turner Macan (Calcutta: 1829), vol. II, p. 559, line 9, to p. 564, line 27. This passage contains a substantial number of additional verses compared to Ferdowsī, *Shāhnāme*, ed. Khaleghi-Motlagh, vol. III, 17–23, vss 240–353. Macan's text has been reproduced in Dabīr Sīyāqī's edition, 6 vols (Tehran, 1335/1956–1957).

34 Marjolijn van Zutphen, 'Lithographed Editions of Firdawsī's *Shāhnāma*: A Comparative Study', *Oriens* 37 (2009) 65–101, at 77 and 81–99.

35 *Farāmarznāme-ye bozorg*, eds Van Zutphen and Khatibi, 3, n. 1, refers to the relevant *Shāhnāme* sections from which all three texts have borrowed, but does not cite the introductory section of the lithographed text.

36 *Farāmarznāme-ye bozorg*, eds Van Zutphen and Khatibi, 368, vs. 5442, n. 2, cites the final six verses of MS RSPA 176.

37 The *Garshāspnāme*, for instance, appears as an interpolation in London, British Library, MS IO Islamic 3263 (fols 13r–104r), the same manuscript that includes a version of the *Large Farāmarznāme* (see note 26), whilst the *Bahmannāme* can for instance be found in London, British Library, MS Or. 2976 (Shiraz, 1249/1833), fols 62r–123r, the second half of the same *Shāhnāme* of which the first part (MS Or. 2926) includes an interpolated shorter *Farāmarznāme* (see above, at note 21).

38 Four of the manuscripts are *Shāhnāmes* that include interpolated later epics: Berlin, Staatsbibliothek, MS or. fol. 4252 (end-Safar 1042/mid-September 1632), fols 194r–203v; New York, Public Library, Spencer Pers. MS 3 (Shiraz?, Rajab 1025/July–August 1616), fols 164v–172v; St Petersburg, National Library, MS PNS 65 (20 Żīʾl-qaʿda 1031/1 July 1630), fols 165v–170r, and

MS Dorn 333 (Mashhad, 1061/1651), fols 319ᵛ–330ʳ. The fifth one, Hyderabad, Salar Jung Museum and Library, MS 929 (early-11th C./*c.* 1600), fols 120ᵛ–131ᵛ, presents four later epics separately, but the *Large Farāmarznāme* follows a piece of text from the *Shāhnāme*, at the same point as in the other four manuscripts (after the verse equivalent to Ferdowsī, *Shāhnāme*, ed. Khaleghi-Motlagh, vol. III, 24, vs. 355). The version of the Hyderabad MS 929 is the longest, consisting of 843 verses. The versions in both the Berlin MS or. fol. 4252 and the St Petersburg MS Dorn 333 consist of 830 verses. The versions of Spencer Pers. MS 3 and MS PNS 65 largely agree with the others, but each misses out a different section of the text, consisting of about one and five folios, respectively. On the texts and contents of the four interpolated *Large Farāmarznāme*, see Van Zutphen, *Farāmarz, the Sistāni Hero*, 323–326 and 450–462, and for the Hyderabad manuscript, see pp. 329–330, although this information is not fully correct, since at the time of writing I had not yet examined this manuscript and was still under the impression that it might contain the complete *Farāmarznāme*.

39 Ervad Bomanji Nusserwanji Dhabhar, *Catalogue of the K.R. Cama Oriental Institute* (Bombay, 1923), 151 (no. 76); Sayad Abdulla Brelvi and Ervad B.N. Dhabhar, *Supplementary Catalogue of Arabic, Hindustani, Persian and Turkish Mss and Descriptive Catalogue of the Avestan, Pahlavi, Pazend and Persian MSS in the Mulla Firoz Library* (Bombay, 1917), xxxii [no. 22]; Ervad Bomanji Nusserwanji Dhabhar, *Descriptive Catalogue of All Manuscripts in the First Dastur Meherji Rana Library, Navsari* (Bombay, 1923), 91 (no. 65).

40 Dehkhodā, *Loghatnāme*, s.v. *qīrwān*, available at www.loghatnaameh.org.

41 M. Streck, 'Ḳāf', *Encyclopaedia of Islam*, 2nd ed., vol. IV (1978), 400–402.

42 There is some contradiction surrounding the duration of Farāmarz's voyage: when he is in Qīrwān, geographically about halfway through his entire journey, his men say he has been away from home for 14 years ('twice five and four years have passed'; vs. 3191), whereas some time later Sīyahdīw informs the fairy king Farṭūrtūsh that Farāmarz has been travelling for more than 13 years (vs. 4603), but when Farāmarz leaves Farṭūrtūsh's country to go back to Iran, we are told that 15 years had gone by since he had left there (vs. 5255).

43 These passages describe, in turn, a number of unreal creatures Farāmarz and his men see during their first voyage across the ocean (vss 2051–2056); mountains of ruby and crystal on the island where Farāmarz slays a dragon, before going to the Zangīs (vss 2975–2976); plants that resemble humans and other creatures of different species and that seem to vaguely resemble mandrakes, on the same island that contains Hūshang's tomb (vss 3780–

3784); and a people of 'innocent' demons that run too fast for any mounted man to catch them, which live near Mount Qāf, where Farāmarz and his men come after dealing with the king of Farghān (vss 3979–3992).

44 Asadī, *Garshāspnāme*, ed. Yaghmā'ī, 286–304, and *Le livre de Gerchāsp*, vol. II, trans. Massé, 133–146.

45 *Garshāspnāme*, ed. Yaghmā'ī, 127–148 and 312–319, and *Le livre de Gerchâsp*, trans., Massé, 23–37 and 152–157.

46 *Garshāspnāme*, ed. Yaghmā'ī, 178–183, and *Le livre de Gerchāsp*, trans. Massé, 58–61.

47 Shaul Shaked and Zabiollah Safa, 'Andarz', *Encyclopaedia Iranica*, vol. II (1987), 11–22.

48 Ferdowsī, *Shāhnāme*, ed. Khaleghi-Motlagh, vol. V, 518–565 (episodes of kings Dārāb and Dārā), and vol. VI (2005), 3–129 (episode of Eskandar). Richard Stoneman, *Alexander the Great: A Life in Legend* (New Haven and London, 2008), 27–48 (chapter 2), deals with several Persian versions of the story of Alexander and, at 28–31, discusses the extent in which Ferdowsī's episode of Eskandar, especially his dealings with Dārāb, goes back on the Greek romance.

49 Elyās b. Yūsof Neẕāmī Ganjawī, *Sharafnāme* and *Eqbālnāme*, ed. Wahīd Dastgerdī (Tehran: Aramghān, 1316/1937 and 1317/1938). The precise date of composition of the *Eskandarnāme* is unknown.

50 *Eskandarnāme*, ed. Īraj Afshār (Tehran, 1343/1964). See also *Iskandarnamah. A Persian Medieval Alexander-Romance*, trans. Minoo S. Southgate (New York, 1978). Afshār, 23, and Southgate, 3, discuss the work's possible dates. Most likely, the core of this work was written around the eleventh century, but it was later expanded to its presently known form.

51 Abū Ṭāher Moḥammad b. Ḥasan b. 'Alī b. Mūsā Ṭarsūsī, *Dārābnāme*, ed. Żabīḥollah Ṣafā, 2 vols (Tehran, 1374/1995–1996). See also Abu Tāher Tarsusi, *Alexandre le Grand en Iran: Le Dārāb Nāmeh d'Abu Tāher Tarsusi*, trans. Marina Gaillard (Paris, 2005). Gaillard, 83–85 (introduction), believes that the present version of the work dates from the twelfth century, although there are indications that it first may have been written down in the eleventh century.

52 Ferdowsi, *Shāhnāme*, ed. Khaleghi-Motlagh, vol. VI, 74–78.

53 *Eskandarnāme*, ed. Afshār, 95–97 (Dawāl-pāyān) and 702–704 (Fīl-gūshān), and *Iskandarnamah*, trans. Southgate, 36–37 and 152–153. Ṭarsūsī, *Dārāb-nāme*, ed. Ṣafā, vol. 2, 570–572 (Dawāl-pāyān), and 395–398 and 573–575 (Gelīm-gūshān), and *Le Dārāb Nāmeh d'Abu Tāher Tarsusi*, trans. Gaillard, 381 (Dawāl-pāyān; part of a summarised episode), and 295–299 and 381

(Gelīm-gūshān; second episode summarised). Ferdowsī, *Shāhnāme*, ed. Khaleghi-Motlagh, vol. VI, 82 (*narm-pāyān*) and 114–116 (*gush-bestar*). Evangelos Venetis, 'Islamic Lore and Supernatural Creatures in the Persian Prose *Book of Alexander* (*Iskandarnama*)', *Persica* 21 (2006–2007), 75–87, at 76–79, briefly discusses the Dawāl-pāyān and the Fīl-gūshān in the prose *Eskandarnāme*, and includes a reference to the Dawāl-pāyān in the *Dārābnāme*.

54 Ferdowsi, *Shāhnāme*, ed. Khaleghi-Motlagh, vol. V, 534–540 (Dārā), and vol. VI, 57–64 (Qeydāfe) and 106–111 (Faghfūr). *Eskandarnāme*, ed. Afshār, 15–21 (Fūr), 192–195 (Qeydāfe), and 256–270 (Faghfūr), and *Iskandarnamah*, trans. Southgate, 17–19, 48–50, and 67 (the latter episode only summarised).

Works Cited in the Introduction

Primary Sources

Asadī Ṭūsī, ʿAlī b. Aḥmad. *Garshāspnāme*, ed. Ḥabīb Yaghmāʾī (Tehran: [n. pub.], 1317/1938).

——— [Asadī Junior de Toūs]. *Le livre de Gerchāsp*, vol. I, ed. and trans. Clément Huart, and vol. II, trans. Henri Massé (Paris: Paul Geuthner, 1926 and 1951).

ʿAṭāʾī Rāzī, ʿAṭāʾ b. Yaʿqūb, and Anon. *Barzūnāme* and *Dāstān-e Kok-e Kūhzād*, ed. Seyyed Moḥammad Dabīr Sīyāqī (Tehran: Anjoman-e āšār wa mafākher-e farhangī, 1382/2003).

Bānū Goshasb-nāme (*Bānūgoshasp nāmeh*), ed. Roohangiz Karachi (Tehran: Institute for Humanities and Cultural Studies, 1382/2003).

Eskandarnāme, ed. Īraj Afshār (Tehran: Bongāh-e tarjome wa nashr-e ketāb, 1343/1964; re-publ. Tehran: Cheshme, 1389/2010).

——— [*Iskandarnamah. A Persian Medieval Alexander-Romance*], trans. Minoo S. Southgate (New York: Columbia University Press, 1978).

Farāmarznāme, ed. Rostam pūr-e Bahrām Sorūsh-e Taftī (Bombay, 1326/1907).

Farāmarznāme, ed. Majīd Sarmadī (Tehran: Anjoman-e āšār wa mafākher-e farhangī, 1382/2004).

Farāmarznāme-ye bozorg (*The Large Farāmarznāme*), eds Marjolijn van Zutphen and Abolfazl Khatibi [Abūʾl-fażl Khaṭībī] (Tehran: Sokhan, 2016).

Farrokhī Sīstānī, Abūʾl-Ḥasan ʿAlī b. Jūglūgh. *Dīwān*, ed. Moḥammad Dabīr Sīyāqī, 4th edn (Tehran: Zawwār, 1371/1992–1993; 1st edn 1335/1957).

Ferdowsī, Abūʾl-Qāsem [Abool Kasim Firdousee]. *The Shah Nameh: An Heroic Poem, Containing the History of Persia from Kioomurs to Yesdejird*, ed. Turner Macan, 4 vols (Calcutta: [n. pub.], 1829).

——— [Abouʾlkasim Firdousi]. *Livre des rois*, ed. and trans. Jules Mohl, 7 vols (Paris: Imprimerie Nationale, 1838–1878; repr. Paris: Maisonneuve, 1976).

———. *Shāhnāme*, ed. Moḥammad Dabīr Sīyāqī, 6 vols (Tehran: Enteshārāt-e ʿelmī, 1335/1956–1957).

———. *Shāhnāme*, ed. Djalal Khaleghi-Motlagh, 8 vols (New York: Bibliotheca Persica, 1988–2008).

Īrānshāh b. Abī'l-Kheyr. *Bahmannāme*, ed. Rahīm ʿAfīfī (Tehran: Sharekat-e enteshārāt-e ʿelmī wa farhangī, 1370/1991).

Īrānshān b. Abī'l-Kheyr, *Kūshnāme* (*Kūsh-nāmeh*), ed. Jalāl Matīnī (Tehran: Enteshārāt-e ʿelmī, 1337/1998).

Jahāngīrnāme, ed. Ardashīr Bonshāhī Farzand (Bombay, 1325/1907–1908; 2nd ed.).

Mojmal al-tawārīkh wa'l-qeṣaṣ (Mudjmal at-tawārīkh wa-l-qiṣaṣ: eine persische Weltgeschichte aus dem 12. Jahrhundert), eds Seyf ad-Dīn Nadjmābādī and Siegfried Weber (Edingen-Neckarhausen: Deux Mondes, 2000).

Mokhtārī, ʿOṡmān. *Dīwān*, ed. Jalāl al-Dīn Homā'ī (Tehran: Bongāh-e tarjome wa nashr-e ketāb, 1341/1962).

Neẕāmī Ganjawī, Elyās b. Yūsof. *Eskandarnāme* (*Sharafnāme* and *Eqbālnāme*), ed. Wahīd Dastgerdī (Tehran: Aramghān, 1316/1937 and 1317/1938).

Sāmnāme, ed. Ardashīr Bonshāhī (Bombay, 1319–1320/1901–03), 2 vols.

Shahmardān b. Abī'l-Kheyr. *Nozhatnāme-ye ʿalā'ī*, ed. Farhang Jahānpūr (Tehran: Mo'asse-ye moṭāleʿāt wa taḥqīqāt-e farhangī, 1362/1983).

Tārīkh-e Sīstān, ed. Moḥammad Taqī Bahār (Tehran: Zawwār, 1314/1925–1926).

Ṭarsūsī, Abū Ṭāher Moḥammad b. Ḥasan b. ʿAlī b. Mūsā. *Dārābnāme*, ed. Żabīḥollah Ṣafā, 2 vols (Tehran: Sharekat-e enteshārāt-e ʿelmī wa farhangī, 1374/1995–1996; 1st edn 1344/1965–1966 (vol. 1) and 1346/1967–1968 (vol. 2)).

——— [Ṭarsūsī, Abu Ṭāher]. *Alexandre le Grand en Iran: Le Dārāb Nāmeh d'Abu Tāher Tarsusi*, trans. Marina Gaillard (Paris: Editions de Boccard, 2005).

Secondary Sources

Arberry, A.J. *Catalogue of the Library of the India Office*, vol. II, pt 6, *Persian Books* (London: By order of the Secretary of State for India, 1937).

Āydenlū, Sajjād. 'Manẕūme'ī pahlawānī az sedde-ye panjom-e hejrī', *Jahān-e ketāb* 21:7–8 (1395/2016), 18–23.

Bosworth, C.E., and I. Afshar. "ʿAjā'eb al-maḵlūqāt', *Encyclopaedia Iranica*, vol. I (1985), 696–698; an updated version is available online at http://www.iranicaonline.org/articles/ajaeb-al-makluqat-the-marvels-of-created-things-the-name-of-a-genre-of-classical-islamic-literature-and-in-part (accessed on 25 May 2016).

Boyce, Mary. 'Gōsān', *Encyclopaedia Iranica*, vol. IX (2003), 166–170; an updated version is available online at www.iranicaonline.org/articles/gosan (accessed on 25 May 2016).

Brelvi, Sayad Abdulla, and Ervad B.N. Dhabhar. *Supplementary Catalogue of Arabic, Hindustani, Persian and Turkish Mss and Descriptive Catalogue of the Avestan, Pahlavi, Pazend and Persian MSS in the Mulla Firoz Library* (Bombay, Mulla Firuz Library, 1917).

De Blois, François. *Persian Literature: A Bio-Biographical Survey*, vol. V, *Poetry of the Pre-Mongol Period*, pt 2, *Poetry ca. AD 1100 to 1225* (London: Royal Asiatic Society, 1994).

———. 'Epics', *Encyclopaedia Iranica*, vol. X (2001), 474–477; an updated version is available online at http://www.iranicaonline.org/articles/epics (accessed on 25 May 2016).

Dehkhodā, ʿAlī Akbar. *Loghatnāme*; available at www.loghatnaameh.org.

Dhabhar, Ervad Bomanji Nusserwanji. *Catalogue of the K.R. Cama Oriental Institute* (Bombay: The K.R. Cama Oriental Institute, 1923).

———. *Descriptive Catalogue of All Manuscripts in the First Dastur Meherji Rana Library, Navsari* (Bombay: Commercial Printing Press of the Tata Publicity Corporation, 1923).

Edwards, Edward. *A Catalogue of Persian Printed Books in the British Museum* (London: British Museum, 1922).

Ethé, Hermann. *Catalogue of Persian Manuscripts in the Library of the India Office*, vol. I (Oxford: Clarendon Press, 1903).

Hanaway, Jr., William L. 'The Iranian Epics', in: *Heroic Epic and Saga: An Introduction to the World's Great Folk Epics*, ed. Felix J. Oinas (Bloomington: Indiana University Press, 1978), 76–98.

Khāleghī-Motlagh, Jalāl. 'Farāmarznāme', *Irānnāme* 1 (1361/1982), 22–45.

———. 'Moṭāleʿāt-e ḥamāsī 2. Farāmarznāme', *Nashrīyye-ye dāneshkāde-ye adābīyāt wa ʿolūm-e ensānī* 31 (1362/1983), 85–121.

Khaleghi-Motlagh, Djalal. 'Farāmarz-nāma', *Encyclopaedia Iranica*, vol. IX (1999), 240–241.

———. *Notes on the Shahnameh* (*Yāddashthā-ye shāhnāme*), 2 vols (New York: Bibliotheca Persica, 2001 and 2006).

Naḥawī, Akbar. 'Molāḥeẓātī dar bare-ye farāmarznāme wa sorāyande-ye ān', in: *Majle-ye dāneshkāde-ye adabīyāt wa ʿolūm-e ensānī-ye dāneshgāh-e tehrān* 164 (1381/2002–2003), 119–136.

Rieu, Charles. *Supplement to the Catalogue of the Persian Manuscripts in the British Museum* (London: British Museum, 1895).

Ross, E. Denison, and E.G. Browne. *Catalogue of Two Collections of Persian and Arabic Manuscripts Preserved in the India Office Library* (London: Eyre and Spottiswoode, 1902).

Rührdanz, Karin. 'About a Group of Truncated *Shāhnāmas*: A Case Study in the

Commercial Production of Illustrated Manuscripts in the Second Part of the Sixteenth Century', *Muqarnas* 14 (1997), 118–134.

Ṣafā, Żabīḥollah. *Ḥamāse-sarā'ī dar īrān* (Tehran: Mahfūz, 1333/1954–1955).

Shaked, Shaul, and Zabiollah Safa. 'Andarz', *Encyclopaedia Iranica*, vol. II (1987), 11–22; an updated version is available online at http://www.iranicaonline.org/articles/andarz-precept-instruction-advice (accessed on 25 May 2016).

Stoneman, Richard. *Alexzander the Great: A Life in Legend* (New Haven and London: Yale University Press, 2008).

Streck, M. 'Ḳāf', *Encyclopaedia of Islam*, 2nd ed., vol. IV (1978), 400–402.

Venetis, Evangelos. 'Islamic Lore and Supernatural Creatures in the Persian Prose *Book of Alexander* (*Iskandarnama*)', *Persica* 21 (2006–2007), 75–87.

Zutphen, Marjolijn van. 'Lithographed Editions of Firdawsī's *Shāhnāma*: A Comparative Study', *Oriens* 37 (2009), 65–101.

———. *Farāmarz, the Sistāni Hero: Texts and Traditions of the Farāmarznāme and the Persian Epic Cycle* (Leiden: Brill, 2014).

The Large Farāmarznāme

Part One – Farāmarz Leads an Army to India

In the name of God the Bountiful; He is the Merciful, the Beneficent, the Just Lord, the Distributer of justice.
This is the book of the *Large Farāmarznāme*. On the unity of God, may He be honoured and glorified, and in praise of wisdom

In the name of the Lord of the soul and of wisdom, higher than Whom no thought can ascend, Lord by name and Lord by position, the Lord Who provides our daily bread and Who is our guide, God Who travels upon the heavenly wheel, Who made time and the world appear, the Lord of the body and the Lord of the mind: you must strive to worship Him. No one knows how to praise Him like He is. You must gird yourself for servitude. Wisdom and the soul are weighed by Him. Who can contain Him in their thoughts or reason? Who is capable of praising the Creator with his means, his intellect, his soul, or his tongue?! You must confess to His existence; stand aside from speech or opinion. Since you are running and seeking the way, you must look deeply into His commands. The Lord of Saturn and the turning heaven, He Who lights up the moon, Venus and the sun, He is more exalted than any name, identity, or imagination, He is the essence of a superior depicter. With your eyes you will not see the Creator; do not strain your two eyes. Nor will any thought find its way towards Him, for He is higher than any name and any place. Whichever words may be uttered about His essence, no soul or intellect will find any path to Him. If wisdom selects the words, it will praise those that it sees. Anyone who is knowledgeable will be powerful; the heart of an old man will become young through learning. There is no way for you beyond this veiled secret about why I have no deficiency in my existence.

Now, wise man, with regard to wisdom, it is appropriate to speak of it in this place. Come and produce what you hold in wisdom, so that the ear of the praiser may take enjoyment from it. Wisdom is better than anything that God gave you. Praise of wisdom is better than the path of justice. Wisdom is our guide and wisdom is exhilarating, wisdom acts as an assistant in both worlds. Wisdom is better for a man than a dear soul. Nothing lies beyond wisdom. From it comes happiness and it produces manliness; it also leads to excellence, as well as to pleasantness. A wise man is a light in the world; wisdom is a harness upon a man's body. What did that eloquent wise man say, so that a learned man might reap the fruits from his speech? 'If a man has no wisdom in the world, he will not be happy for one moment: a sensible person will call him mad, his own relative will call him a stranger. Because of wisdom, a man will be noble in both worlds, but when it is broken, he will be in fetters.' Wisdom is the eye of the soul, when you observe; for without eyes you will not travel the world happily. Recognise wisdom as the first creation; it is the keeper of the soul and those three guards: your three guards are the ear, the eye and the tongue, because through them you achieve goodness without a doubt. Whoever acknowledges wisdom and the soul will praise them. After this, say what has been created. You, who will not see what amongst the makings of the Creator of the world is open and hidden, seek a path by means of the speeches of knowledgeable men, rush across the world and tell every person. When you hear words about every piece of knowledge, do not rest for one moment from learning. As soon as you gain sight of the branches of speech, know that knowledge will not reach its origin. From the beginning you must correctly see the worth of the essences from their commencement.

Beginning of the story

The episode in which King Keykhosrow mounts the throne and orders the champions to seek revenge for his father and the champions answer him

Now I will return to the story and recount something that originates in ancient times. An eloquent landlord recollected as follows: one day at dawn, Keykhosrow was seated upon his throne, full of grace and, according to his wishes, attended by all the famous men of Iran, such as Rostam, Gūdarz and the brave Ṭūs, as well as Gīw, Farīborz and Gostaham the lion, and also Gorgīn and Zange-Shāwrān, in addition to Farhād and Bīzhan from amongst the heroes. A banquet had been laid out like a field of produce, it was as if Sorūsh had brought it from Paradise. All kinds of things were said, about every subject, about every famous man and every country, about kings of the past, both just and unjust, whilst they abundantly sang the praises of the munificent king.

The king then spoke: 'O brave men of mine, my male lions at a time of honour, I have traversed this country of Iran on horseback, and from this region to the house of Āżargoshasp I did not see anyone whose heart was happy, whose breast was strong or whose land prosperous. They have all been wounded by Afrāsīyāb, all their hearts are filled with blood and their eyes with tears. The first liver he wounded was mine, so that my body and soul were full of pain because of him. How evil was that bad deed that he performed against me: he nullified his protection of Sīyāwakhsh's life. Because of him, his daughter was affected by suffering and hardship; he cut through his brother's waist with his sword; with his sword he also severed the head of Nowżar, that king of the free men, from his body. About the behaviour of that tyrant king I can say many things without ever coming to an end. In Iran, women and men are all lamenting because of him, because of so much killing, pillage, war and turmoil.

'Now, I will gird my loins to avenge my father, and I will torment the soul of that dark man: if you all are sincere supporters of mine, if each one of you in his heart is my friend and if you now also are of a mind to go to war, you must strive and provide the counsel of leopards. What do you say and what answer will you give me? You must all at once give me noble advice. He excelled in this evil: retribution for this evil should not be kept waiting. If there is justice in this speech, you must take to the road. But if not, you must give an answer about this matter.'

As the nobles prepared their answer, they got up from their places, filled with pain, and said, 'Your Majesty, may the world be happy and may it be freed from grief and from every sorrow. Our bodies and souls are completely at your service; our greater or smaller grief and sorrows are yours. We were all born of our mothers to die; we are your servants, even though we are free men.'

When the king had received such an answer from the gathering, from Gūdarz, from Ṭūs and from Pīltan, his face became like a deep-red flower, since his power was young, as the monarch was young. He praised them abundantly: 'May the land be prosperous for the warriors!'

Keykhosrow reviews the army and he sends the champions to Tūrān to seek revenge for his father and appoints champions to each land; an account thereof

The heaven kept on turning for a while after this, and when the sun showed its face from a corner, the monarch ordered the paymasters to call out the names of the men, high- and lowborn. The names of the warriors were written down properly, as was worthy of champions. As it accorded with the new moon, there firstly was Farīborz, the general. Next, Ṭūs with the famous clan of Nowżar, all mace-bearers and all soldiers. Thirdly, there were the likes of Gūdarz son of Keshwād, whose counsel caused the army to be well-organised – his grandfather had eighty-eight sons, brave men from the mountains and horsemen of the plains – and the margrave with the select champion: Zawāre and the praiseworthy Farāmarz. It came about that the registrar did not know how he could write down the names of so many famous men of splendour and glory onto the emperor's roll as befitted them. They were ordered to leave the city and to go from the town to the desert and the plain. The soldiers one by one bowed down with their heads to the ground and said in praise, 'We are servants, whilst the kingship is yours; the earth is yours, from the bull's head to the orb of the moon.'[1] He opened the door to his treasury of coins and said, 'The treasure of great men should not remain concealed.' He distributed the hidden treasures amongst the soldiers and sent one of the great men out in every direction.

After that, the victorious world-ruler sat with his sceptre upon his golden throne and had his flock, from every place where they were roaming, gathered all together in a crowd at the army camp. He bestowed gifts on the soldiers one by one, so that they would gird their loins for war. He spoke as follows: 'O, renowned men of mine, friends of mine both young and old, deny your eyes and bellies food and sleep, and delight the soul of Sīyāwakhsh. Someone taught them a suitable lesson: if an eminent and fortunate son is not in pain about avenging his father, his heart will become soft through sleep and through food, his constitution will not be purified by water, and a sword will be his helmet and soil his crown.'

When the army was completely arranged, he distributed riches to every person. First, he ordered Gūdarz to block the road to Khotan and make an unexpected assault upon that region to rob the crowns and thrones from the nobles, since Tūrān obtained its worth from that region and Pīrān was the commander of those lands. Towards the region of Khwārazm Ashkash would go, so he quickly made preparations to fight Shīde, for Shīde was a son of Afrāsīyāb, a proud young man with power and vigour. On the field of valour, at the time of battle, he could even bring a war elephant to destruction. The fortunate king ordered Lohrāsp to go towards Ghūr in order to attack the army. He entrusted the Ālāns and Georgia to him and said to him, 'Lion-like valorous hero, at the time of battle you must destroy Garsīwaz, the evil-doer of our times, for that malicious, defamed, wretched man shed the blood of my dear father. You must exact vengeance by mace and by sword upon everyone you find from the Tūrānian army who agreed with the killing of the king, and you must bring his head with its crown down to the dust. Because from now on, by the strength of the Creator of the world, I and my mace and sword upon the terrain of war will not enjoy rest or pleasure by night or day. My throne is my saddle and my cup my sword; neither night nor day will I take sleep or food, nor will I open my two lips for feasting or entertainment. Perhaps, with the power of God I will bring my enemies down into the dust with my battle-sword and I will brighten the soul of Sīyāwakhsh and with goodness transform the world into a rose-garden. Sīyāwakhsh's soul should not be in pain whilst evil people take pleasure, rest and food. Now his son has placed the crown of glory upon his head, the exalted people will not laugh at this.'[2]

When the colourful peacock lit up from behind the mountains and burned the feathers and wings of the black crow, the warriors of Iran all departed in such a manner as the king had ordered his flock. When the king had sent the army in every direction, he himself and the faithful Rostam returned and he sat upon his throne with music and wine, drinking to the memory of Kāwos the Keyānid king. When his head had become heavy with palatable wine, the illustrious king went to his sleeping quarters.

Rostam speaks with Keykhosrow about the province of Khargāh; Keykhosrow's answer to Rostam and his speech about sending Farāmarz there, to which Rostam agrees

When the night had traversed the face of the earth and the light of morning opened its lips, so that the land was refreshed, the mountain turned the colour of sandarac and you would say that the world became like the eye of a cockerel, the world-champion Rostam came to the court and said to the king of exalted stock, 'Adjacent to the province of Zābolestān lies a land more pleasant than a rose-garden. There is an abundance of cities like paradises and many villages with gardens and tillage, as well as castles, palaces and high fortresses; nothing in the world is so exquisite. It is a world adorned with good things, containing boundless soldiers and riches. An experienced landlord had gained success in that region, which is called Khargāh. On one side that province gives passage to India, and to Qannowj and Kashmir; on the other side, the road leads towards the border of China, adjoining the kingdom of Tūrān. In former times, that province belonged to us and we received its tribute in its entirety. When Kāwos became devoid of power and lustre and he went without food and sleep out of pain for his son, the Tūrānians took that region and no Iranians remained there. Now the king of the land of Tūrān has his share in that prosperous region, in its lands and cities. Since you are now the king of Iran, eminent, illustrious and seeking vengeance, we must not let the Turks rise up and also take profit from the lands belonging to Iran. We must put together a large army under a renowned, strong champion and send it there on the command of Your Majesty, with his elephants and with his drum, throne and crown, so that they can empty that land of them and settle there in hundredfold magnificence. With the strength of his valour he will bring to ruin Sind, Kashmir and India, as well as the margraves of Jādūstān, so that the world will become obedient to Your Majesty. When we have taken hold of that region in its entirety, we will bring defeat upon the land of Tūrān.'

The king replied to him, 'You elephant-bodied hero, you enjoy high standing with me. You are that celebrity in whose fortune both the Iranian army and the court rejoice. You were the educator of my father, of which you are well aware, famous nobleman. I gave you your country and its cultivated lands, as well as treasures and soldiers whenever they were depleted. A land that lies next to your country, why should someone else take it and settle there?! Tell Farāmarz, the celebrated lion-slayer, to gird his loins for this war. From Khargāh to the land of India and from Kashmīr to the borderlands of Jādūstān you must entrust him with the kingship of every region that he conquers and that is submitted to his command, for he is a hero, proud and celebrated. The matter will be resolved in his hands; his snare will be at the throats of the crocodiles.'

When Rostam had heard the king's speech, his heart became fresh like a pomegranate flower. He praised the king abundantly and said, 'May wisdom be joined with your good name, may also your crown and throne be prosperous and may the revolving heaven be at your service.' After that, a messenger mounted, to summon the son who had been appointed to this task.

Farāmarz comes before Keykhosrow and the king orders him to take the province of Khargāh; he accepts and gives an answer; an account of the king bestowing gifts and giving him counsel

When Farāmarz, the army leader and strong warrior, came before the great king, he kissed the ground in front of his throne and spoke in eulogy of the king of the Iranian army: 'May you live for ever with an enlightened mind, may you be exalted upon the Keyānid throne! May your enemies be diminished and destitute and may the hearts of your well-wishers be upright!' The king of kings made much of that warrior and said to him, 'Perfect man of good fortune, you are an offshoot of that famous hero from whom a formidable lion learns his skills. You will remain with this strength and these arms and shoulders, as long as the world continues as a result of the actions of Zāl.'

Next, he let him sit beside the throne and sent for the renowned men of the army. The king of the country lined up two rows of ten thousand selected horsemen and gave them to him, together with elephants and trumpets, drums and banners, as well as a crown and a throne, and a sword inlaid with purple. He entrusted those renowned commanders to that celebrated young man and said to him, 'March towards India, to that region of Khargāh, as far as the Jādūān, and clean out Qannowj, Kashmir and India. Take your sword to India, army leader, and of any of the Tūrānians that may be there, whether they are a champion or someone's sweetheart, of any person who might seek to fight against you, you must drag his head completely into the dust. When you have conquered it, that kingship is yours: rule it with munificence and along a straight path. But you must not be severe with your subjects or make them wretched and abject. Be a friend to the poor in every place; act in accordance with your reputation amongst your own people. Do not be an acquirer of riches during your youth; take treasures but do not cause anyone any trouble. Your reputation must remain unsullied. Take care that your heart will not be perturbed in this world. It is a transient dwelling, which will not last forever; no one remains powerful in this world.'

Farāmarz kissed the ground and eulogised the king of illustrious stock. He said to him, 'O, example of the Keyānid kings, I keep my loins girded at your command. I will travel upon that road as you have ordered and I will obtain all my honour from your speech.' Having said this, he returned to his home and made necessary preparations for his battle against the enemy.

Rostam gives his son counsel for his journey

His father also gave him several of his brave men, lions of pre-excellence. He further gave him a lot of advice and counsel: 'Do not molest any person without reason. In every place where there is a warlike person, send a swift messenger at a gallop to him. First you must speak gently', he said, 'for with softness you can bring a snake out from its hiding place. When your work does not achieve anything good through kindness, you must apply harshness and, after that, seek battle. When you have brought your inferior to obedience, you must forgive him in accordance with justice and worship of God. When you have become victorious, you must not order bloodshed or provocation of the people. Every day you must inform me of your actions and conduct, of the battles and quarrels, of good and bad things, of peace and of war, so that we will not be sorrowful.'

All night the man of enlightened mind loosened his tongue with counsel for his son. And when the father had completed his counsel and advice, the heroic man put his head down to sleep.

The beginning of the story of Farāmarz setting off for the province of Khargāh, Rostam travelling two stages to send Farāmarz off and Farāmarz's arrival there

When the sun upon the azure dome spread yellow rubies from its face, as it shone radiantly from the constellation of Aries, so that the earth all over became like golden water, Farāmarz the army leader, conqueror of countries, came out and mounted his swift horse. He beat the drum and set out for the road, whilst the world filled with soldiers and hubbub. Rostam, the famous world-champion, rode out for two stages along with his son, after which they in parting gave each other many kisses on their cheeks and heads. Rostam like a lion turned back from the road, whilst Farāmarz, the brave warrior, for his part led his army towards the province of Khargāh, having dipped the tip of his sword of glory in vengeance. He urged his army on fast as the wind, as he happily approached the border, and after a three-day journey the exalted Farāmarz and his army dismounted there.

There was a champion there, a celebrated hero of enlightened mind named Ṭoworg, valiant, proud, strong and rugged, who was the margrave of that province of Khargāh. He was also a kinsman of Afrāsīyāb and commanded an army endowed with rage and power. Whilst Farāmarz stayed there, he called for a scribe who had elegance and understanding, and told him to write an agreeable letter to that renowned man, filled with advice and lessons and written with pomp and pride, and inform him about his business point by point.

Farāmarz writes a letter to Ṭoworg and has it delivered by Kāhū

As the scribe prepared his reed, he first cut off its end at a slant. Now that its head had been cut off, the reed became eloquent and like a polo stick immediately played ball. First, as the pen touched paper and made notations upon it with black musk, it wrote: 'In the name of the Lord of life and of the world, Who reveals things open and hidden, the Lord of Mars, Venus and the sun, because of Whom hatred exists and because of Whom love exists. He is the world-ruler, the sovereign of the heavenly wheel, He is worshipped from high to low. From him comes repose, fear and hope, and because of Him black and white are visible. May His benedictions be upon the king of Iran, who has been His warp and woof since Āfrīdūn. You should know, distinguished, pugnacious Ṭoworg, what our great king said to us: "Formerly it would not happen that the Tūrānian army could pass through the province of Khargāh. Since the times of the God-worshipping Manūchehr, when Tūrān was crushed by his sword, no one, neither king nor the warriors from the army of Tūrān, had access to this province. But now, how come that the Turks have settled in this province and how come they have taken hold of those lands?! As soon as the lion had abandoned the woods, the fox bravely entered the forest. You must go and quickly empty the country of them, hack off their heads with your sword of vengeance."

'I have come now on the order of the king to this province, with my elephants, drums and soldiers, for I will not allow anyone from the land of Tūrān to pass through these lands. I will clear Khargāh of the Turks. It is with goodness that I have shown you the way. If wisdom shows you the right way, you will know by contemplating good and bad that by the covenant of the pure-minded Keykhosrow you have no foothold in this province. It will be better for you if you leave behind in this province your treasure and army, as well as your throne, diadem, crown and tiara, and if you depart. May you not receive any retribution for this evil. Heed this advice of mine filled with dread and fear: you must not stretch yourself beyond your limits. For if you rebel against my speech, I will not allow your body to keep its head. I will also lay the province of Khargāh to waste and I will make a trapping-place for you out of the mouths of lions; I will turn your entire army, the lower and higher ranks, into food in the bellies of lions and wolves.'

When the letter was completed, it was rolled up. The ambitious conqueror, filled with anger and dispute, ordered a courageous and intrepid man, whose name was Kāhū the lion, to gird his loins tightly for the journey and go to that pugnacious man. The noble Kāhū made preparations for his journey and quickly left, hurrying to Khargāh.

Ṭoworg is informed about the arrival of Farāmarz's messenger, he sends out Mahāwar to receive him and they come before Ṭoworg; Ṭoworg's answer to Kāhū

When he arrived close to the border of Khargāh, he selected a commander from amongst his warriors and told him to go happily, cheerfully and with an enlightened mind to that margrave and tell him: 'An exalted, sharp-witted man has come with a message for you from Farāmarz, who is full of conflict and bustle, and he will not stand around for long upon the road.' The messenger went like the raging wind, or just like an arrow that had sprung from a bow, and when he arrived beside the river on the border of Khargāh, he saw a mountain: it was a fortress rising up from the depths of the water and reaching up into the heights with its top in the clouds, where the sun acted as its gate-keeper and Saturn kept watch over its roof. It had been raised up so close to the heavenly wheel that it scratched the cheeks of the moon with its bricks. A learned wise warrior has said that the son of Fereydūn suffered his affliction there. It was filled with palaces and gardens and full of running water. Here, a decrepit old man would become young. It contained arms and soldiers in abundance and provided the desert plain of Tūrān with colour and fragrance.

The envoy approached the foot of the fortress and requested admittance from the gate-keepers there. He said, 'The exalted Kāhū is this very moment coming towards your renowned leader from Farāmarz, who is making preparations for war. What will that bold knight Ṭoworg say? As we were travelling, he told me, "Go ahead and bring them information about us."' One of the warriors went inside and spoke to the army leader, who was amazed when he heard this. He ordered them to grant him access, and when the envoy had entered the court, he made his tongue like an arrow and his heart like a bow and told him that Kāhū was coming in a hurry. When the warlike, intrepid Ṭoworg heard this, he selected a man like a lion from amongst his warriors to go and receive the hero Kāhū, and ride towards him with banners and drums. That renowned man, who was called Mahāwar, arranged his affairs to go like the wind with several chiefs, shouting and raging, in order to receive the bold man.

He crossed in a boat and rode in haste towards Kāhū, like an arrow from a bow. When the lion-slayer Kāhū saw him, he drew up ranks opposite Mahāwar. The two nobles approached each other and Kāhū asked the other about things great and small. After that, they travelled towards Ṭoworg, so that he could convey the message from the great warrior. He laid that letter before him and a scribe read it, whilst Ṭoworg listened. That intrepid man became agitated and exclaimed, 'Why should I keep my words hidden? Even if Farāmarz is skilful with a sword, I am no less than he in bodily strength. Nor is my king less than his king; at a time of war he is a hundred times greater than he. No one in the world will ever see in his dreams a fortress, an army, a people and a river filled with water like these. Who is he to tell me to relinquish this fortress and depart, so that he can be the new army leader?! Since that young man sees great power in himself, he will undoubtedly rely on his own strength. Does he not know that even though an elephant is brave, he will weaken in the claws of a lion? I will not cast aside my reputation and honour and I will not turn away from him at the time of battle.'

For three days he entertained Kāhū as his guest, among his own eminent men and companions. On the fourth day, he told him to go to that renowned hero and say to him, 'O, man without understanding or intellect, a person of clear insight would certainly not say this. You in your impetuous actions do not know that I have raised my head in every gathering. And then you tell me to abandon my homelands and my court and to go to the army of Tūrān?! Arrange your affairs and take no rest at all, for I will make preparations for battle. Certainly, you will not stay alive; fate has led you from Iran to this province. I will make you the guest of my mace and sword, I will shower you with arrows like rain from a cloud.'

Ṭoworg leads his army to war against Farāmarz and Kāhū takes his letter of reply to Farāmarz; Farāmarz leads out his army against him and Ṭoworg devises a plan to make a night attack

When Kāhū turned away from there, he swiftly travelled along the long road. The bold Ṭoworg arranged his affairs and led his army out of the fortress to the plain. He also brought out his apparel of war and his arms, together with his trumpets and drums, while the desert became dark as ebony. Such an army came from the mountain to the plain that the earth-bearing bull[3] was stupefied by its agitation. The hooves of the horses caused the heart of the mountain to tear and dirt was scattered up to the face of the sun. The dust of the army transformed the surface of the water into such a state that a camel could run upon it at full speed. The king of the stars became astonished at the noise of the warriors on those mountains and plains. Ṭoworg quickly crossed the river and set off, wending his way towards Farāmarz in haste.

In the meanwhile, when Kāhū had arrived at a gallop with Farāmarz of enlightened mind, he told the great champion what he had heard from

Ṭoworg in its entirety. When the army leader heard this, he jumped up and said, 'I will join my sword with that malignant Turk!' He immediately blew the horn and led his army out, his steed scattering dust up to the sun. As they in one body approached the enemy, the world became as obscure as the dark night. He ordered his celebrated army to dismount at the water's edge and they set up the pavilion of the select champion on the plain of the Tūrānian land.

Between the two armies were two parasangs and, as they alighted, night came on. It was a night darker than ebony and the stars were shining like sandarac. Farāmarz ordered a patrol to go around the desert and go behind the watch of the other army. The Turkish horsemen became aware of this and hurried towards their army leader. They told the warlike lion Ṭoworg, 'The feisty warrior Farāmarz has arrived, he has dismounted in these plains and valleys, but he surely has no information about us. It would be advisable that we perform a night attack upon them and turn the grass the colour of jujube fruit.' The ill-advised Ṭoworg then said, 'Great men and bold warriors, we must this very moment strike against them and with our swords pierce their hearts and eyes!'

Ṭoworg makes a night attack upon Farāmarz and Farāmarz fights him and kills Ṭoworg's champion Qolūn; Ṭoworg flees

Two ranks of ten thousand suitable warriors moved out of that innumerable army, with their weapons of war and equipped for the fight, brave horsemen, strong and powerful. He spoke to them as follows: 'Go off road and quickly ride along a shortcut. You must suddenly throw yourselves upon them and tear out the hearts and eyes of the enemies.' They set their minds to it, prepared themselves and galloped away. There was no sound of the horn and no beating of the drum during the night that was turbid at the time of cock-crow, as they approached the Iranians, all with their loins girded tightly for battle.

The patrol of warriors from the Iranian army amounted to more or less a thousand on the road, whilst the other illustrious men had one by one lain down, tired from all their galloping. All the tired and sleeping men still wore their coats of mail on their chests; no one had even loosened his belt. All the horses of the warriors stood strong in their horse armour and saddled-up. As Ṭoworg's army approached the army camp of the great champion during that night as dark as dirt, the patrol all of a sudden engaged with those warriors. A clashing of swords, maces and arrows erupted, and the desert turned into a pool of blood from the heroes. That tumult and hubbub and those shouts that the pugnacious men directed at each other caused the Iranian warriors to jump up from their sleep, their hearts all filled with war and their heads with expedition. They mounted their swift horses like lions, whilst a cry rose up from the brave heroes. Because of all that tumult and hubbub and all the capturing and killing, no strength or understanding remained with the commanders. The night was dark and the blades of the swords were flashing like lightning from the heart of a dark cloud.

The army leader Farāmarz, the hero, mounted, full of anger and with his shimmering sword in his hand. Appearing like a mountain, he made an attack, all by himself, single-handed and without any companions. In one movement he uprooted them from their places and threw them into his own army camp. In each direction in which he performed an attack, he unhorsed two hundred intrepid men, as that tall champion moved about with his sword and with his mace, lance or lasso. Many of those pugnacious men were killed; above their heads a heaven of affliction had appeared. He then told his chieftains, 'You must handle the reins of your steeds as lightly as smoke.' Because of the actions of an unwise army leader, bad things happened to his army upon that battlefield. At that moment the moon showed its face, so that, although the night was dark, the moon showed the way.

There was a champion, Qolūn by name, rugged, ill-tempered and a spiller of blood, with the strength of an elephant and with a body like a mountain, so that a mountain would become helpless in a battle against him. He quickly went towards the champion and let out a cry: 'Hey, wicked man! You will now experience how real lions fight; if you can hold out, you will sacrifice your head!' Farāmarz filled with rage about Qolūn, clenched his fists and rode out from his army. On his own, the champion went in a gallop up to him, turned his reins towards him and then said to him, 'Hey, malevolent, useless man, you try and hold out awhile upon the battlefield!' When the large, bold Qolūn saw him, he came up roaring like a rapacious wolf, and as he arrived at a gallop next to the army leader, he drew forth his heavy mace from the saddle of his large horse. He lifted it up and struck the head of that lion-like man. The army leader turned his battle-horse, quickly came up behind him and grabbed him by the belt as if he was a polo-ball, then lifted him up from his leopard-skin saddle; it was as if he weighed no more than a gnat. He threw him head first with such force to the ground that his buttocks could not be distinguished from his neck.

He took his soul-robbing sword in his hand and once more showed his superiority over the Turks. He roared like thunder and let out such a loud cry that the mountains and the sea started agitating. His sword made the earth sodden from end to end, and the dust from his fights caused the heavens to bend, as he with his head-scattering sword and his battle-mace brought those famous men to annihilation. In this manner, until the dark night tore apart and the sun threw its reflection from the sky onto the ground, the army leader and his champions did not rest, whilst their swords were scattering the heads of their enemies.

When Ṭoworg, the oppressor, saw what kind of bad things happened to his soldiers, he took flight from the large army, like a gazelle from the claws of a wolf. Behind them maces and swords and in front of them the river, their fortune had put its head to sleep: they at once set off from there and spilled into that deep river. Such are the workings of battle and war: they put one person's body at ease and another one's in pain. Ṭoworg and a group of noblemen arrived at the river like insensate men and in fear entrusted their lives to the boats. It was not a day for battle, war or tricks. They entered the fortress and shut the gate, their heads without helmets and their waists without belts.

Ṭoworg writes a letter to Afrāsīyāb and explains the circumstances of his situation

In pain and grief he wrote a letter to the land of Tūrān, addressed to Afrāsīyāb. He first praised the Creator, the victorious and omnipotent Lord: 'May His blessings be upon the Tūrānian king, the lord of Māchīn and of the land of Tūrān.' He next said, 'From the country of Iran an army has come, filled to the brim with anger and vengeance: Farāmarz, the noble-born son of the elephant-bodied hero, has come here with his troops. First, he sent a message to me saying: "Leave your province and forsake your reputation. Move from there to Tūrān without delay, and if you do not, come and prepare for war." I became fearful that I would have to flee from my domains, that I would have to leave this settlement of falcons for the owls, so I lined up my renowned soldiers, worthy men, suitable for combat. When that army opposed Farāmarz's army like a planet in the heavenly orbit and the moon, I conceived the idea first to attack by night, because in my heart the thought was steadfast that I would turn the desert into a sea with their blood when I would attack the heights by deceit. I led my army with verve during the dark night, at a time of drunkenness, rest and sleep. But when my soldiers drew their swords of vengeance, no assistance was proffered by fortune. The Iranians had laid an ambush, so when my army came in their midst, they at once opened their arms to receive us, killing many of us and defeating us. Now I am sitting with a thousand horsemen in my fortress, until the king gives me my orders, which I then will execute. Because I fear that that evil-conceiving man will prevail.'

As his messenger he sought a brave man, whom he told, 'You are a man of understanding, intellect and reason; you must not delay anywhere, if you are to deliver my letter to the king.' The messenger jumped up like the wind and headed for Tūrān, his head filled with thoughts.

Farāmarz distributes the booty amongst his army and takes counsel with his soldiers, and the soldiers' answer to Farāmarz; Farāmarz blocks the road in three places against the army coming to assist Ṭoworg

Farāmarz for his part, endowed with strength and force, looked over the battlefield from end to end: he saw the world filled with the corpses of the enemy and he saw the valleys and plains piled with heaps of dead men. Of the courageous Iranian men of battle also a thousand heroes were killed. The entire plain of Khargāh was strewn with riches, like a Chinese bazaar. There were also herds of Arabian horses in every direction where the Turks had abandoned them. He bestowed all those things upon his soldiers, upon each one in such manner as was to his liking.

He then said to his brave men of war, 'You brave men of understanding and worth, I have heard that the malevolent Ṭoworg and a number of horsemen have gone to the fortress, having found a passage across the river by boat after they had turned away from the battle against us. Since the enemy has fled into the fortress, this matter cannot be resolved by fighting them. I suspect that he has sent news to Tūrān about my doings, from beginning to end. Any moment now an army will come to him and raise its head up from the hollows to the heavens, so we must cross that water before an army from Afrāsīyāb arrives and matters will be different, because then the fortress will again be full of soldiers. We must quickly have recourse to a scheme to deal with him and bring that army and that fortress to ruin.'

His renowned men spoke in reply, 'Celebrated man and world-champion, we have girded our loins at your command and counsel, whether we are in good health or wounded. Do such as is your opinion on this matter.' When he had heard the answer of his courageous men, he galloped to the river's edge, crossed it by boat and performed his business: he circled the foot of the fortress and was amazed as he looked in every direction. He was hoping to find a place from where he could capture that fortress like a fish in his net, but as much as he went round it, there was no way into the fortress, behind or in front; he saw no space for a falcon to fly over it. Helplessly he turned back from that place.

The soul of that brave man was filled with reflection as he sat long devising a plan how he could bring about that battle by means of a scheme and perhaps overthrow the enemy. He had thirty thousand men of war from Iran and Zābolestān, both cavalry and infantry, and he divided the entire army into three parts. He selected two exalted men, endowed with power, and entrusted two companies to them. He then said, 'Renowned warriors, there are three roads from here to the country of Tūrān, upon which we must lie in wait. I entrust you with two of these three roads and you must at all times avoid any negligence. You must now march quickly and drive thoughts of sleep and food from your minds. Night and day there must be a patrol with watchmen to keep you informed around the clock, so that an army will not unexpectedly arrive and cause trouble for you. Because I have no doubt that this fortress cannot be taken in a hundred battles, I hope that the pure God will be our guide and I can obtain this province through force and intellect.'

After that, the two champions departed along those roads, having girded their loins for war. The other company he took upon himself, all the while amazed at those fortifications. Having mounted, he rode along the third road, as he reflected with his heart full of wisdom. In each direction he sent a thousand patrolmen, so that they would inform him about the fortress. The young intelligent man of glory and understanding kept his eyes and ears open to wise thoughts.

Ṭoworg's letter reaches Afrāsīyāb; an account of him conceiving a plan

Meanwhile, as the letter arrived in Tūrān, the king was informed in a fitting manner that a messenger had come from Ṭoworg to the exalted great king. Afrāsīyāb called him before himself, in order to hear what he would say about the mountains and the water. When he came, he kissed the ground and said, 'May fortune be joined with the king of Tūrān!', then gave him the letter. When the king had read it through, he was filled with anger and vengeance about the pain of the army. He thundered and remained confounded about this matter. He reviled the messenger and sent him away. Then he spoke as follows, 'O foolish man, who cannot discern a good thought from a bad one! Someone who has such a fortress of which the height is adjacent to heaven, and all he may need in victuals and food, more than can be counted, is stored in that fortress, which also contains running water and even cultivated fields, as well as proud knights that can capture demons, when he lets his army go to the plain to do battle, will he not undoubtedly make matters difficult for himself?! May that foolish man be cursed, that unworthy, malevolent man of bad descent!'

Next, he ordered a lion-like man to gird his loins tightly to seek revenge. He was a renowned and exalted warrior, who had seen many highs and lows during his acts of valour. He was called Shīrmard, as he continually performed battle against lions.[4] To that lion of a man he entrusted two ranks of ten thousand selected men of war, and he told him, 'Be insightful in your actions and protect the army against the enemy.'

Afrāsīyāb writes an angry letter to Ṭoworg, sends Shīrmard with an army to assist Ṭoworg and gives him counsel

He dictated a letter to Ṭoworg, reproachfully saying, 'O blustering wolf, who had told you to allow your army out of that fortified place onto the plains?! You should have stayed in your place, for there was no need to put one foot outside the fortress, because even if the evil-doing, malevolent enemy had settled down in those lands for years, they would not obtain anything but a mountain of bedrock and they would not even have to undergo a defeat. Because of your foolishness, O wicked man of bad stock, you in this manner led your army to ruin. Now that Shīrmard is coming over to you, do not make a tour of your army or your fortress, but entrust the army, fortress and people to him. Turn round and do not do battle against anyone.'

When he had sealed that letter and given it to that renowned lion from the family of Shīrū, he said to him, 'O brave Shīrmard, exalted, proud man and strong lion, you must go to the province of Khargāh and you must not take any rest along the way. You will be the protector of that province and army, you will be the leading king of those lands. As you travel, you must be vigilant that the warrior Farāmarz with his army does not block your way, because there are few horsemen like him in the world and he is a son of the elephant-bodied warrior Rostam. I hope by the Distributor of justice on the day of reckoning that you will be victor in this battle.'

When the brave Shīrmard, exalted, proud and a true lion, had heard this from him, he did not stop day or night from marching with the renowned men of his army. For three days and three nights he urged them onwards like the wind, in a manner that no one could remember before. On the fourth dark night he arrived and let his soldiers dismount beside the road.

The episode in which Farāmarz fights Shīrmard and Shīrmard is killed at Farāmarz's hand; an account thereof

They alighted in that region where Farāmarz's company was. When Farāmarz's patrol became aware of this, they went onto the road to look at that army, in order to find out who they were and why they were hurrying so in the middle of the night. When they had seen them, they told their champion, and the heart of that famous man became happy because of this. He knew that that army had come in the dark night to that place to seek revenge, that they were soldiers who had hurried from Tūrān towards the fortress in search of battle. He ordered his soldiers to mount and to gird their loins for an attack. In the dark night resembling a mountain, they came up like a black cloud over the heads of that army, from which cloud a shower of arrows rained down. Everyone was shouting in the clamour and bustle.

When Shīrmard awoke from his sleep, he confusedly made his way to his steed. He mounted his swift horse, spurred it on from its place like fire and let out a roar in the manner of a lion; you would have thought a whole body of men had come down from the universe. With his mace, his javelin and his sharp sword he brought down the day of resurrection upon the Iranians. Many of the Iranian soldiers were killed and no one was left with any power on the battlefield.

On the other side, Farāmarz had remained uninformed, so he felt rancour about the fight by the enemy when the heroes who had been on the battlefield said to the champion of the army, 'Many of our celebrated men have been killed at the hands of that demon without fear or trepidation.' The army leader spurred on his grey war-horse and attacked Shīrmard, with his mace in one hand and his bow on his saddle. When he saw him, he said to him, 'Hey, malevolent man, you saw the woods empty of feisty lions, so that you now could bravely come to fight. You will experience a battle against men of war; if you remain alive, you need not fear a crocodile.' Shīrmard answered, 'Bad-natured Sīstāni, you will be taught courage, strength and skill. You have placed your own foot in a snare; as you sought a reputation, you came to disgrace.' He came close to the champion, holding his battle-sword in his fist. They fought with each other in such a manner that you would think they had merged with each other. When a sword swung at the head of the champion, the young warrior lifted his shield above his head, so that the sword that was aimed at his head hit the shield. The army leader spurred on his horse from its place, lifted his iron mace to his neck and from his full height hit

Shīrmard on the head in such a manner that he, wearing his helmet and clad in his coat of mail, was broken in pieces and was thrown down onto the ground of the battlefield.

Farāmarz drew his sharp sword from its scabbard, roared like thunder and called out his name. He threw himself upon the large army as if he were a lion and the enemy a herd of cattle. With his shimmering, fire-sparking sword, he like the wind kept on rendering them abject. Then the leaders of the Iranian horsemen, as they saw their famous champion, all drew their sharp swords in vengeance, so that it was like the day of resurrection for the Tūrānians. When they saw that their celebrated commander had been killed, the renowned men all turned their heads and started to flee in a herd, leaving their goods and chattels behind. After the horsemen of the Iranian army had put many of them to death, they pillaged their army camp, all their tents, horses and pavilions. When Farāmarz, the army leader of enlightened mind, and his renowned and courageous men were done with their fight against the enemy, they marched towards their own encampment.

An account of Farāmarz finding Afrāsīyāb's letter that he had sent via Shīrmard to Ṭoworg and of Farāmarz devising a scheme and taking Shīrmard's clothes

At that moment, one of the illustrious Iranians came before the champion and said, 'Among the tents of the combat-eager Turks I found a letter that had fallen to the ground.' He handed it over and it was read by a noble secretary. It was a letter written on silk, filled with anger and vengeance and full of effervescence and passion, from the army leader of Tūrān, King Afrāsīyāb, addressed to the noble, pugnacious Ṭoworg, saying: 'When the large army has reached you, you must entrust your province and your men of war to this renowned Shīrmard.' When that letter had been read to the champion, his champion's heart filled with thoughts about this. Through what plan could he grab hold of the fortress, even if this were to bring him honour by means of a ruse? But a wise man has said: 'When matters become tight at a time of turmoil and when one's hands are about to remain devoid of skills, it is better to set your heart on finding a stratagem. By means of a scheme, a wise man of great insight will catch the head of a wicked demon in his noose.'

He wrote a letter to each of the two companies that had settled near the main roads and told them, 'O intelligent, skilful and expert knights, you must know that through the twists of fate an army came from the land of Tūrān towards us on the battlefield and we drew our swords of vengeance at each other. Eventually, God came to my assistance and their luck was turned upside down. I thus believe that that famous army was going towards the fortress and I now hold a thought in my heart to let my company pass in that direction. As soon as you are informed about the position of me and my great and glorious company, you must march along the road according to the customs of war and battle, and raise the dust. When you have come close to my company, you must for a while fight ardently. Then you will start fleeing from me, so that I can pass in front of you. When the army leader Ṭoworg sees from the fortress that you are afraid of this large army, he will believe that my brave company has come from Tūrān, sent by the king. They will open the gate of the fortress, and I will immediately lead my army at a gallop into that fortress. Perhaps I can seize the fortress by means of this stratagem, for I have no plan other than this one.'

The messenger left and the army leader, that warrior, counted each one of his soldiers. He ordered them to don tunics and helmets according to the custom of the Tūrānian army, as well as take coats of mail, horses and even battle-swords of the same kind as they have in the land of Tūrān, and then to arrange themselves on the road while wasting as little time and effort as possible. Farāmarz dressed himself in Shīrmard's coat of mail and also his helmet, took his horse and war-banner, and then mounted, even holding his blood-shedding sword in his hand. Galloping with his army, he headed for the road, with the intention of razing those fortifications to the ground.

Farāmarz devises a stratagem, takes counsel with his soldiers and tells them an anecdote; Farāmarz goes to the gate of the fortress and gives the letter to Ṭoworg

Meanwhile, the champion's messengers had reached those generals, and as soon as they had read the letters, they got up and hurried towards Farāmarz the hero. When those two companies had come close by and darkened the day with their dust, the three companies engaged with each other in such a manner that they all hit each other on the head with their maces and swords. For a while both companies went fleeing from the battlefield, whilst the proud, exalted man followed them in reproof for half a parasang, before he turned round. When the warriors in the fortress saw this from afar, those lion-like men of the fortress started shouting. They believed that the Iranian horsemen who were fleeing from the battlefield in this manner were Iranians running in flight from the army of the king of the Tūrānians, and they said, 'We, too, should make for the plains and eradicate the Iranians root and branch.'

As the soldiers and their commander were talking, the army headed for the fortress. The young, exalted man of sun-like glory, that wise and eminent famous man, loosened the reins around the neck of his horse and went galloping in the manner of Āżargoshasp, arriving in a rush at the fortress's court. He told them, 'I have a letter from King Afrāsīyāb for the great warrior, the army leader and commander-in-battle Ṭoworg. The exalted king also privately talked to me about the army and spoke as follows: "My head has filled with anger and my heart has become heavy because of the doings of the Iranians," and the king was distressed and his soul was disturbed because of that trouble with the province, the fortress and the army. Having selected an army for this purpose, which the prescient king of kings gave to me, he said to me, "You must go to the fortress with your army to be of assistance to them and give them good advice. Be the guardian of the fortress, as well as its supporter, and make sure that no harm comes from Iran."' The letter was handed over, and when they had read it, all their souls lifted up with happiness.

Ṭoworg opens the gate of the fortress because of Farāmarz's deceptive scheme, Farāmarz fights with Ṭoworg and kills him and his army and takes the fortress; an account thereof

They opened the gate of the fortress and the strong lion immediately entered the height of the fortress. A pugnacious leopard once said to its cub: 'O skilful, sharp-clawed child, never unknowingly make haste with your business; reflect and observe it from top to bottom. Do not consider yourself safe with a stranger's sweet speech, especially at a time of dispute and battle, and do not submit your head to disgrace. At such a moment you must distinguish delay from haste. Perform an examination and fear for a trap; investigate in depth the nature of the speech, for behind a veil of friendship an enemy will show his power when it is time to overthrow his opponent.' Since the foolish leader did not inquire about the stranger in this surprising affair and did not suspect any ruse of the enemy, he thus gave his fortress up to ruin.

The noble and strong Farāmarz by means of this stratagem threw himself upon the fortress. The army leader and his warriors as one man drew their swords on the mountain ridge and put many of them to the sword, without any means of delay or a road to escape. The entire mountainside was strewn with heaps of corpses and the rocks and soil became entirely smeared with blood. The commander Ṭoworg quickly came up to contend with the great champion, but Farāmarz hit him once on the head with his sword, so that his body at once fell into two pieces: by means of this blow to the head, both the renowned man and his horse were brought to perdition. The wave of blood that rose up from the sea of swords at its highest point reached the moon. As the blood started flowing through the diamond-bright river, the souls started flowing from the bodies together with the blood. This blood made the skirt of the mountain become like the river Jeyḥūn, so that the mountain stood up to its middle in blood.

In this manner, by the time the dark night arrived, neither the fortress nor its guardian and warriors remained. They razed all the walls of the fortress, dug them up and wholly removed them. The women and children came lamenting to the army leader and begged for protection: the famous leader spared them and then ordered the baggage to be loaded. They departed and, now the fortress had been razed to dust, those decimated fortifications became flat as the plain. That lion-hearted man happily came down, having turned the black rock into mud with his sword.

A wise, learned warrior once said this: 'You must not entrust an army to an ignorant man. Never consider yourself safe from the enemy, for you will be scattering dust over your own head.'[5] When the army leader was finished with the fortress, he was happy in his heart and his face was like the new spring. He had fulfilled his heart's wishes by means of that battle, sewing the eyes of sorrow shut with cheerfulness.

Farāmarz writes a letter about his victory to King Keykhosrow with an account of his taking of the fortress and his killing of Ṭoworg and Shīrmard; the letter is received by King Keykhosrow

He dictated a letter in accordance with the rules and customs to the king about his victory over that province and fortress. Like a black-faced, silver-beaked bird his words took flight through the air; from its beak the pearls of style were mixed with musk onto the surface of the dry paper. They rained fluidly onto the paper's surface from the sea of thought, as they were completed by the pen's nib in one swift movement just like night appears out of the day. He opened his lips in the name of God: 'The Lord who possesses all power, the soul-bestowing and omnipotent Guardian of the world, Who created the sun, the heavens and the world, and Who created place and time and our state of being, may His blessings be upon the king of Iran, who holds the warp and woof of the tapestry of the world.

'World-ruler and famous conqueror of lions, king and monarch in all seven climes, by whose glory my army on an auspicious day marched in vengeance towards the province of Khargāh: the king with his sun-like glory will have heard that there was a fortress in those lands, over which the constellation of the Eagle, if it made haste, could with difficulty find a passage. As far as the world-leader has looked around the world, no one had seen such a fortress or ever heard of it. There was a champion, whose name was Ṭoworg, an exalted man, intrepid and strong, a world-ruler and a remembrance of monarchs, a crown-bearing king going back through the generations. He was from the stock of the praiseworthy Fereydūn all the way down to Sīyāwakhsh of pure religion, who was commander of the province of Khargāh and guardian of the army with his manliness. That renowned leader sat in that fortress as the protector of the province, fortress and lands. When he received information about our actions, he crossed the river and came to face us. He had put together an army and prepared for war, having cleared his heart of fear and anguish. He plotted a night attack and came galloping, but by the glory of the king of kings with good intentions, I uprooted him from his place in such a manner that I could launch him senseless into the river, and I lifted up so many soldiers from their places that I could fill the river with them. At the end of the matter, that evil-doing bad man crossed the river in reproof and rebuke, ensconced himself with several of his men in the fortress and shut the gate. We made many tours of the fortress, but there was no place for a skirmish or battle. When I had become hopeless about that difficult place, our pure God became my guide. An army sent by Afrāsīyāb suddenly arrived, twisting and turning.'

In the letter he also gave a full account of the actions of their commander Shīrmard and of his stratagem for the fortress and on the battlefield, and then he dispatched a messenger fast as the wind. He further said: 'Since I am finished with matters here, I will prepare my army to go to the Indians. I will dwell in this province until Your Majesty gives me orders to take to the road.' A large amount of tribute and taxes from those lands, such as ten cowhides filled with pearls and rubies, which had been placed in the treasury of that fortress and had been gathered with effort from every place, he sent to the king of his country. The tongues of the heroes were full of praise for him.

The messenger travelled the long road with a caravan loaded with spoils and treasures. When he arrived at the court of the auspicious monarch, he was brought straight from the road before the king. He touched the ground with his face, recited many praises of the crown and the throne, and then gave the king the letter from the champion. When it had been read, the king became happy and of an enlightened soul and bestowed many praises, straight from his heart, upon that famous warrior, protector of the army, as well as upon Rostam and Zāl and their family, for the manner in which they had raised their young offshoot.

King Keykhosrow's letter of reply to Farāmarz son of Rostam; Farāmarz receives the letter and he is pleased

He told his secretary that very moment to prepare a letter of reply on silk to that honourable descendant of champions, who had removed the heads from his enemies with his sword, that exalted, eminent and famous man who had raised up his head amongst the warriors of the world, that army leader and son of the elephant-bodied warrior, a pillar for the warriors and an exaltation for the people: 'Blessings from the Lord Who provides our daily bread upon Garshāsp as well as Sām and Narīmān, who had such an offspring and lineage. May the family never be without sons and descendants. We received your blessings and salutations, may this message from us reach you in a similar manner. From beginning to end I have read all the things that you related in your letter, O man of skills. It suits you thus, son of a champion, that no bad actions are caused by your behaviour. As soon as you have read this letter, you must without delay set in order and lead your army towards the Blacks! Go quickly and move onwards to the Indians; wash their entire country with your sword! Empty that land in its entirety of the sorcerers and rescue the world from the hands of evil people! Ask for what you need in terms of treasures or soldiers; no one will block the way for your request.' Upon the letter he placed a seal like pitch, containing ambergris mixed with perfume. The king gave the messenger a robe of honour, about which the entire army became amazed, as well as a horse, armour, a tiara, a belt, horse's tack, a saddle-cover and a golden hatchet. In all goodness he gave him many best wishes, so that the messenger's heart became happy with the king. He kissed the ground and then jumped up and left. He made his preparations and hurried towards Farāmarz.

He quickly reached the champion with his letter from the monarch of all monarchs. He kissed the letter and placed it before him, passing on the salutations from the king and his army. When the exalted man had read the letter, he praised the world-ruler at length. He laughed and became happy with the king of kings, saying, 'May his throne and his justice forever stay with him!', whilst the leaders and heroes of the army also expressed their praise of his court. In that mood of happiness they got up from their places and arranged a pleasant feast. The wine was purple and their hearts were happy; the world had changed and its rule was rejuvenated. The voices of the musicians changed the plains and valleys of the world into another Paradise. The cheeks of the fairy-faced servants who held cups of wine in their hands had obtained their colour from the wine cups; their faces were reflected in the wine cups and there were roses, tulips and narcissi at their feet. During the long days the heart of the exalted man did not take repose for one moment from the banquet and the presents. For one month he bestowed and drank in this manner, whilst no memory of fear and pain entered his heart.

Farāmarz sets off for India and he entrusts the province of Khargāh to his deputy and gives him counsel; several words of admonition are spoken

At the end of the month, the exalted young man with insight and design ordered the trumpet to be blown and he moved the army on from its place. He entrusted the entire province of Khargāh to one of his champions, named Nastūr, and he gave him an army of brave warriors. He told him: 'Be continually on guard and protect the army from the enemy! If the Turks come and attack, you must not abandon your position and you must inform Dastān in Zābol, because of whom the great throne lasts: he will send you help in any situation and elevate your head to the turning heavens. Since he is the leading champion, what then can you fear in Zābol from evil people?' Having said this, he turned to face the road, from which road he raised the dust up to the moon. He went galloping to India and saw that country of Jādūstān.[6]

Hey, wise, alert-hearted man, who has entrusted his intelligent heart to knowledge, see what a learned man said, when he joined his speech with counsel. He spoke as follows, as he made his tongue loquacious: 'People must, both publicly and privately, arrange themselves in accordance with ten qualities, because through those ten, their souls will be adorned. Firstly, one shall be in concord with the Creator of the world, openly and secretly. Next, he shall be intelligent when opposed with good or bad, and he shall not take one step towards injustice. Whoever performs justice with glory and equity will call justice to mind in his actions. Thirdly, he shall treat his desires with oppression, because if he wants a sweet drink, he will be given poison to drink. Anyone who suppresses his own desires will not obtain anything bad from his actions. Fourthly, he who discourses with a king shall live with respect and pious wisdom, for anyone who is arrogant towards a king will in the end experience nothing but the sword and basin.[7] Fifthly, a man of a pure religion lives with compassion with regard to his subjects, because when he exercises compassion towards a subject, he will catch the head of a good reputation in his snare. Sixthly, he shall suffer the load of his malevolent enemy without thinking of a reproof, because a man who endures patiently has foresight and will win over the enemy at the time of dispute. Seventhly, when he has power, he shall be wise, clear-sighted and a seeker of the right way. He shall display liberality towards a poor man and keep harshness and stinginess away from his heart. Eighthly, he shall extinguish for himself any association with ignorant and common people and with men who are ignoble and imperfect, so that he will swiftly escape from them. Ninthly, he will be a friend to men out of wisdom, because in friendship he holds the chief substance and not the shell. In his goodness he will not withhold counsel, even if swords are raining from the clouds onto his head. And tenthly, he shall consort with a man who worships knowledge and through humility gain pre-excellence over him: when he sees that he is lowly next to him, he will be famous through that lowliness. If these ten qualities are brought to pass for a man, all his desires and hopes will be fulfilled. In this world he will be amongst those who do good deeds and at the last judgement he will also be amongst the bountiful. May God, the Creator of the world, Who has brought forth the moon, Saturn and the sun, be content with His mute servant. May wisdom be of profit for his foundation and his soul!' O, man who is fond of knowledge, I will now continue with the story about Farāmarz the lion!

Beginning of the episode in which Farāmarz writes a letter to the Indian Raja and has it delivered by Keyānūsh; an account of him giving the letter to the Indian Raja and his speech

When the skilful hero, prince of Sīstān, took his army to India, there was a man, the army leader of India, whose authority reached as far as the borders of Sind. By name and by title that man was 'Raja'; he was an illuminator of knowledge and had pure insight. He also had an army with elephants and apparel, and night and day he was occupied with warfare and power. He always said, 'No one on the face of the earth is like me in terms of valour at a time of anger and vengeance.' Thirty-six kings in India paid him yearly and monthly tribute and the number of his soldiers was unknown, since their measure was larger than could be said or heard.

When Farāmarz the hero arrived there, he had a wise secretary brought before him and dictated a letter to the Raja, so that he would get to know him through his pure insight. As he opened the door of justice and knowledge for him, he first made mention of the Creator of the world, the Lord without assistant, companion or partner; because of Whom secret and hidden things are visible: 'The Creator of the world is without need. Know that everything high and low is at His command. With His power He created things out of nothing and He even made gems appear out of the soil. The sun and the moon are at His command and because of Him the dark earth finds its rest. He is the Lord and we are His servants, who bow our heads at His order and command.' He further said, 'O powerful king, you have both a seal and a treasure, and a throne and a crown, you are king of the proud men of India, who from the borders of China to Sind stand at your command. You will certainly have heard that the pure Ruler of the world created the world and our dwelling-places from water, soil, wind and fire, and that He brought forth man from His bosom.

'Amongst the great men in the world no king has appeared like the pure-hearted Keykhosrow, with such a face, love, goodness and justice, with such strength, culture, glory and lineage. Because of his glory the world became fully secure and the actions of Ahrīman were destroyed. All the kings of the world are his servants and have bowed their necks at his command. Since the time when the Protector of the world chose him from amongst the great men and entrusted the land in its entirety to his kingship, no other name than 'Key' was used to indicate the kingship. Nobles and kings across the surface of the earth from end to end have sung his praises. This world-ruler was begotten by Sīyāwakhsh and is from the lineage of the insightful Fereydūn, who killed Ẓaḥḥāk of evil essence and bad stock and destroyed his offspring.

'You have never paid a visit to his court and you have never gone to his homelands. It would be appropriate if you submitted to his command, since he is the monarch of the world from beginning to end. Send tribute and taxes to his court and you will know that you will not have any trouble with him. But if you do not, I will with my sharp sword set fire to this land of India, these provinces on the plains of Jādūstān, and I will tear them out by their root and foundation from this land; I will make all the mountains and plains like a sea and I will turn the heights of this regions into flatlands. I remember a saying the king told me, when he loosened his tongue to give me counsel: "A man is wise and of a pure religion if he chooses to step aside from injustice and dispute." I have told you this, so that you will not say: "I am the sovereign of the people in India." If you do not heed all that is written in the letter, you will be sorry and you will be left with nothing but the wind. Now, if you are wise and insightful and take care in all your actions, you will step aside from war and strife and you will slumber at ease in the world.

You will keep your lands, treasure and army, your greatness and kingship and your throne and crown. A wise, learned man with insight knows that reproach is better than praise. It is also good to free the heart from pain and sorrow and make it happy in this transient world.'

When the letter, which had been written down more swiftly than the wind in musk on a camphor surface, had fully dried, Farāmarz placed his seal upon it and called a learned man with insight and justice. He was a renowned hero, named Keyānūsh, an experienced warrior endowed with intelligence and ambition. The commander then told Keyānūsh, 'Separate a sweet drink from poison. Take my letter to the supreme Raja, king of India and Kashmir and Rāy-barīn.[8] After reading the letter, you must speak words of such a kind as you judge right, as long as they are of use to you.' The intelligent Keyānūsh made preparations for the journey and opened the door of wisdom and sagacity. He set off and travelled to India, hurrying towards the Raja of enlightened mind, whose residence was in Qannowj, as were his treasure, army camp and chattels.

From the place where the champion of the army was staying it was a month's journey to reach Qannowj, but the brave Keyānūsh of auspicious intellect arrived at the Raja in ten days' time. He sent someone ahead on the road to inform the king and the army that a renowned messenger was coming from Farāmarz of majestic offspring. When the envoy of Keyānūsh, who was joined with purity, reached the master of ceremonies, he conveyed his message, and the chamberlain went to tell the king that a messenger with a crown was arriving. When the elect king was informed about him and about the business of Keyānūsh of pure religion, he ordered in accordance with custom that drums and elephants be arranged for five miles along the grounds. The brave men of India, bold horsemen and lions of Sind, went to meet him. The elephants carried brass drums, as well as golden cymbals and trumpets, and the heads of both the elephants and their drivers were decorated all over with golden bells and golden sparks.

The worldly-wise man entered the city and arrived at the court accompanied by pomp and pride. He walked in a stride towards the Raja and pronounced his blessings upon the court and the heroes. After the men of enlightened mind had sat down, he gave the king the letter from the champion, then conveyed him his salutations, showed his reverence and pronounced benedictions for a long time. A throne just like heaven had been placed there, made of gold and inlaid with pearls and gems. The entire foundation of the golden throne was of crystal and on it were paintings of lions, gazelles and onagers. Upon it the monarch of the Indians was seated, a young king with his ornamental bracelet and necklace. The king ordered a golden seat to be placed in the throne-room for Keyānūsh, who sat down on the golden seat, his belt fastened around his waist and his hand open.

At that moment, a wise secretary of enlightened mind came before the king and read the letter to him such as it was, reciting it in the Indian language whilst the monarch listened. The eminent Raja was upset about the letter and in anger knotted his eyebrows in a frown. In the Indian language he said to the translator, 'It has never been seen that the Iranians performed such boldness upon India, that they showed themselves quarrelsome and displayed ferocity! Even if Keykhosrow is the king of Iran, my crown is not new in this age. From father to son, down to my kingship, the king of India has had notoriety in the world, so by threat, counsel, fear or hope, should I not expect the tribute from India!? He certainly does not know who I am and in whose footsteps I follow in this country. If I lead my army to battle, with my elephants I will bring Iran to destruction!'

Keyānūsh gave the following answer: 'Astringency does not become an exalted man. I have some words to say to you, so listen for the sake of justice; there will be a time when you will remember this speech. You are a king and the leader of the Indians, but those foolish words will produce difficulties. You know, or perhaps you will have heard, that Keykhosrow, that victorious king, is a world-conqueror and a king with a fortunate star, whose wisdom is higher than the supreme heavenly wheel. On his own accord he came all by himself from the land of Tūrān to the country of Iran in the manner of lions, whilst two Tūrānian armies were chasing after him and without anyone to help him but fate. Those two armies had to turn back from him in such a manner that the gazelles on the plains were crying over them. The earth was a servant and the sky a slave to the glory of his greatness and emperorship. He crossed the river Jeyḥūn on horseback and arrived in Iran like Āżargoshasp. There was a fortress in the land of the Iranians which caused pain and affliction to the free men there because in that fortress upon a tall mountain sorcerers had grouped together in a multitude with demons. Not one man in that region dared pass by there to perform his business. With his Keyānid glory and his auspicious star, with his valour, warriorship and leadership, he emptied all those lands of them and exalted his noble crown to the heavens. He killed all the sorcerers, from beginning to end, then with his courage he grabbed the world in his fist. From the lands of the West to the region of the East, everyone has girded their loins for him. An army leader like Ṭūs of royal descent and a general like Gūdarz with his glory and justice, or two brave warriors like Lohrāsp and Ashkash, went like elephants and lions to fight a long-lasting war to avenge his father, in order to bring Tūrān entirely to destruction. It has not been very long since the news reached you of how they turned that country upside down.

'In this country, the son of the world-champion, the army leader Farāmarz of enlightened mind, has sent a message to you in goodness. Perhaps the sword of vengeance will stay in its scabbard, because a wise man at a banquet or feast does not unjustly seek a quarrel or a fight. But you talk to him in a quarrelsome way?! I see no end or conclusion to these words.'

The Indian Raja gives Keyānūsh, the messenger of Farāmarz son of Rostam, an answer; an account thereof

The king of the Indians in return gave him this answer: 'I have no need for these words. You must turn around from here, go quickly and take this answer of mine to that parvenu commander: "O warrior, upstart of an army leader, you have seen superiority amongst your relatives, but you have not measured the strength of real men and only praised your own force. You have performed battle against gazelles, but I am not an onager of the plains, nor are you a lion of prey. You will experience from me on the day of combat how a man at such a time performs manliness. I will not delay upon my royal throne, but I and my Indian sword on the field of war will in one thrust turn away Farāmarz and his knights and warriors from these lands."' A robe of honour was prepared for Keyānūsh, and a tiara, a tunic and a belt were sent for, after which the brave Keyānūsh with his golden tiara directly left the presence of the king.

The Indian Raja leads an army to fight Farāmarz, puts Tajānū at its advance guard and gives him counsel with regard to the battle against Farāmarz

The Raja moved from his palace to the fields and ordered the trumpet to be blown. Soldiers from China, Kashmir, India and Sind gathered at the gates of the Raja of India, who ordered the brave men to leave the city and go towards the valleys and plains. The army, of which each company came from a certain region, left India: there certainly must have been three hundred thousand horsemen, illustrious lance-bearers.

There was one champion, with the name of Tajānū, whose fame because of his valour had spread throughout India. He was like a demon, that formidable ugly man who had obtained his complexion from the smoke of the heat of hell. In height he was taller than thirty cubits, his teeth were like those of an elephant and his eyes were bloodshot. He had arms like an elephant's legs, the strength of a tiger and claws just like those of an intrepid lion. His speed was like the wind and his body was like a mountain. The ground became stupefied whenever he passed over it. The Raja gave him fifty thousand mounted warriors and brave men of war from his army, to go with the elephants, drums and tymbals and receive Farāmarz. He said to him, 'Champion of the army, night and day you must keep a patrol on the road. If the Iranians arrive quickly, you must with your lance take out every person who has designs on this kingdom. You must not leave any one of them in his place.'

Tajānū went fast as the wind and headed towards the Iranians, filled with vindictiveness. With all the roaring of the drums and the battle-horses, the noise of the warriors and the dust from the soil, you would think that the day of resurrection had arrived. The horses' hooves pounded the soil as in an assault, so that the dust collected in clouds, whilst the earth became like the mouths of a crocodile and a lion.[9] The world filled with tumult and shouts, so that the hearts of the depraved flowed from their bodies. In such a manner he led the army like a mountain, onwards until he reached the Iranian forces.

Farāmarz leads an army to fight the Indian Raja and the armies come to face each other; a description of the fight against Tajānū and them speaking with each other

Meanwhile, Keyānūsh the warrior in a hurry delivered the message such as he had carried it. When the army leader had heard the message from thence, his heart raged like fire about that answer. He ordered the drums to be tied to the raging elephants and he himself mounted his fast steed. The mountains were calling for help, as the trumpets blared and the drums and Indian bells brayed. He drove his army on like a strong wind, in his fist his Indian sword and his bow and arrows.

When the two armies had arrived close to each other, their hearts brimming with hatred and their heads full of war, the soldiers on both sides drew up in ranks, swords in their hands and foaming at the mouths. Farāmarz arranged the centre of the army, placing to his left Keyānūsh, the protector of the army. In the left wing was the lion of war Tokhwār, before whom at a time of battle a lion was humbled. At the front were forty huge elephants with harnesses draped over their bodies. On the backs of the powerful war-elephants sat brave, pugnacious archers, whose arrows could make a mountain fearful, with their chests thrust out and their belts tied tightly. And on the other side, Tajānū, the Indian commander with his coat of mail, mace and Chinese sword, arranged that battlefield from end to end with pugnacious warriors and feisty elephants, the elephants in front of the army, and behind them troops who had raised a blockade like a mountain.

When the right wing had come level with the enemy's left wing, a roar arose from the horsemen of war. Shouts from both armies reached the heavens, whilst the ground started boiling like the sea, as a result of the many maces raining down, from the arrow shafts and from the heat of the horsemen in their bustle. You would say that the world had turned into the mouth of a large dragon and that affliction was pouring down from heaven onto earth, because of all the dust from the horsemen and the heat from the swords. The arrows had become like rain and like a thunder cloud: there was a shower of arrows and a hailstorm of swords, whilst death was pouring out of the lightning from their rain showers.

The commander Farāmarz, that defeater of armies, with his soul-robbing, enemy-overthrowing sword made an attack upon the Indians, roaring and raging like a powerful elephant. As he brandished his sharp sword, he brought the day of resurrection down upon the Indians with his arms. With one blow he hacked two heads from their bodies and with his roars he levelled an entire group of men. Because of his mace the heart of the sky tore apart and because of his actions heaven laid its face on the earth. The world remained stupefied when his feet were in the stirrups and the earth strewed blood from its eyes out of terror for him. When his arrow travelled from its bow towards its goal, the heart of a valiant lion would tremble before it, and when he threw his lasso in a straight line from its coils, he would draw in heroes like a dragon with its breath. In this manner, numerous men from that famous Indian army were felled on the battlefield.

Tajānū for a while observed that lion of a man, as he annihilated the Indian warriors, then he cried out, 'Hey, feisty lion, army leader, overthrower of men and conqueror of heroes! If you can hold out on the battlefield, you will experience the fight of a pugnacious leopard!' The champion, that raging lion, replied to him, 'Hey, evil-doing, dark-souled demon! In one of my fights against a hundred impetuous demons just like you, their legs turn weak and their swords blunt. When I grab my lance at the time of action, I will bring the demons of the world to destruction. You dare speak these words in reproof to me?! You will experience my mace and my head-scattering sword! You now have surely walked into a snare, as you spoke immature words in haste.' Tajānū said to him, 'O, intrepid man, why must we talk like this about fighting? If you seek a fight, come and do battle. And if not, leave this place this very moment! I will grant you passage so that you can reach your country. May you not be washed in the blood of the army. You do not have the strength to fight me; a lion would flee from my attack. I have conceived pity for you, my heart is full of ease with affection for you. I feel regret for your youth and for your valour and heroics, since you with your army will all at once be killed on my plains and your enterprise will come to ruin. I command the lion-like men on this earth, exalted sword-wielding horsemen who display valour at a time of war and vengeance and who number exactly thirty thousand. It is contemptible for me to wrap up your army and it is a disgrace for me to even seek a fight with you. I will presently show you some skills that find approval with every champion.'

Tajānū kills Farāmarz's war-elephant and the Iranians are afraid of him; Farāmarz becomes angry with his soldiers and talks to them about the battle

There was a war-elephant at the front of the ranks which burned the ground with its ferocity and power. The brave Tajānū briskly ran towards the valorous elephant and roared like a fierce lion. Since the powerful elephant was disposed for battle, it threw that man like a raging elephant down on his face. The pugnacious man jumped up on the spot and grabbed the elephant's trunk in his fist. The huge elephant exerted itself greatly to free its trunk from the young man, so that the demon's striving and the elephant's resistance kicked up dust that turned the air to the colour of indigo. The elephant was seeking a path of flight away from him, so Tajānū, full of strife and anger, exerted himself with his strength and his power, making it seem as if the earth would tear apart, and he eventually tore off the elephant's trunk, causing the elephant to go running off for several miles. He grabbed another elephant by its leg and back, lifted it up and threw it onto the hard ground.

After that, he set himself upon the army like a lion upon an onager in the hunting grounds. He tore the centre of the Iranian army apart and by means of his fighting blew up a dust-cloud, so that the clear day became like a sea of tar that covered the faces of the sun and Mercury. The Iranian army scattered out of terror of him, and no one remained standing on the battleground. The army leader Farāmarz, that brave warrior, roared in the manner of an angry lion, his head filled with anger and wrath over his warriors. He let out a loud cry towards his army and shouted at his soldiers as follows: 'Are you not ashamed of your behaviour and your actions, of how your hearts filled with fear for that demon and you became dispersed amongst the hills and valleys?! What will you say to the king of Iran when you return to him tomorrow; what answer will you give him?! That the hands and feet of you all weakened in such a manner out of fear of an evil, dark-minded demon?' When they heard the shouts of the exalted lion-hearted man, the warriors became ashamed. Their faces burning from that reprimand, they hurried back to Farāmarz.

Farāmarz fights Tajānū, captures him in the noose of his lasso and ties him with chains to a tree; Tajānū escapes from his fetters and Farāmarz fights him again

Next, the famous knight went towards the demon and said to his opponent, 'Hey, blundering demon with your dark soul, you will now see my soul-scattering sword.' The fierce lion contended with the champion and a neighing rose up from both stallions. The God-fearing lion wanted to tie the hands of that malignant demon, so that he could take him alive before his king and thus bring him a new present from India. They made many attacks against each other, and eventually the son of the famous hero threw his lasso around the other's neck and pulled his dark body to the ground. The formidable demon strove hard to free himself from the lasso's noose: he inserted his arms and pulled, in his effort tearing the ground apart. The army leader up in his saddle spurred his horse on and encouraged the large animal to move. He took his cow-headed mace in his hand and hit the other hard on the head, so that it broke in pieces. That blow made Tajānū lose consciousness and he fell to the ground and became powerless.

The army leader requested the Iranians to tie him up immediately. They brought forty lengths of iron chains and a lasso of fifty loops, tied up his hands, head and feet and dragged him by those chains away from that place. There was a large tree of seventy cubits, and the vengeful lion-slayer ordered them to tie that demon tightly to the tree with those iron fetters and chains. He appointed a hundred feisty men as his guards, noble-born warriors of pre-excellence.

When the sun had set and the night was drawing close, the strong men of war separated from each other and Farāmarz, after his victory and his superiority on the battlefield, sent a patrol from his famous army into the mountains and valleys. After half of the dark night had gone by, that litigious warrior without fear or dread scattered soil to heaven in his anger. He strained his hands and broke his chains and fetters, then pulled out that large tree by its roots, roared, and with his fist killed a few well-known men from that famous army in their sleep. As he held a branch of the tree in his hand, the soldiers were afraid of that creature of obscure fate. A clamour arose to the left and to the right; no one knew why those cries were produced. The soldiers jumped up from their places because of that clamour and arranged the ranks and the centre of the army.

The army leader abruptly awoke from his sleep and in a hurry put on his coat of mail. He mounted his dun-coloured charger and, in one hand his mace and in the other his lasso, his helmet upon his head and his body dressed in an iron corselet, rode off in the manner of a roaring lion. He went to fight the demon like a fierce lion, or like an elephant of war against an intrepid crocodile. He put loops in the lasso in his hand, and he wore a frown on his brow and rage in his heart. He rode towards the demon that had escaped from his fetters and threw the lasso over that unfortunate devil. The ill-starred creature jumped out of the lasso's noose and threw the branch at that lion-like man, hitting the head of his horse, so that his steed fell on its side in pain. The army leader grabbed his heavy sword, raised it up and hit the warrior-demon on the head. But the blow from the skilful hero did not affect that pugnacious demon, who this time lifted up a rock from its place, a black stone that was heavier than a hundred weights. He threw that rock at the champion, so the young warrior lifted his shield above his head: the rock hit the shield and broke it into small pieces, but the heroic commander suffered no fracture. Farāmarz became distressed about that fight, having become involved in combat with the demon in such a manner, so the famous man brought his fist towards his quiver of arrows, took out an iron-pointed arrow of poplar wood and aimed that arrow, which could pierce through iron, at the contemptible Tajānū. As the back of the bow was curved by the bow-string and the loops on the crook of the bow met each other, the lion's roar descended from that new-moon curve in the manner of rain from a cloud. Again, that warrior of victorious fortune shot arrows at the chest of that dark-fated creature, letting a shower of death rain down on him, in the way springtime hail rains down. The shower of diamond-tipped arrows turned the ground around the unfortunate demon into a tight spot. His demonic body became like the body of a porcupine, as he was killed by the diamond-tipped poplar arrows.

When the Iranians saw Farāmarz's fight and how he had brought the demon of such a height down on his face, they all together took their swords in their fists and made matters tight for the Indians. They rode in a gallop towards that army, and when its famous warriors became aware of this, they unavoidably arranged themselves for the battle and prepared anew for the day of resurrection. On one side of the army, the warrior Keyānūsh performed an attack on that Indian army and put many of them to the sword, not holding the blows of his swords back from the soldiers. On the other side, the pugnacious lion Tokhwār, a cow-headed mace in his hand, threw himself upon the centre of their army and turned the ground beneath the Indians red and black. So much blood was spilled onto the ground that it produced a deep river. The mountains and plains became level with each other because of the blood, in which horses and warriors were swimming. The bodies of the dark-souled Indians had fallen about and blood was flowing from them like wine from a leather bottle. The night was dark and the dark-coloured Indians had no road to flee along and no place to delay in. In this manner, an army of such a diversity of experienced men brought them to destruction.

Such are the ways of the battleground. You must be bold when you want to obtain a crown. O wise man of exalted essence, if you want fame, you first must say: 'Forsake your head'.

The Indian Raja becomes informed about Farāmarz's battle; a description thereof

Any of those Indians who survived left, whilst their misfortune was crying over them. They brought the news to the Raja that the world had been emptied of Indians and that because of this newly arrived brave knight the heads of his illustrious men had become sated with battle. The king questioned them in depth about the doings of the army and about the battlefield: 'About whom are you so worried and full of talk; what kind of man is this war-seeking warrior?' They told the Raja, 'This champion who came in vengeance to the Indians is a young man who has not yet seen the world, whose musk-like nature has not yet been covered by mud. No wild lion has such strength and he can roar like a cloud. His two arms are like the legs of a huge elephant and he has the chest, shoulders and neck of a ferocious lion. His face is like spring, in height he is like a cypress, his body is like a mountain and his waist is as thin as a reed. No one has seen, or had ever seen before, such skills as that brave man displayed. Tajānū, from whose hands in combat no raging elephant could find a way to flee, was in the grasp of that brave lion-like man like a mountain sheep fallen into the claws of a lion. Whether by mace, by lance, by javelin or by sword, there is no fleeing from water or from fire: one cannot flee from fire or water, nor from earth, wind or an intense cold breeze, any more than from his sword or his arrows. That experienced lion causes amazement. Perhaps

Your Majesty should receive him. After this, we do not know what that man of skills will bring about in this country and these homelands. Who will fight against him at a time of battle? For he considers fighting a feast and a banquet.'

An account of the Indian Raja leading an army to fight Farāmarz and Farāmarz being informed; Farāmarz talks with his soldiers about going to the Raja in the manner of an envoy and their answer

When the astonished Raja had heard them talk, he thundered and quickly stood up in his place. He ordered his endless army of pugnacious and renowned knights from Kashmir and Qannowj and from India and Sind, with their Indian swords and their Chinese scimitars, to assemble at his gate as soon as possible and to trample the bodies of their enemies underfoot, and he ordered seven hundred elephants, raging like the river Nile, to be brought. Harnesses were draped over them, so that they, together with the swords and lances, became like huge mountains. The armour of the horsemen and the massive elephants caused the mountains to sink as low as if they were plains and the ground started shaking like a ship on water, whilst the day darkened with the black dust. Such an army marched from India, as well as from the margraves of Jādūstān, that if an engineer were to count it, he would find more than five hundred thousand. As they set foot outside the city, a clamour rose up from the drums and the Indian bells. The roaring of the drums and the trumpets and the noise of the horses with their iron hooves was tearing apart the heart of the bedrock mountain, and as their sound reached the wheel of heaven, you would wonder if the nine verdigris-coloured heavenly spheres might turn upside-down from the noise of the clarions. They travelled for three stages in that manner like a black mountain, making the world dark with the dust of the army, and then they alighted, the soldiers spreading out along seven parasangs over the ground.

On the other side, Farāmarz of heroic stock was driving his army onwards as fast as the wind. When he arrived close to the Indians, he addressed his nobles and warriors as follows: 'I need an envoy with good judgment, so that he can learn about the circumstances of the Raja. For they certainly are informed about us and they must be preparing their affairs or already be on their way.' Farāmarz the lion sent out a brave renowned man with experience, and when he had reached the army camp of the Indian Raja, whose army accoutrements were joined with those of the raja of Sind, he observed the knights one by one, then he quickly returned to the champion and spoke with that famous man: 'There must be more than five ranks of a hundred thousand war-elephants and men of battle, a lot of renowned men about to go to war.'

When the army leader had heard these words from him, he drew up a different plan and said to his illustrious nobles, 'From my experienced soldiers and knights I sent a man to quickly go and return, with the purpose of gaining information from the spies. He told me that the ground was filled with the maces and Chinese swords of the men from India, Kashmir and Sind, that seven hundred huge elephants were prepared and that the earth stretched for seven miles beneath the army. He himself does not know the number of soldiers and he talks about nothing but their excess. I now have a plan in mind to go and explore that army a while: I will go to him as a messenger, a warrior and nobleman from the land of Iran. I will see how and with how many the soldiers are and I will look around a bit on the battlefield. I will converse with him about the good and bad things of olden days of every kind. I will regard him with valour and wisdom, after which I will block his path to war.'

The nobles prepared an answer to him, jumping up from their places with love in their hearts: 'How can this wish be fulfilled? May our eyes not be filled with bloodied tears because of this. We do not see any reason for this wish; do not run bedazzled into the environs of calamity. A wise man would not judge it right to place his foot in the mouth of a dragon and he would not acknowledge any of those sorcerers, those malevolent Indians of evil stock. If any of them recognises you, you will not stay safe for long in the world. If you are destroyed at their hands, what will we say tomorrow to our king? Or to our world-champion? Whose soul will remain in his body?! We do not see any wisdom or solution in this action and it will not find approval with the king.'

He gave them the following answer: 'Have no fear, for in the end we have no other bed than the ground. Even if I have another hundred thousand years left, my business will eventually end in the earth. It is certainly better that I leave behind my good reputation, if I in my valour nevertheless am to be slain. No life lasts for ever, so it is better that courage is remembered. A brave man told an aphorism, when he came face to face with a fierce lion: "When a young man chooses a reputation of valour, he will not fear a fight with a raging lion." A valorous man who seeks to abstain from calamity will be afflicted by a bad reputation.' Whatever his renowned men would say, that young champion would not listen.

Farāmarz entrusts his army to Homāyūn, son of Zawāre, and gives him counsel with regard to his army

Homāyūn, the famous defeater of warriors, who was a son of that intrepid knight Zawāre, who was the same age as and of a similar appearance to Farāmarz and whose heart always was full of love for him, this brave and exalted man with widespread ambitions had with his valour spread his fame around the world. The proud and pure-bodied Farāmarz appointed him commander of his army and said to him, 'O man with glory and intellect, whilst I am gone, you must keep an ear open for me! I am entrusting you with the drums, the elephants and the soldiers. Stay all the time informed about this place. You are now the foremost man of this army, protector of the soldiers from any fight or attack. Always keep a patrol on watch in every direction and be informed about the actions of both armies. Keep your head aloft night and day, prepared for war and with your loins girded.' When he had told him this advice and counsel, he left to make his undercover observations.

Farāmarz goes to the Indian Raja in the manner of an envoy and a patrol brings Farāmarz before the Indian Raja

He led out a thousand men of war, experienced mounted warriors, and travelled in the manner of an envoy, riding with noblemen behind him. They rode for three stages, and when they arrived at the fourth, they saw an illustrious man on the road, who was a scout from the Indian army, a proud commander and champion. As he advanced, he saw the exalted man and he said, 'You mustn't keep your words hidden from me. Tell me where you are from and what is your name and lineage; where do you want to go, with justice or injustice?' He answered him, 'I am an Iranian and I will tell you, since you do not know me, that I am a servant of the champion of the army, the ambitious Farāmarz, protector of the forces. I am taking a message from Farāmarz of enlightened mind to the Raja of India. The exalted and famous sword-brandishing hero, who is from the lineage of the elephant-bodied warrior, comes from Keykhosrow, who as king and ruler wears a crown that has been handed down the generations: at his command he has come to this country. What can a pugnacious man say about his counsel?

'You must go to the king and tell him, "An exalted man from that army is bringing a message addressed to you, so that he can gain some insight into your subtle judgement."' The scout quickly turned round from there and went from that wide plain towards the Raja. He told him what he had heard from that renowned man, and the Raja ordered, 'Bring him to me.' The scout went like the raging wind to that famous champion and brought him before the Indian king. When Farāmarz the hero had come close to him, he dismounted and laid his hand on his chest. The Raja looked at that lion-like man and he saw a hero like a huge mountain, the sight of whom refreshed the soul: his face was like a rose-bed in the garden of Paradise; you would say that heaven had created him out of valour. The Raja's heart filled with affection for him, because of his stature, his appearance and his face. When he had approached closer, he bowed down before the king and spent a long time in obeisance before him. The Raja ordered his servants to prepare a good place for him: they placed a golden seat before him and the champion of good religion sat down upon it. The king of the Indians remained amazed about him and in the Indian language invoked God's name upon him.

Farāmarz speaks with the Raja in the manner of an envoy; an account thereof

Next, the Raja said to him in the presence of the gathering: 'Tell us what you have to say.' That famous hero showed him his obeisance, and then he unloaded his treasure-box of words and said to the monarch of the Indians, 'Famous king of enlightened mind! Farāmarz son of Rostam, the praiseworthy hero, told me to go to the eminent king and say to him: "O great famous man, it would be proper if you would not become quarrelsome so quickly, because the king of kings of the land of Iran, the world-ruler Keykhosrow of pure religion, gave me the following order: 'March on to India and Sind with the power of your Chinese sword, and when you have arrived, you must first tell the Raja: "Do not withdraw yourself from manliness. You know that the kings of the land of Iran, since Jamshīd and the praiseworthy Ṭahmūraṡ, since king Āfrīdūn of noble stock and from him until Manūchehr and until Keyqobād, each were ancestors of mine, great men of the world in every gathering. Their commands had currency in the world, whether in China or Rum or amongst the Indians. By the glory of God, the Ruler of the universe, the Creator of the world and our Guide, I am today greater than them all and I am more powerful in intellect and grandeur. I am always increasing my treasures, my glory and my skills on behalf of my pugnacious warriors. Now, O king of kings and ruler of India, I am distinguished amongst all the commanders. You will be prudent if you come to my court in servitude and put wisdom to work. You must abandon your excess and leadership and choose to be servile to this superiority. Then you will lawfully keep your lands and your treasures and the sword of the champion will stay far from you. But if you do not, my soldiers will, by the power of war and of the pure God, in the lands of India, as well as from Kashmir to the region of Sind, raise up the dust towards the turning wheel of heaven. Then there will be no use for regret, when your lands and soldiers have been brought to destruction."'

'"When I travelled from there towards you, in such a manner as would suit one of your renowned relatives, I first sent Keyānūsh, a wise and alert man with insight. With kind speech and warm words and with gentle counsel and a soft voice he tried to turn your head away from this arrogance and set you free from quarrelling and warring. But you did not speak any words in a correct manner; you did not give an answer in such manner as was requested. And then, after he had come back from your presence, his heart pained because of your speech and your beliefs, you put together an army and prepared for war. You will get what you wished for. I am telling you, leader of the Indians, the thoughts that I hold in my enlightened mind: levity of mind and expediency, O prince, find no approval with smart people. You surely have heard what has been inflicted upon your army, as well as your territories, your homeland and your country by the mace of the world-champion and by his famous, auspicious heroes?! You have seen all good and bad things, when they happened; now, choose what is suitable to your wisdom. As you house a bold man under your skin, you should judge this in your head: from what you now know about this battle, if you were elevated at the end of the matter, it would be acceptable that you had performed a fight and a battle and after the fight and strife held a feast. But you had cleared those fights from your mind and arranged your affairs according to your wishes, in order to lead out your army another time and raise your banner of greatness. Since your thoughts about the matter have shown their face, I do not see in you any love for your own body. A fierce lion once said to a leopard, when fate had become dark and constricted for a mountain sheep: 'If he looks at the good and bad side of his actions, he will come running straight towards me.' I see you in a similar situation, but I do not see any wisdom in your head. Now you must let your thoughts work over this matter and you need wisdom to help you provide an answer."'

The Raja recognises Farāmarz and speaks with him; Farāmarz's answer

When the king, the Raja, had heard this speech from him, amazement started a deliberation in his heart. He started contemplating that acuteness and elegant smooth speech and that illustrious heart and pure mind, how he without fear or anguish spoke these words in this assembly. For a long time he studied his face: it pleased him, and he said to himself, 'this is a brave man!' A thought arose in his mind: 'I believe that this lion-hearted, proud warrior is an army leader, that the commander himself is acting as his own envoy. He has come with the purpose of observing and both seeing my army and taking its measure. Because such sharp words, upon which a diamond sword would be blunted, would not be uttered by a man of humble descent; a lowly man would turn weak before a king. He cannot be but a champion's son or a descendant of monarchs of independent means. There is no error in my thoughts on this, that he is the army leader from the land of Iran.'

The Raja then spoke to him, 'O exalted man, the thought has arisen in my mind that you are the son of the formidable lion Rostam, descending from Dastān, son of Sām, and from Narīmān. You are the army leader who has come from Iran for this war, you are the exalted man amongst his warriors and lions. For the sake of valour and wisdom you must not keep your intentions hidden from this famous court.' Farāmarz answered him, 'Do not say this, for your honour will be darkened by these words. If you apply the name of the army leader to me, your body will be rid of its dear soul. Farāmarz son of Rostam is too great for this; he will not stoop as low as delivering a message. There are a thousand men like me at his court and they do not command his army camp. I am one of the lesser men at his court and I am also lower ranked than his illustrious men.'

The Raja said to him, 'O honourable man, as I speak these words, do not turn away from my guidance. I feel affection in my heart for your countenance, as well as your glory, your face and your speech. Assign your heart to this land of India, in this place with these friends of yours. I will not refuse you any treasures or jewels, nor a crown, a country, a throne or a sword. You will be commander over the whole of India, a world-leader, a general and a king. I will be like a father to you, and I will further keep my loins girded at your command. And I will even give you my own daughter; you will live in goodness in a pleasant palace.' Farāmarz gave him the following answer in return: 'A wise and proud man will not find it acceptable to go against justice and religion and turn his head away from the king of the land of Iran, especially since he has received horses, apparel and treasures from him in this transient world. Do not speak these words, O exalted king, but provide a reply to my message.'

The king of the Indians answered him, 'O famous champion of the world, I will give an answer to your message when I have auspiciously deliberated a reply. I have ten warriors amongst my soldiers who are the crown of my army. At a time of action each one of these ten warriors can compete with ten thousand men. Now, I will put you to the test and I will observe with benevolence and under a good star: if all of these ten warriors flee from you and fall down like leaves before your mace, we will bow our necks at your command and we will accept a covenant from you from our souls.' The Indian commander was looking for a pretext, so that he perhaps could deflect this lion-like man from a battle in Sind against his own men, by having him perform his heroics against that group of men. The army leader said to the Raja, 'Yes, I accept. It is appropriate that you want me to display some of my skills. The agreement is that if I am defeated, if I am wounded by the swords of your heroes, I and this company of mine will be your servants and we will keep our heads bowed to you in abjectness.' They made this pact and then got up, whilst the field was arranged for the tournament.

The Indian army leader went to the plain with thirty thousand horsemen from Sind. In front of them rode ten lion-grabbing heroes, with their maces, javelins, swords and arrows. The knights of Iran drew up in ranks, their lips foaming with blood coming straight from their livers. The champion warrior stood at the front, with behind him the experienced war heroes. The roaring of the drums and the battle-cries rose up as the men came forward to oppose each other. The dust from the soldiers put the heavens in such a state that the sun lost its way on the heavenly wheel. After those ten heroes had strutted about, they galloped up before Farāmarz.

Farāmarz fights the Raja's ten champions and he kills them; the Raja speaks deceitfully to Farāmarz and Farāmarz's answer

The army leader moved forward in the manner of a lion and roared like a valiant dragon, his head-turning mace in his hand and his light-footed steed beneath him. When he came close to those Indians, growling in the manner of a fierce lion, he dug his spurs into his battle-horse and made an attack on those ten warriors. He grabbed one of them by his waistband and back, lifted him up and, as he threw him onto another one, killed him. Another man he grabbed by his shoulders and head, twisted him and threw him on top of the first one. He grabbed the tail of the horse of yet another knight and turned it round around his head, how amazing! Farāmarz launched him promptly as if from a sling, so that he landed on top of a heroic warrior full of strife. In one blow two of those four men were killed and the other two returned to their king. Until nightfall, when the sun went down, the men galloped now to the left and then to the right. Those ten brave men, who would oppose ten thousand at a time of battle, all in search of valour, fame and honour, one by one had to submit in the fight. For no reason at all the king without insight or justice had sent such illustrious men to perdition.

The Raja's heart filled with hatred for the exalted man. After his feat, the proud Farāmarz said, 'O Raja, seeker of knowledge, uphold our pact in the presence of these people! Now accept the responsibility of paying tribute and taxes, for no bull can escape from a rapacious lion.' When the Indian king heard these words from him, he became sorrowed because of that elephant-bodied champion and he devised a plan of what he should do so that he could fill the plains with the blood of the Iranians. He applied sleight and deceit and filled his heart with malice, fraud and expedition. Sweet-voiced he said to the champion, 'O lion-hearted warrior of enlightened mind, dismount, sit down and accept my entertainment. Take a cup of wine in your auspiciousness. I will not at all turn away from our pact and agreement; I will travel along that path as you command. When the land is lit up by the sun and the leader of these illustrious men wakes up from his sleep, our hearts will be refreshed at the sight of you and we will perform your business according to your wishes.' Although his words were sweet, there was a lie inside the heart of that famous man without splendour. The lion-hearted man dismounted from his steed with his soul-breaking sword in his hand. He did not know that the old fox was laying a trap for the feisty lion by means of a ruse.

What did that wise, alert-minded man say? 'When your enemy has been injured at heart, you must not put your trust in his smooth words, because from that pleasantness bitterness will rise to the surface.'

Then Farāmarz and his famous men, great and small, sat down together with the Indian Raja.

Farāmarz sends for Homāyūn and gives him counsel; an account of the Raja devising a ruse with his army to lay an ambush for Farāmarz

The army leader sent two brave noble men towards Homāyūn the lion, in order to tell him that he should quickly move his drums, elephants and soldiers from their place close to the Indians, in case the malicious, bad-intentioned enemy by means of trickery and out of malice and fraud had laid a trap upon the plains of war: 'He must be aware of our situation and quickly come to our aid with his army.'

After they had left, the Iranians sat down with their champion to hold counsel. The army leader spoke as follows to his companions, his brave warriors and knights: 'Auspicious, lion-like men, you must drink wine in moderation, so that your awareness remains in your bodies. You must not feel safe from the enemy.' His honourable father with his enlightened heart had said, at the time when had given him counsel: 'Lion-like man, sensible warrior, do not consider yourself safe as your enemy's guest. You must be cautious of your enemy at the moment when he addresses you with friendship.' After he had spoken, he sat down and took a goblet, amazed at the workings of the world and wondering how the heavens would turn above his head, how his fate would show him its face.

The Indian army leader arranged a feast in accordance with the customs of Qannowj, Kashmir and Sind. Royal gold tissue had been laid down with a spread of Chinese silks and painted fabrics. The whole plain, filled with the noise of music and song, held the world in its warp and woof with pleasantness. Fairy-faced and musk-scented beautiful girls, like silver-breasted and sweet-faced images, were standing with cups of wine in their hands and with roses, hyacinths and tulips beneath their feet. The wine was digestible and the ground was filled with paintings, whilst the silks sighed under the crowd.

Then the king of the Indians ordered his warriors, intimates and illustrious men to prepare an ambush on the road of the tall champion for the purpose of his ruin, so that when the lion-hearted son of Pīltan set out for his own army, they would come out of their ambush and trap him, and perhaps the hero of pure religion would be killed. For the purpose of the battle, the Raja selected three noble champion warriors, and for each one thirty thousand fighters, horsemen who knew how to draw their swords in battle. He told them to take several flying birds with them to the ambush, and by means of counsel he said to the illustrious men, 'The soldiers, divided into three parts, must remain hidden. When it is time to open the trap, you will not be able to inform each other about the action, so the sign amongst the three companies will be the birds going up in flight to the sky. The companies will see them and come out into the open, so that the soldiers and their leader can be killed.' In this manner he made a plan and it was executed, as they went off with their heads held up high for battle.

Farāmarz for his part opened both his lips at the feast in enjoyment until the middle of the night. When the time for rest arrived, the knowledge-enlightening hero of ambition and elegance went from the feast to his own tent, his heart filled with worries about the day of battle. Not one of the Iranians rested, and all night they kept their loins girded for the fight.

Farāmarz comes before the Indian Raja and speaks with him about paying tribute; the Raja gives Farāmarz a deceitful answer

When the sun in its rusty orbit had left the dark pavilion of the night and settled on the turquoise-coloured wheel of heaven, rising up with victory towards its burning sphere, the army leader came to the Indian king and said to him, 'O noble ruler, quickly give an answer to my message, as well as agree to the tribute and complete our business. Observe our pact and do not turn away from it! For a pact-breaker will soon fall into the dust. You will have heard what that old landowner said when he discovered a hidden path: "A pact-breaker is a man full of lies and he will not obtain any lustre from a wise man."'

The Indian commander gave the following answer: 'O famous tall champion, I will accomplish for you all that you say. I will not deviate from our agreement, just as I judge right. Take this answer from me to the champion: "O elephant-bodied warrior of enlightened mind! I will accept the demand for tribute and taxes from the illustrious king, since we do not have the strength for a war against Iran. But you must rest for two weeks in these lands and not depart from here any sooner, because in our region there are hunting grounds upon the plains and mountains, on and off road. There are such birds flying in the sky that your affection for this country will be kindled. In every place there are panthers and falcons in flight; your spirit has a need for this country. You must know that I will make an effort to collect all the best treasures from the lands and cities, which I will send to the king of the land of Iran, whilst I will set aside my anger, fighting spirit and vengeance. Since the world is deceitful and full of empty pride, why should we make our souls abject out of love for it? A noble man of wisdom has said: 'Everyone who distinguishes a good way from a bad one will know that the world is deceitful and empty and he will not introduce a memory of pain or trouble into his heart. It certainly is better for man to live happily in this fleeting world, without pain or trouble.'"'

He opened the door of beneficence at his loss and gave Arabian horses, Chinese swords, twice three thousand slaves with golden belts and two hundred camel-loads of jewels, silver and gold as a messenger's reward for the warrior army leader. He further decked the illustrious men with pre-excellence, old and young, who had accompanied the champion in robes of honour, and he happily gave each one according to his worth horses, slaves and servants. In this manner the commander satisfied them, whilst he blocked their way with deceit and trickery, believing that that lion-like man would be reduced to dust on the day of ambush.

Farāmarz returns from the Raja and the Raja's army lays an ambush for Farāmarz; an account of Farāmarz and Homāyūn's fight against them and a description of that battle

Farāmarz with glory and strength mounted the back of his horse in order to return, as did the thousand renowned lion-like men that had come with him to that battleground. He drove his company along the road like the wind, unaware of the king's action of setting an ambush. From the other direction, Homāyūn and his proud men, in response to the words of the exalted army leader, had set off and travelled towards the Indian Raja, not aware of the doings of the men of Sind. Whilst they were arriving close to the ambush, Farāmarz was approaching it from the other side, and when the horsemen of the enemy became informed of this, they all came onto and next to the road to receive them. All three companies opened the trap when the birds rose up from the road in flight. They drew up their ranks for the battle, with the purpose of annihilating the Iranians. Farāmarz said to the warriors of Iran, 'Today your valour must not remain hidden. Exert yourselves and fight like lions. Perhaps you may obtain a good reputation. Anyone amongst great men who has accomplished a good reputation in the world has not died.'

The bustle of the warriors at war swelled, and the world became dark and narrow for the Indians. Matters were different from what had been expected, but no profit is produced by caution. By necessity, the men from Iran and India engaged with each other and they threw themselves upon each other. When glory is auspicious and the warrior young, even if he is given grief by an ambush and a large army, especially when wisdom is his friend, he will exalt his head to the turning heaven.

When Homāyūn the heroic champion saw Farāmarz, he said to his warriors and illustrious men, 'Lion-like men with strength and pride, a courageous man will appear out of a coward here, because a good reputation is to be sought in battle, where the blades of your Indian swords should be washed in blood. All of you, draw your swords of vengeance and fill the entire plain with the blood of the enemy. For when the enemy displays deceit, a courageous man cannot reckon them amongst celebrated men. Ambush and trickery are actions of despair; these actions of theirs are cause to make one weep.' He spurred on his horse and stirred up the dust, whilst his brave men produced battle-cries.

A dust cloud as black as the face of an Indian rose up and covered up the sun and the moon: night appeared instead of the bright day, whilst heads were carried off by the swords. No one could have believed that on that day they could have so many lances and maces. On one side, the son of the elephant-bodied warrior and on the other, the sword-drawing Homāyūn let loose the reins around the necks of their horses and with the blows of their hatchets and heavy maces killed countless of those Indians and rained down fire onto that battlefield. Every time that they, from atop their horses, pounded down their maces in the battle, heads, helmets and coats of mails, together with horses and men, were shattered to such small pieces upon the field of war that they could not be distinguished from the soil, even if someone were to observe them at length and in depth.

Such is the conclusion to a bad action. An evil thought without doubt comes to a bad ending. An aged man, wise and decisive in action, told an aphorism about this: 'Anyone who lays a trap on the road will himself first fall into that snare. When you unjustly dig a pit in a road, you will throw the head of your own fate into it. As long as you live, you must be a faithful friend. Behave with valour in wartime.'

In this manner, until the sun turned yellow, the army did not rest from fighting and warring. Of so many shield-bearing Indian horsemen only a few remained to be counted. The rest had been felled in groups at a time, forming heaps and mounds in every corner.

The Raja is informed about the fleeing of his army and he once more puts together an army; Farāmarz sends out a patrol and gives them advice

When the darkness of the night appeared and the army was left with nothing to do in terms of fighting, when the ravens hid the feathers of their crops and Saturn lit its lamp from the stars, Farāmarz rested with his soldiers, his heart satisfied about that country of his.

In the meantime, the Indians that had been put to rout went towards the Raja with weakened souls. They said to their famous monarch, 'This battle turned out badly for us. Farāmarz came upon us in a rush with his illustrious and brave men, and the way in which we fought was not according to our wishes, as pugnacious soldiers from our side were killed. Surely, our fate has been reversed, going by the manner in which the entire army was killed.' When the Raja of ignoble fate heard this, he sharply flared up and got up from his throne. That famous man prepared an army of five ranks of a hundred thousand renowned men, with elephants, drums and his war apparel, as well as famous leaders with glory and majesty. Company by company the soldiers went on their way, instilling fear into the mountains and plains. A patrol was sent ahead, a troop of ten thousand pugnacious men.

And on the other side, Farāmarz like a mountain, whilst his army was tired out from all their attacks, sent a patrol towards the Indian side, lest the lowly born men of Sind came and attacked in the dark night and a defeat from every side befell the lions. He did and said all that was necessary, and then went to his sleeping quarters to sleep a while.

Zāl has a dream and talks to Rostam; Rostam comes to help Farāmarz because of the speech of the white-haired Zāl

That night, by the divine decree of the Omnipotent, Zāl of good fortune during his sleep saw in his dream Farāmarz of enlightened mind, who was in a region of the country of the Indians, on a mountain top and involved in a fight, whilst his entire army was held back from him. He was captured by the hand of someone whose excellence was not greater than his valour. Like a far-flying arrow the vision of the white-haired Zāl was launched from afar, and he saw a fire burning that had set the plain alight. A great war-engine appeared, a catapult that was set up on the mountain: Farāmarz was placed in it and was slung like a ball towards the fire. All around, the fire had become like a sea, when suddenly Tahamtan became visible. When he saw his son in the air, whilst the fire was coming closer, he judged this was not right and then stretched his hand up into the air and snatched him by his chest away from there.

When Dastān son of Sām awoke from his dream, he immediately sent someone to call the renowned Rostam. When he had come, Zāl told him this story, saying to him, 'I saw a strange dream of a kind that I have never heard of. I saw Farāmarz just now in my dream, and my heart started racing because of his situation: he was a prisoner in the hands of Ahrīman. If you do not find him, his cause will be ruined. You must now hurry quickly and leave without delay; perhaps you may rescue your son from his claws.'

Tahamtan started agitating like the sea and emitted a roar like thunder. Like the wind he put on his Rūmi coat of mail and knotted the iron rings of his harness together, then pulled his tiger-skin cuirass over his head on top of the coat of mail on his chest.[10] He laid the horse armour on Rakhsh and stuck his world-distributing sword in his belt. He ordered twelve thousand illustrious horsemen with maces and cuirasses to gallop to the country of the Indians and bring the hearts of the sorcerers to destruction. He did not rest day or night from galloping, whilst his heart was all ready to deliver battle.

A worldly wise man may say that you will experience no greater pain than the pain over a son, for God has mixed the love for him with his father's soul like milk with wine. Of everything in the world nothing is sweeter for a father than his child.

He kept on galloping towards the battle in such a manner that he loosened the dust from the bedrock mountains.

The Raja leads his army to fight Farāmarz son of Rostam and Farāmarz is informed and fights the Raja; a description of his battle

When the sun raised up its head from the east, spreading out its golden shimmer over the mountains and valleys, so that its reflection turned the world into a mine of ruby and the tarlike night became food for the day, the army leader of India set off towards Farāmarz, the conqueror of countries. The supreme Raja set in order his army, with leaders from every place in India and with seven hundred elephants and five hundred ranks of thousand illustrious men of war. The elephants had bodies like Mount Bīstūn and fire shot from their eyes. Onto them were loaded the apparel of war and the weapons of the powerful and strong knights, such as maces and swords of the finest steel, as well as war-tunics and battle-swords. The world became like Mount Qāf because of all that iron, into the heart of which the kettle-drums caused a breach. When he had come close to the Iranian army, he arranged his soldiers like a black mountain. They drew up in ranks for battle, some just like lions and others like panthers.

When Farāmarz the army leader saw the enemy with such an appearance, he charged up a hill and lined up the ranks. He gave Homāyūn, brave and exalted on a day of battle, a position in the centre. In the left flank stood the warrior Shīrūy, who was a courageous and pugnacious horseman, and in the right flank was the warrior Keyānūsh, who with his sword could remove the colour from the face of the sun. Behind them, the warlike warrior Tokhwār arranged matters for himself in the interior. When the centre and the wings of the army were set in order, the face of the sky turned black with the dust, the heavens were quaking in their marrow and the bodies of the bad-hearted men took leave of their souls. The mountain roared, the plain shook and the world changed its appearance out of fear. One army marched up towards the other and a tumult erupted on the battlefield.

The army leader looked at his soldiers and said, 'Smallness and greatness should not be hidden. If we consider our opponents, the size of their army and the number of enemy soldiers, which resemble a sea with a deep bottom, I do not know how I can set to work or which route to take. Perhaps our auspicious fortune will lend assistance and give me power over our enemy. Five hundred thousand men from India, warriors and knights, have been assembled, with seven hundred huge elephants in front of them. The earth has become dark-blue as indigo from their dust. Now, my knights, you must be courageous and fight these illustrious great men! It is better to leave behind a reputation in this world: we will exert ourselves with valour and we will stand firm.' All the illustrious men from the land of Iran sung Farāmarz's praise: 'As long as we have not lost our lives or souls in this battle, we will not turn away from the Indian army.'

When the son of the elephant-bodied hero heard this, these words brought happiness to his heart. He shouted out at the king of kings of India, 'O ignoble, lowly-born man of Sind, you laid a trap on the path of lions; see how I now will administer justice. I and my mace and sword will on the battlefield turn the face of the earth red with your blood. At the command of the pure God I will bring the souls of your soldiers one by one to the ground.'

The commander of the Indians was enraged because of him, and he said to him, 'O Sīstāni with your dark soul, where is the limit to this talk of yours? This very moment I will let a river of blood flow out of you.' The king and his army moved from their place like a black mountain and attacked. Like a sea in which the waves are agitated by the wind and throw out fish from the water to their summits, they launched their lances at the Iranians and pressed the army towards the mountains. They drove them to the foot of the mountains and crushed them underfoot. The Iranian horsemen suffered a defeat by the elephants and those countless soldiers, who killed ten thousand men from the Iranian army, illustrious and proud knights. The heads of those famous men became distressed about that, as the face of their fate darkened: they all at once gave up their places and tore their feet away from the battlefield.

But auspicious Farāmarz of pure intellect stood firm upon the battlefield. He kept turning round the renowned Indians, so that the tall mountain got tired of his fight. On one huge elephant was placed a golden throne inlaid with pearls and jewels, upon which the monarch of the Indians was seated. He said to his renowned warriors,[11] 'You must exert yourselves and perform such a battle and a fight that you perhaps can grab hold of my enemy and bring Farāmarz as a prisoner before me with his hands tied like a madman.' When the soldiers had heard these words from the Raja, they took up position around the elephant-bodied hero, so that the Indians joined together like a wall around him, enclosing him in their midst. They pointed their many lances at him and pressed him with the points of their spears. When Farāmarz saw the fight had turned in such a manner, he roared and raged like a lion. As he shouted, he drew his head-scattering glittering sword from its scabbard and he called out his name, then he threw himself upon the large army and slew many famous men. In one attack he threw down ten thousand of those innumerable soldiers into the dirt and blood.

As he removed his body further from the centre of their army, he did not see any of the Iranian warriors. He shouted out at the warrior Homāyūn, making a reproach about their supremacy and saying to him, 'Hey, famous champion, bring a company towards me in a hurry!' Homāyūn gathered all his soldiers and rode towards the champion as fast as a dust-cloud. When Farāmarz saw them, he said, 'O commanders, this is not a time for swords or heavy maces; no one shall perform this fight except with arrows. You shall turn the ground into a pool of arrows. When you draw the arrow's notch and the string to your thumbstall, you must as one man direct your hands at the elephants and string together their trunks with your arrows, so that you will make the elephants captive with your arrows.' The men of war took hold of their bows and their arrows of poplar wood with iron points. After they had knotted the strings onto their bows and the strings had made the bows bend when they pulled the notches next to their ears, the vault became clad in iron by the arrowheads: at once, thirty thousand arrows left the bows in the manner of hail in spring. They passed through the trunks of the elephants and their tips bored through their chests into their livers. Three times they fired in this manner and cleared the ground of the elephants, which turned their heads away from the battlefield, as they sought an escape from the iron arrowheads, turning the soldiers upside down from beginning to end, trampling, killing and giving them a beating.

When the battlefield had been emptied of the elephants, Farāmarz ordered that they this time should take up their maces and scimitars and inflict a defeat upon them with their swords. They grabbed hold of their clubs and swords, and a hubbub rose up like a fury. The clashing of the swords, maces and hatchets and the battle cries from the horsemen tore apart place and time, whilst heaven gathered its skirts in fear. The army leader, with his lasso on his saddle-straps, his heart full of anger and his head filled with fight, killed many Indian knights with his sword, lance and mace, as well as with his fist. Keyānūsh the lion-killer at once advanced from the left wing with his company like a cloud full of maces and swords, from which cloud javelins and scimitars rained down. His left wing defeated their right wing, so that the Indians abandoned their weapons and baggage. When the warrior Shīrūy from the right wing saw Keyānūsh obtaining such a victory, he galloped with his company out from the right side, as they directed their lances straight at the hearts of the Indians. In a short time not one brave or rugged man from that large army remained. Whether they were killed or thrown down abjectly onto the road, they all were overturned like drunks. Farāmarz the lion-killing champion was galloping in every direction like a raging tiger: heads were whacked off like balls by his mace and blood was made flowing into rivers by his sword.

Farāmarz captures the Indian Raja in the noose of his lasso; an account of Farāmarz's fight

He saw the banner of the king of the Indians, which was visible on the other side in the centre of the army, and large as a mountain he galloped off from his place towards the army leader, the Indian Raja. He arrived at his formidably huge elephant, on the back of which sat the monarch of the Indians, and as he approached, the famous hero laid down his cow-headed mace on his saddle and briskly unwound his lasso from the back of his saddle. When he had come next to the man of sorcerer stock, he threw his twisted lasso and caught the head of the Indian king in its noose. He launched him down from up high onto the ground just like a ball, the crown of his head covered in dirt and his face full of dust. The brave lion dismounted from his steed, roared like a fearful dragon and tied up both his arms in a loop of his lasso.

Such are the customs of the high heavenly wheel: it may have nurtured someone for years and regarded him with nothing but goodness, but when it has kept a man safe for a while, it thereafter may not grant him protection for his life. It will take him down from his throne and set him on the ground, having neither any fear in this action nor any solicitude. In such a manner it will let a king of exalted fate, with his crown, his ambitions and his throne, be captured in a lasso at nightfall and his head and shoulders be kept abjectly in fetters for half a day. I do not know what the firmament is thinking, that it will not provide anyone protection for their lives. O brother, do not set your hopes on its affection, even if it brings you happy tidings without limit, because in the end you will not see any loyalty from it, even if a few people have escaped from deceit.

When Farāmarz had tied up the hands of the king, he entrusted him to his warriors and then remounted. Next, he demanded an arrow from his servant-boy and aimed it straight at the Indians who were frightened out of their minds. Like the wind he tore them out root and branch and knocked them down, either killed or wounded. With his lance he made the ground like a mine of rubies, as he reinforced doomsday with their souls. Not one warrior from amongst those renowned men from India, nor those from Sind or the kingdom of Jādūstān remained in this place, whether they were killed or trampled underfoot, whilst a part of them went fleeing, tortured by fear for Farāmarz.

An account of Rostam arriving at Farāmarz and embracing his son and of Farāmarz bringing the Raja before Rostam and Rostam giving the Raja counsel

In the meantime, by the decree of the pure God, the Creator of man from wind and earth, a clamour rose up from amongst the Iranians, which Farāmarz and his renowned men heard. At the same time, such a dark dust-cloud drifted up that one would think the earth had become level with the mountains, and the banner of Tahamtan appeared on the road, together with the famous men of the Zāboli army. That same moment Pīltan arrived, and when Farāmarz saw Rostam's face, he dismounted from his horse, kissed the surface of the ground and praised his father. When Rostam saw the hero Farāmarz alive, it was as if he saw the firmament as his servant next to him. He kissed the face of Farāmarz the lion and said to him, 'O offspring of the brave Sām! Thanks to the Protector of the world on the day of reckoning that I could see you alive on the battlefield. My heart rejoices because of you, famous man, who is both a champion and of a good essence.' Farāmarz kissed his father's feet, whilst he made his heart happy and joyful at the sight of him.

At that moment, the king of the Indians, with his head bared and his feet in heavy fetters, was led before Rostam, and he kissed the ground and made his obeisance. Rostam said to him, 'O famous man, you did not listen to the speech of the king, who said that everyone who seeks fame and honour must first have washed both his hands in blood. I take pity on your stature and your height and I will refrain from ruining your country and your position, because your father, that man of enlightened mind, was my friend in his time of strength. But I will take you in your fetters to the king, so that you will learn the worth of his crown.'

After that, the army leader of enlightened mind looked the desert over from side to side. On the entire plain of India from beginning to end he saw gold and jewels scattered in every place, as well as crowns, thrones, tiaras and belts. There further were maces, coats of mail, swords and hatchets, as well as horses, camels and war-elephants, and also clubs, javelins and horse armours. Rostam ordered that they should be gathered and one by one be counted before him. They were accumulated in large heaps, so that the eye tired at the sight of them. In the presence of the nobles Tahamtan first extracted from the lot a share for the king of the world. Next, he ordered fetters to be prepared, long chains of precious gold, which were placed on the feet of the Indian commander, the exalted king and army leader of Sind. He was sat on the back of a huge elephant and the army set off from there towards the Iranian king.

Rostam and Farāmarz return from India to the land of Iran and have an interview with King Keykhosrow; an account of Rostam talking about Farāmarz's fight and the circumstances of the king's feast

While the army leader led the soldiers from the mountains, the dark night tore her black veil, as a golden banner appeared on the mountain slope and raised its head ever higher with its golden light. The ambitious hero headed towards the king of the land of Iran together with his auspicious son, and he travelled along that long road in happiness, his heart having become pleased about his son's actions. The entire way they used their falcons, panthers and dogs to capture animals of prey and birds, running and flying about: now the champion's son with skill pierced the heart of a male onager with his arrow, then a panther, running from his ambush at a distressing pace, caught a mountain goat fast as the wind, and then again a gazelle was running from a dog, and the dog would swiftly overtake the gazelle. In such happiness Tahamtan drove the army along the road for more than two months.

When they had arrived close to the land of Iran, news of them was brought to the eminent king. He sent out his warriors to receive them, all his famous men of Iran. They travelled with drums, soldiers and banners, as well as golden tymbals and golden shoes, and they filled the world with clamour and the sky with noise, as the shouts of the champions tore the ears. They reached the exalted champion and one by one showed him their respects. Tahamtan praised the nobles, each one in such a manner as suited him. After that, they rode on to the court to pay a visit to the famous and just king. When Tahamtan came before the throne of the king, the world-ruler stood up and stepped down. He embraced him and kissed his face. He became happy at the sight of father and son, and he kissed the face of that lion Farāmarz, the young world-conqueror and courageous warrior. The monarch asked them all about the exertion of the long journey and about the battle, as did the famous men that were with him, who were exalted and without any blemish of evil. They all laid their heads on the ground before the king's throne and praised him.

He ordered a banquet to be laid out with all kinds of food, better than what they could have wished for. When the great leaders had eaten the food, the king of the world arranged a feast. The music of the flutes and the resonance of the songs, as well as the melodies of the lutes, the tinkling of the harps and the scents of the beautiful roses and tulips caused Venus to bid her soul farewell. The air was filled with sounds and the ground with pictures, whilst jasmine-bosomed, fairy-faced servants were serving wine.

The famous king of kings Keykhosrow questioned the excellent Rostam about the actions and the skills of the youthful army leader, Farāmarz of enlightened mind. Tahamtan loosened his tongue to give an answer and he recounted Farāmarz's battle to the king, talking about the fights he had performed and about the matter of Tajānū, of whom he had disposed, about the matter of the Indians setting up an ambush and about the deceit and trickery of the king of the sorcerers. The king of the world praised that renowned young champion at length. They drank wine until the middle of the night, their lips opened at ease and to their desire. When everyone's head was heavy with wine, they went drunk to their sleeping quarters.

Farāmarz presents himself before Keykhosrow to request a pardon for the Indian Raja and to have him placed in Farāmarz's charge

When the dawn had hoisted its flag up high and made the face of heaven turn as purple as camphor, when the earth became refreshed and the mountain like sandarac, the sound of the drum rose up from the court and Farāmarz went with Rostam the champion towards the king of the world. Farāmarz spoke to the elevated king on behalf of the Indian king: 'He has given me a lot of counsel out of goodness and he has given me a place in his heart. During the time when I had gone to him, to see his power, crown and country, I experienced many good things from him and I approved of his greatness. Now I have set my hope on the king of the world that he grants him the kingdom of India. Since he has shown me friendship, he must not be treated with affliction or vileness.'

When the just king of kings heard this, he replied, 'I completely place him in your charge. Take him such as he is to India, towards his homelands of Jādūstān. Place him with goodness on the royal throne and take many champions from here, for I have given you, man of pure religion, the kingship of those lands until the sea of China. Manage it with goodness, do not harm anyone or exert the workers too much and let agriculture come to prosper. Your reputation must remain upstanding.' Farāmarz kissed the surface of the ground and said to him, 'O, you are a monarch with elephants and drums! I am standing before your throne as a servant; whatever you command, I will set in order.'

The monarch sent for the king of the Indians and gave him a robe of honour, an adornment of his status. He made much of him and gave him counsel, so that the Raja was troubled by the behaviour of the king. He said to him, 'I am a servant to the king, to whose command and judgement I bow my head. I will not turn my head away from your servants, if they will regard me, O renowned man!' He kissed the ground and left the court, his belt girded tightly for the journey to India.

After the king of India had come outside, the army leader Farāmarz, approver of goodness, took him to his own pavilion and held a gathering with his renowned men. They sat down happily to drink wine and spent the night like that until daybreak.

Farāmarz goes on his way with the Raja of India and he hears about the circumstances of Mahārak the Indian; the Raja and Farāmarz speak with each other

When the sun had set its foot on the heavenly wheel, the sound of bells rose up together with the blaring of trumpets, and Farāmarz set off with the Indian Raja towards his own land by way of the province of Sind. When they had arrived close to the Indians, someone informed the champion: 'Another monarch rules over the Indians. He is a king of kings and a famous hero, a proud man named Mahārak, an arrogant and self-willed army leader. During the time that the brave champion had gone from here to the great king, the nobles of India in the meanwhile chose a courageous and young king. They placed him on the throne with the golden crown and all girded their loins at his command. All the men of India, the nobles, the lions and the warriors of Sind, made a pact, saying, "Even if swords rain down upon us from heaven, we will not side with the Raja on account of our affection. Surely, Keykhosrow, as part of his war of vengeance, will have made him disappear from the world, but even if he comes alive to this court, he will obtain neither the crown nor the country or the diadem."'

When the valorous lion heard this speech, astonishment arose in him and he became distressed about this. He repeated these words to the Indian Raja, and when he had heard him out, the Raja said in answer: 'That malevolent, demonic Mahārak of evil stock, who has set his mind on my throne, was a servant to my father, a worshipper of my earth and water. At my command he was king of Kashmir and governed that country and its lands. I held him dearer than my own life and exalted his head higher than any person. Now, out of foulness and through demonism, he has made devilishness appear, and now he has sought my place and taken my position: as he displayed his bad nature, he lost his way.'

A wise teacher has said it well: 'Do not hold someone of bad essence in a good regard. If someone nurtures the poison of hatred with sweetness, he will for months and years undergo suffering and hardship. He may develop a constitution of wine and honey, and milk and water may be flowing in his mouth, but eventually he will reveal his secret and make his true nature appear.'

Farāmarz said, 'O honourable king, do not let your heart lose its way because of that evil-doer. By the power of the victorious God, I will pull him upside-down onto his head from his throne. We must write a letter to him, and our speech in this letter can be short. If he turns obedient, he will come to this court and relinquish his place to you.[12] And if he does not, I will incite the day of judgement upon his soul with my mace and my sharp sword.' The Raja replied, 'I will do as you say; I have set my heart on your counsel and your treaty.' The raging lion ordered a scribe to bring his pen and musk and amber, and write a letter possessing pureness addressed to that foolish man.

Farāmarz's letter to Mahārak the Indian and Mahārak's answer; the circumstances thereof

Like a musky tongue of a sweet-voiced bird scattering pearls from its mouth onto the page, as the waves were thrown up from the sea of thought, he gathered the groups of pearls together with his reed. At the top of the letter he put the name of God, the Creator of man from earth and wind: 'May the blessings of the Lord Who rules both worlds, our Guide in victory and greatness, be upon the king of Iran, so that Iran and Tūrān may soon be his. May the Ruler of the world and the Bestower of the pure religion be praised for as long as the world exists. This letter is from the warrior of enlightened mind, Farāmarz, son of the world-champion, addressed to the evil Mahārak of a bad stock, who should not put his father's reputation to ruin. In your foolishness you sought a higher rank. You are of a bad essence, lower than dogs; it is very much a sign of your bad nature that you, of no high reputation, sat down on the throne of exalted men and were not ashamed of yourself. You have not yet experienced the heat and cold of this world. When someone takes the crown and the throne from his own master, and sits down upon it, is this proper?! I have made you aware of this cause: you shall at once take the road of lowliness. And if you rebel against my counsel, you will see your head removed from your body. You should know how I execute my plan of war: my sword will burn a water-monster in the sea.'

He sought a messenger swift as the wind and sent him on his way towards that man of evil lineage. He himself sat down with the Raja and the warriors of the Iranian army, enjoying wine and music in the hunting grounds. Sometimes he hit a ball, whilst at other times he galloped after prey; now he took rest in sleep, and then he organised a feast.

The messenger arrived at Mahārak and saw him upon the throne with his crown, around him renowned nobles, the leaders of India, lined up in ranks. He gave him that heart-breaking letter, and a scribe read it to him before the gathering. Mahārak flared up like a demon because of that letter from the celebrated hero. He directed a fierce cry at the messenger, whose feet were paralysed and whose tongue was numbed: 'How dare Farāmarz act as if he is my superior, displaying greatness in such a manner in his letter?! Perhaps he considers me in the same manner as the Raja, with my victorious fate, glory and honour. When I head for the battlefield, I will make the bright day black in his eyes.' He reviled the messenger and banished him, sparking with the fire of anger and hatred.

He immediately assembled such an army that the bright day turned into a dark-blue night. The soldiers were all lance- and mace-bearers, proud heroes and sword-drawers from Qannowj and Kashmir, and from the provinces of India, from China and Māchīn and from the land of Sind. Four hundred ranks of a thousand warriors, suited for war, gathered around him, as well as elephants with chains and carrying golden thrones, and there were more than twice five hundred tent-bearers. The army of such a large extent went on its way, brimming with the anger and vengeance of the warriors. The noise of the drums and the dust of the brave men of war made the world dark and the land constricted.

Meanwhile, when the distinguished messenger returned to Farāmarz, he told him bit by bit what Mahārak had said and did not in any way keep anything hidden from him. When the famous champion had heard him out, he flared up like a raging elephant. Full of anger and vengeance he took an oath on his seal and his ring and by his religion and his justice, by the Ruler of the universe, of Jupiter and the sun, by his feasts and fights and by his fears and hopes: 'I will seize the whole country of India from that malevolent, dark-souled dog. In a fight on the battlefield I will make him twist; I will roast him like a bird on a spit.' He ordered the soldiers to mount and he quickly rode towards the battlefield. A deep river appeared in front of him, which in width came to more than one mile. When he had come close to that deep river, he ordered the army to dismount.

Farāmarz crosses the water to fight Mahārak and Mahārak's army lays an ambush

When Mahārak heard that the army was coming, had moved from its place towards the deep river, he sent a message to the champion: 'Cross the water at dawn, or otherwise tell me to cross this deep river myself, with my army. When I have arrived on the plain, prepare to do battle for a while, and you will see a fight by a leopard.' His message reached the ear of the army leader, whose heart was beating out of anger with Mahārak. He gave the following answer: 'Give way, for I will let my army cross the water. I must come with valour towards you: because of your speech bad things will happen to your army.'

When Mahārak heard this, he gathered his army, while the dark night descended. The edge of the river was full of shrubbery and trees, and the trees had many branches, while the terrain was rough. He ordered trenches to be dug on the edge of the river, for the purpose of the battle, so that when the champion with his soldiers went down to the river in order to cross it, at the moment when they left the water, they could quickly block their way. They plotted thus and then got up and prepared traps in every direction.

Farāmarz takes counsel with the Raja and Farāmarz battles Mahārak the Indian

When the sun made its appearance on the heavenly wheel and made the world bright with the colour of spring, Farāmarz the hero made preparations to go, whilst he started cultivating a thought in his mind: 'If they prepare an ambush for us and put wrinkles on the cheeks of the water, things will happen wholly at the wish of the Indians, and because of this cowardice our souls will fly away from us. A wise man says: "At the time of war, acting in haste when the occasion calls for delay will produce only sorrow and pain and will result in regret and grief."'

He spoke his thoughts to the Raja, in order to see what his opinion in this matter was. The Raja said to him, 'O exalted warrior, do not underestimate these sorcerers, for they have evil intentions, are bad-natured and perform their battles with trickery and deceit. We must think deeply about this matter and ask everyone about a way across the water. We must conceive a plan, so that you will not be reviled about this. Perhaps that great army with expedition will be further away from the edge of the river, and then you can quickly cross this water, so that the enemy will flee before you.' The army leader gave him the following reply: 'O great man, prominent king, you must know that everyone who has sought fame first has washed his face in blood. He wouldn't hold back from either water or fire and he wouldn't allow himself to flee from the swords of destruction. When his time has come, he can't fend it off with valour or caution. A guide of enlightened heart has said: "If you seek a reputation, you mustn't fear affliction." I will provide a solution for this battle, so that I can cross this water without a trouble in my heart.'

He ordered many of those tall trees to be cut down and gathered. Next, they were tied together and their branches were spread out on top of them. Many rafts of this kind were manufactured and launched like boats on the water, and on each of those sat a thousand archers, shield-bearers and men of war. The horses were dressed in their armour and then they set off quickly like a moving mountain.

When Farāmarz, the famous slayer of heroes, had come close to the other side of the river, Mahārak revealed the ambush amongst the woods, and his army attacked like the wind: they were powerless against their bows and arrows; it was all lances, darts, spears and nothing else. With swords and with javelins of the finest steel they killed countless Iranians. The blood made the water of the river turn vermillion, whilst the shouts of the warriors tore the mountains and the plains. The army leader then said to his proud men, 'You must all together put the strings on your bows and from your cloud of bows rain down arrows like hail upon them in a shower of death.' After the soldiers had brought their fists to their quivers, they released the poplar arrows from their thumb-stalls, and the ground along the water's edge became like a tulip-garden of iron, mail-piercing arrowheads. As they executed this abuse with their arrows, they cleared the water's edge of those men.

The army leader came from the water onto the plain, his soldiers all following him in haste. Like lions they mounted their steeds and in one body drew their swords. The soldiers from both sides threw themselves at each other, now striking with lances and then with swords, whilst the Indian soldiers were like ants and locusts, spread out on the plain like ice on a mountain. Proud Farāmarz, eager for the fight, arrived on the battlefield with his lance, and in each attack he threw down two hundred lion-hearted men in one flow with that life-robbing lance. He slew many men and beasts and inflicted terror upon the Indian army.

One lion-hearted man at the front of the Indian ranks, foaming at the lips in the manner of a wild animal, a brave horseman with a stature like a mountain and a heaviness that put fear into the earth, roared when he saw the champion, and he drew a shimmering sword. He rode up and turned around the champion like a raging elephant or a fierce lion. He thrust his glittering sword with the intention of cutting his face entirely from his body, but the tip of his sharp sword got caught in the mail covering his head, which was twisted and because of that thrust broke into pieces. The army leader hit him on the head with his lance, the force of which caused his helmet to fall from his head. The Indian lifted up his mace from the saddle of his huge horse, swung it like a mountain from the top of his height and struck, breaking the champion's lance into pieces. The army leader took his heavy mace in his hand and smashed it on the top of the head of the other's horse, so that the light-footed beast fell on its face in pain. On foot, the Indian with his darkened soul litigiously engaged with the champion: he came up close to the army leader, that hero, and at once laid his hand on his waistband, hoping that he maybe could pull him down from his saddle. The army leader grabbed him by the chest and shoulders and the head, and twisted him like the neck of a sheep or like an onager in the claws of a fierce lion. He tore his head from his body like a ball, whilst the two armies stood rooted in stupefaction over of him. He threw that head towards the Indians, whose souls all were fearful in this terror.

When Mahārak saw such superiority, he attacked the Iranian army. The day's face darkened with the dust of the army and the world-lighting sun went fleeing from the wheel of heaven. At the same time, the dark night arrived and the world pulled her musky veil over her head. The two armies separated from each other, since the time for the battlefield had passed.

When the dark night had appeared, Mahārak assembled his army in the mountains. He had the idea of making a surprise attack that night and filling the plains and valleys with the blood of the enemy. He sent a horseman from his camp onto the road to gain information from among the Iranian army, a scout who should learn the ins and outs of the army and see who was asleep and who was awake. The scout came and looked about much in every direction, but he did not see anyone from Iran. Farāmarz, on his own, was riding along the river and over the plain, in search of the sentinel of the other army, whilst the Indian spy wasn't aware of that exalted man in the long night. The night was very dark, like ebony, and there was no sound of neighing horses or of drums. When the army leader had come close to the Indian, his horse neighed as it strutted by, and at the same moment as the noise escaped from the Indian's steed Farāmarz pricked up his ears. In the manner of Āżargoshasp, he launched an arrow in a straight line at the sound of the horse: it hit the head of the dark-souled Indian, and that same moment his soul left his body.

Mahārak had been waiting for a long time and became fed-up with this business of his envoy. When the Indian did not return to him, his dark soul filled with pain, for he knew that he had been harmed by the Iranian army and that his cause had been ruined. His head filled with pain and his heart with hatred, whilst anger put a frown upon his brow.

Farāmarz fights Mahārak and Farāmarz kills seven champions of Mahārak; a description of his fight

When the sun with its sword and golden shield and with its golden crown had taken a seat on its throne and made the entire earth resplendent, both armies took their places on their saddles. Mahārak led his soldiers out to the plain, making the world invisible with the dust of the army, whilst the drums roared like thunder in spring, the earth became dark and the heaven ebony-coloured. Fire raged during that battle, for lances were flashing and swords sparking. Dust was whirling up like a smoke cloud and the face of the moon turned blue with wretchedness.

Mahārak set up his ranks like a mountain, turning the ground in dread of his army. He had seven young courageous warriors, all experienced and like formidable elephants; each one had a body like a black mountain and in courage each exceeded a hundred soldiers. They were fast as the wind, had a pace like lightning and from top to toe were covered in iron. He fetched them, placed them at the front of his army and appointed a company to each one of them. Then he arranged the right wing with elephants and placed the baggage train behind his army. He arranged the left wing like the right one, entirely with elephants that had been tested in battle. He himself stood in the centre, together with a company of renowned men.

The army leader Farāmarz observed them and stood rooted in amazement, evoking God's name in his heart. He said, 'No one in the world has ever seen an army of such a kind, nor will anyone have heard of it.' The Raja said to him, 'O world-champion, wait while I this very moment with my enlightened mind will send a noble man to each corner, to every place where a man rules a province. I will once again call the famous men that sided with me but now have joined that bad-seeded Ahrīman, and I will give them one by one a reward in the form of treasure or land out of the goodness of my hope that they will come over to me and light up my darkened judgement.' The army leader answered him, 'May it not happen to me that I ask for help from a man of Indian descent. I have set my hopes on the day of battle – or is there maybe no real man left in the world?! Don't disregard this small army of mine, for honour behoves a man at the time of battle. You, renowned king, be happy of heart and free yourself from fear for that army.'

After that, he arranged his army with selected suitable horsemen: in the right wing was the lion-hearted Ashkash, who with his sword would turn dirt to mud, and in the left wing, the hero Nastūr, whose sword would make the heart of a demon sorrowful. When he had delegated them to the right and left wings, he kept the Raja in the centre to assist him, and chose a place for himself at the front, as the dust of war was kicked up from the battlefield.

The soldiers on both sides lined up in ranks, all with swords, maces and lances in their fists. They clashed and contended in such a manner that they mixed dirt and blood into mud. One of those seven warriors came forward to display his superiority by means of his skills, and the lion-hearted hero rode up to him, his life-robbing sword in his hand. That demon engaged with the champion, and shouts arose from both young men. The Indian, with a sword in his hand and a corselet of mail on his body, roared like a thunder cloud, raised his sword and lifted it above his head, so the army leader in the manner of a thundering fog brought his shield over his own head and like a fierce lion stretched out his fist to his waistband. He grabbed, pulled and threw him to the ground. The Indian Raja praised him.

When he was killed, another one, just like a demon that caused the world to fill with tumult out of fear for him, approached the famous champion and threw down his heavy mace onto his saddle. He pointed his lance straight at the heroic army leader, scattering dust to the turning heaven, and stabbed his lance at the chest of the champion, that honourable knight of enlightened mind. The coat of mail on his body tore completely, so Farāmarz the hero drew his sword of vengeance. He swung his sword at the Indian, who became sorrowful and distressed at heart, as his lance was cut in two. One more time he lashed out and hit the other on the head, so that his back, shoulders and chest were soaked in blood. A joy rose up amongst the Iranians, because he had increased the pain for the Indians.

Another one came towards him in a hurry, a sword like water in his hand. He let out such a shout at the hero Farāmarz that you would think it would break a mountain to pieces. After that, he lifted his battle-sword and hit that lion-like man on the head and shoulders, but his sword of vengeance had no effect on him. The skilful hero moved forward from his place and smashed his sword onto the crown of that celebrated man, so that the horse and its pugnacious rider were cut in two halves.

Again, an Indian just like a black mountain, in a garment of iron and a helmet of iron, came galloping at the champion, turning the earth feeble beneath his horse, with an iron spear in his hand, his face full of anger and a frown upon his brow. With his spear he performed an attack on the lion-hearted man, his dust turning the face of the sun dark blue. The army leader came towards him in an assault, his lance fiercely aimed straight at him, and when he arrived, he took hold of his waistband and pulled him from his saddle like a ball. He lifted him up from the back of his swift steed and threw him in the manner of a crow. His whole back, shoulders and chest were broken to pieces and his pallid soul was dismissed to hell.

Another Indian like an animal, foaming at the lips and his eyes completely bloodshot, came forward, scattering fire as if from a cloud, whilst his roar would tear the ears of a lion. With a javelin of the finest steel in his fist, rushing and striking like a pugnacious leopard, he turned around the brave champion, under him a fast horse like a mountain. He threw his shimmering heavy javelin, which hit the arm of the tremendous lion. The army leader was angered like a raging elephant when his arm was wounded by the Indian javelin: he picked up his club from the saddle on his huge horse and lifted up his shoulders to the sky, then brought it down and hit the other hard on his helmet. Like a ball his head landed beneath his feet.

From the Indians another horseman rode up, under him a chestnut-coloured fast horse, and he immediately engaged with the famous exalted man in his helmet, coat of mail and shield. In vengeance he drew his glittering sword, he roared, raged and puffed, then hit the steed of the exalted warrior, consigning the horse's head to the ground. As his precious horse fell into the dust, that lion of a hero leapt off the back of his steed, then jumped up and grabbed the tail of the Indian's horse. He turned it over and threw it to the ground, how amazing! He struck out in such a manner that both the battle-horse and its renowned rider broke into pieces upon the battlefield. When the Iranians saw Farāmarz just like a formidable lion on foot, they brought him a grey horse with iron hooves and let the brazen drum sound together with the trumpet. He mounted the horse, took his iron sword and went forth like a thundering cloud, performing an attack on that army of the Indians, of which nothing, large or small, remained visible: his sword turned the earth into a sea of blood from the many horsemen that had fallen upside down.

For the seventh time, another proud Indian came with a life-robbing sword in his hand. He roared like a violent demon and, having lifted his precious sword to his shoulder, brandished that head-turning sword. Farāmarz spurred on his horse from its place, hit the other on the head with his shimmering sword and sliced his shoulders, neck and chest into two halves.

When the lion had felled these seven commanders, his soldiers showed their courage against the Indians: the entire army engaged in battle, so that the soil from the battlefield rose up to the moon. Mahārak for his part sounded the drums and the trumpets, moved forward and drove on his army from its place. The raging elephants, which with their feet could level a mountain, were brought to the front, where the elephants were incited against the Iranian soldiers, so that the sky turned dark as indigo from the dust of the army. The valiant Iranian horsemen, with their bows strung and their loins girded tightly, released a heavy rain of arrows; it was as if a tree was shedding its leaves. That shower of poplar arrows made the earth dark and distressing for the elephants and their drivers, because the trunks of the elephants were pierced with arrows and the surface of the earth turned into a pool of arrows. They turned their faces away from the warriors' arrows and wretchedly they all abandoned the battlefield, trampling the entire army underfoot. Not one man amongst the Indians was left in his place: they were thrown down, killed or wounded, or they were captured, carried off and tied up.

As the Iranians hurried to seek a name for themselves, they found many of the enemy's possessions, such as horses or gold coins, pearls and jewels, as well as elephants or thrones, crowns and belts. Everyone set to plunder all those things that could be found and Farāmarz allowed them all to keep it. When night fell, they returned with joy in their hearts, because their auspicious fate had been awake.

Such are the customs of honour and battle: one's head is on top of the heavens, whilst another one's is beneath the ground. Sometimes you find a throne, sometimes the surface of the ground. Such is the beginning and the conclusion, downright. Since a man's time will reach its end and he will not remain for ever in the world, it is better that he goes with a good reputation and that he departs from the world in valour and without any blemish.

Mahārak flees and Farāmarz is informed and sends Shīrū after him to fight while he himself sits down to a feast with the Indian Raja

In the meantime, as the Indian army was defeated and not one of the Indian famous men escaped, a noble man with thirty thousand leaders, with their elephants and with their swords and heavy maces, went fleeing from Mahārak of bad stock and defected to the Raja of good disposition.

When the dark night arrived and Mahārak could not see one of his Indian warrior-horsemen, the world turned dark before his eyes and his head became stupefied because of the workings of fate. On that dark night he left in flight and with expedition galloped towards the road to Kashmir. He left his pavilion and his tents behind and on that dark night rode off with his intimates.

When the night turned into day, a mounted patrol from the Iranians with their loins girded tightly came to report to the champion and made hidden secrets manifest for him: 'The enemy has gone fleeing from your presence; he feared that soul-biting sword of yours.' The army leader remembered an aphorism: 'When an enemy of bad stock is not killed but has fled away from our presence, a fleeing enemy is better than a litigious one.' He then ordered the warrior Shīrūy, that brave and ambitious knight, to gird his loins for that battle and go after the blundering enemy. He did not allow him to take any rest upon the road, for he should with his sword make the day black for that man, who must not suddenly bring his army and let the entire world turn around in his favour. He gave him ten thousand of his proud men, warlike and vengeful knights, and that famous man arranged his army in order to put the enemy to ruin.

When the proud hero Shīrūy had left, the army leader prepared a feast. He and the king of India set themselves to wine and sat down in happiness at the Indian court. Instead of swords, they took hold of cups, from which cups they drank digestible wine. The brain of heaven came to boil because of the songs of the minstrels and the sounds of the drinking party. In this manner, they drank happily for a week, sometimes playing ball and at other times going hunting.

You too, brother, bestow and enjoy, for old and young men are but passers-by here. Do not suffer sorrow, for your life will come to an end, whether you are sorrowful at the time of death or happy.

At the end of the week, the army packed up from there and took the road towards Qannowj. The entire way they were galloping after prey and onagers, their arrows filling the hearts of the lions with vice and strife.

Shīrū fights Mahārak, Mahārak flees into his fortress and Shīrū writes a letter to Farāmarz; Farāmarz entrusts the kingship to the Indian Raja

Meanwhile, Shīrū like a ferocious lion was riding in the manner of an arrow from a bow, and when he neared the city of Kashmir, the world turned dark for the man of bad thoughts. Mahārak raised his head up from among his soldiers and saw an army disposed for war, brave men who had stretched out their fists for battle, with their exalted leader in the vanguard. The world before his eyes turned dark in colour, and at that moment he did not see any opportunity for delay: he quickly galloped to the city of Kashmir and entered the city of which he was governor. He speedily lined up soldiers before the city gates, who raised up their lances, maces and swords. Shīrū the hero urged his army on and attacked them straight from the dust of the road: as his army fell upon Mahārak's army, a river of blood swelled up on the battlefield. In one attack he uprooted the soldiers from their places and hurled them at the gates of the city. Many of the Indian army were killed, and the corpses formed heaps at the city gates. When Mahārak had launched himself into the city, grief befell him because of the excess he had displayed. They shut the gates of the city tightly and from its ramparts rained down many stones. The army leader Shīrū, the ambitious hero, did not see any use in remaining standing at the gates, so he pulled his soldiers back from the city gates, retired to the fields and led them onto the plain. No one came out of the city to do battle, nor did they seek fame and honour by means of valour.

The wise freeborn Shīrū prepared a letter addressed to Farāmarz: he summoned a writer before him and told him, 'O priest endowed with wisdom, write forthwith a letter of such a kind as is suitable for a world-champion.' Firstly, as he put his hand to the letter, he set the name of God at the top of the letter. Next, he directed many praises and benedictions at Farāmarz the hero: 'May you live forever and may your power remain young. May you remain happy at heart and of enlightened mind.' After that, he recounted in the letter everything about the struggle, the fight and the battle: 'After my fight with Mahārak on the first day, at the gates of the city into which he had sought a way, I am now besieging the city of Kashmir. Perhaps the malignant man will fall into my hands. If the world-champion finds it advisable, he will turn his reins towards the city of Kashmir, for I believe that in the land of China, full of soldiers and filled with select arms, an army of this measure cannot be gathered. Also, the country is a tight spot because of the enemy.' He sent a warrior upon a camel swift as the wind towards the noble-born hero.

Mahārak for his part, on the fourth day at dawn, as the sun placed its crown upon its head, put together an army, so that the sun turned dark-blue from all the dust. He led twelve thousand men of war out of the city to do battle against Shīrū. But haste did not suit the army leader Shīrū with insight and authority at a time of delay.

You must know that a commander with intelligence and passion, when he distinguishes delay from haste, with his intelligence and patience and with insight and wisdom will grab hold of the head of the enemy's fate.

In this manner it came about that the warrior Shīrū did not quickly lead the army towards the battle of vengeance. But he lined up his ranks opposite the enemy, in the hope that they would stand at ease, for he had no hope for that fight. Maybe the champion would arrive soon.

Farāmarz, in the meantime, had gone with the Indian Raja to Qannowj by way of Sind. He brought the eminent Raja into the city, with such praise as was proper. He let him sit on the ivory throne in manliness and he placed the heart-kindling crown on his head: his country of India had been conquered, but the kingdom of Jādūstān was restored to him. They sat down to entertainment with magnificence, at the regal banquet that had been arranged. Night and day they occupied themselves with polo, hunting and wine, all having settled down in happiness.

The letter from Shīrū reaches Farāmarz and Farāmarz goes to Kashmir to his assistance

The messenger from the warrior Shīrū came during the night before Farāmarz in all politeness. When he had given the letter to Farāmarz, the army leader quickly gave it to his reader, and when the champion was informed about Shīrū, he immediately went from feasting to fighting.

One must not sit with entertainment, music and wine when the enemy comes after you. You may sit pleasantly and happily at a time when there is no sign of your enemy in the world.

He at once ordered the drum of war to be tied onto an elephant, and it was tied tightly. When the sound of the drum had reached the ears of the soldiers, their dust turned the face of the sun ebony. While his great black horse lifted its hooves as high as its saddle, Farāmarz had drawn a frown of anger on his brow. He rode on day and night in haste, like a bird in the sky or a fish in water. While he traversed one stage during the night, he travelled two stages in one day: he passed the dark night so fast that he would arrive at the day that had not yet come. In this manner, the raging lion galloped on, not eating and not resting at night or by day. And when he had come close to Shīrū the warrior, Farāmarz straight from the road attacked the enemy.

Shīrū battles against Mahārak and Farāmarz arrives to assist Shīrū

On that day Shīrū like a ferocious lion was engaged in the battle against the Indians. Mahārak's army was spread out like a carpet of ants and locusts over the plain of Kashmir. Many of the Iranians were killed: the heads of the warriors were ruined at that feast. The horsemen were dispersed in the battle, having in one blow discarded their esteem and honour. The heroes had had their fill of fighting and men had fallen on top of other men.

Suddenly the hero with authority, the ambitious leader, the brave and pugnacious Farāmarz, threw himself upon the enemy and in one attack uprooted them from their places. With his sword in his fist, like a raging elephant he killed Indians and laid them low. Moving his hand from his sword to his heavy mace, he let it rain down upon the men like rocks from a mountain. When he let loose his mace upon the group, its fierceness made the world-bearing bull and fish distressed, as he tore the army apart in such a manner that fathers and sons could not see each other.

The exalted Shīrū did not know that that lion-hearted battle-eager nobleman had arrived and that this fight and battle was being performed by him, that the enemy was dispersed by his assault. He was amazed and thought, 'I have never in the world seen any other famous knight of this kind. Maybe Sorūsh has come to our aid, having come clad in iron to exact vengeance.' As he was thinking this, the champion suddenly emitted a roar just like a raging lion and called out to Shīrūy, 'Hey, ambitious warrior, what has been done to you by the men of Kashmir?! Exert yourself this very moment, O illustrious hero, so that you may bring them to destruction.'

When Shīrūy heard the shouts of his army leader, he dismounted from his horse and ran towards him. Out of happiness he kissed the surface of the ground and praised the champion at length. After that, the news reached the Iranians that the raging lion, that pugnacious warrior, had arrived and had shaken up the enemy forces, so that the black dust reached Saturn. When the Iranians heard the name of their own commander, they as one man charged forward, drew their swords and heavy maces and turned the ground into a river of blood flowing from the heads. The other soldiers fell about amongst each other, so that the mountains and the earth were turned upside-down. Many of the Indians were killed with the sword, and for the living also their fortune was reversed. The corpses had fallen in mounds all over the place and the mountain and desert were worn out by those swords.

Mahārak flees and Farāmarz goes after him; Farāmarz kills Mahārak, the nobles ask for mercy and Farāmarz pardons them

When Mahārak saw that army at battle, he started to flee and make for the gates. He wanted to entrench himself in that city: perhaps he would escape from the bustle of the battle. Someone told Farāmarz about his action, so the army leader, surprised at this account, gave his noble grey horse free rein, set off in a gallop and went after the man of bad stock. It happened that the famous man overtook him and like a lion at the chase cut off his path. When the ambitious hero had arrived near Mahārak, he engaged him: the brave commander immediately aimed his spear straight at him and emitted a shout. He thrust his lance and brought him down from the back of his battle-horse into the dust. He then lifted him up with his lance, suspending him like a bird on a spit. At that moment he remembered his oath and threw him down onto the ground just like a heavy mountain. The spear extracted the vapour from his soul; you could say that Mahārak was no longer in this world.

Such are the workings of this acrid celestial globe: one man he gives a crown, another one the din of battle. A wise man will not set his heart on the world, for in the end it will without doubt slip from his hands.

When Mahārak had been killed and was gone forever, the news about him reached the city and its nobles. A group of great men of the city, who each had their share in wisdom, went up to the army leader to ask for mercy. With their insightful intelligence and wisdom, they spoke in lament to the champion, 'O lion-hearted, successful leader! You should know that we are very destitute and all have personally been oppressed. Forgive us and be fearful of your fate. Do not consider yourself safe from the dissonant wheel of heaven, for sometimes it will give you happiness and sometimes sorrow; sometimes it produces justice and sometimes tyranny.' Farāmarz heard them out, made much of them and arranged all their affairs with goodness. There was an Indian whose name was Tohūn, whose insight would turn a lion weak. He made him king of the land of Kashmir and raised his name of greatness up to the moon.

For two weeks he remained happily in those lands, night and day with wine, music and cups.

Farāmarz goes to Qannowj to the Raja, they talk with each other and Farāmarz gives the Raja an account of Mahārak

From there he went to Qannowj with his army, his crown placed on his head in kingship. When the news was brought to the eminent Raja about the approach of that select champion, he went to meet him with his nobles and with drums and elephants, more than could be measured. Beating the kettle-drums for seven stages along the road, they went towards the battle-eager hero. When he saw the face of Farāmarz the hero, he dismounted and delivered his praise. The nobles also came down from their horses and all filled their tongues with blessings. The army leader dismounted from his steed, and when they had completely reached each other, they embraced each other and then sat down to entertainment and wine drinking.

The day passed for them in happiness, and when the world-illuminating sun became hidden in the mountains, they went to sleep pleasantly without grief or pain. And when the sun on the azure blue cupola in happiness adorned the world with colour and with this colour made the mountainside luminous, they mounted upon their way-seeking steeds and headed for the city of Qannowj. The entire city of Qannowj, on and off road, had put up decorations according to the custom of the time. Cheerfully they arrived at the court, coming with joy and friendship in their hearts. The exalted Raja arranged a feast of which eternal Paradise would be envious. There were beautiful girls with bosoms like jasmine and faces like suns and musk-scented idols with faces like fairies, all cheerful with harps and goblets in their hands and half-drunk with heart-ravishing slit eyes. The air was full of perfume and the earth filled with song, so that Venus was blessing her soul. There were roses, hyacinths, narcissi and dog-roses, whilst jasmine was heaped in every place. The army leader sat bedazzled at that feast, his soul scattered by so much pleasantness. They received and drank and became drunk. How pleasant is this life when you can take hold of it. In this manner, they spent one month fulfilling their desires, happy and with their hearts at ease.

Farāmarz writes a letter to King Keykhosrow and sends presents and the Indian tribute; the king receives the letter and an account thereof

At the end of the month, the world-champion gathered all that he could obtain from India, such as elephants, turquoise, ivory thrones, silks and crowns, as well as tribute and taxes in the form of pearls, yellow gems, rubies and carnelians; musk, amber and dry camphor; servants from Kashmir and

Khallokh[13] and beautiful slaves with faces like moons; also, excellent and precious things obtained from China, India and the land of the Berbers, such as potions and saffron beyond reckoning; from India all kinds of cups filled with exquisite musk; further, Indian swords and heavy maces, noble horses and jewels, as well as uncountable numbers of helmets and horse armour and twelve thousand war elephants. This tribute for two years from all over India he sent to the victorious king with a hundred thousand praises addressed to that lion-hearted eminent monarch. In a letter he recounted from beginning to end the fights and struggles on the day of battle.

First, as he set his hand to the letter and the top of the pen was wetted with amber, he conveyed his praises from the pure God: 'From the Lord of Saturn, the sun and the earth, the Lord Who created life and soul, Who created ants' feet and raging elephants, may His blessings be upon the king of kings of Iran. May defect and diminution never be part of his warp and woof. Your Majesty, I arrived in Qannowj with the Indian Raja, the king of the country of the Blacks. There was a man named Mahārak, such an ignorant, malevolent and incomplete person, and that dark-natured foolish and ignoble man had set his hopes on the Raja's position. By the fortune of the king of kings of the land of Iran, I cleared him from the face of the earth and I seated that famous monarch with victory and power on his own throne. Now I stand in service to the king of the world, for whatever he orders me publicly and privately.'

The messenger jumped up and went travelling along the road, onwards until he reached the king's capital. Someone told the king of the world that a messenger from the champion had arrived, and the king of kings of Iran called him to his presence and let him sit near his throne. He placed that letter on the ground before the king and addressed many praises to him. The famous monarch questioned him about the doings of Farāmarz and about the battle, and the messenger told the king everything, about things bad and good, open and hidden. All that had been brought was entrusted in its entirety to the treasurer of the just king of kings, who approved of it all and praised that lion-hearted champion of the land. He gave the messenger a robe of honour and a horse, and he recited many praises of him.

Keykhosrow's letter of reply to Farāmarz and its arrival with him; an account thereof

The king dictated a letter of reply, and the first thing that was written to his faithful servant was: 'In the name of God the Victorious, the Lord of strength, glory and honour, the Lord of Saturn, Mars and the sun, the Lord of the elephants and the Lord of the ants, from Whom comes victory and excellence, deficiency and augmentation, and an auspicious star. May His praises be upon Farāmarz, the lion-killing army leader of pure religion, the exalted son of the world champion, master of the sword and the heavy mace, a noble warrior with intellect and authority, an honourable man endowed with intelligence and with glory and dignity. At a feast he is a cloud scattering jewels and in battle he is a cloud raining swords. Worthy of heaven and a protector of the kings, his loins are girded in valour and warriorship.

'We have taken note of all you have recounted, and it has refreshed our constricted minds. I became glad at heart about your actions and about that alert, honourable soul of yours. Many thanks to the Creator of the world – and this I assent to, O great man of pure religion – that He gave me a knight like you who overthrows lions, an exalted and famous warrior, so that I by means of your mace, your warrior-defeating arms and your shoulders can wipe the traces of my enemies from the earth and on the day of battle can burn the bodies of the people who have gone astray. You are a memory of Narīmān and Sām. May you always remain in happiness in this world.

'Now, O proud conqueror of countries, we have written a covenant with a pure intention. All the lands of Khargāh, Kashmir and India, entirely up to the sea of Sind, we entrust fully to your kingship. Birds and fishes will obey you. Be happy and remain in goodness. Enjoy with prosperity and fortune. Cultivate the entire country with justice, lay a foundation of wisdom in every action. Never torture the heart of a munificent man and do not hover around the door of greed and sorrow. Seek to abstain from troubling a person who does no harm and speak words with goodness and equity. Do not display violence or vengeance against landlords and merchants, for this would cause you to be ruined.' In this manner, the king wrote his mandate together with counsel and advice for the army. The messenger returned with joy, he was like a pigeon returning from the king's glory.

When he happily reached the army leader, he one by one conveyed to him the blessings and the message. He placed that letter and the golden crown from the king in front of that war-seeker's throne. The mighty lion was so pleased that you would think his soul would scatter. He called down praises from God upon the king: 'May he be happy in the land of Iran; may it be prosperous for him for as long as the world exists. May his heart and fortune be cheerful and happy, may he stay clear of affliction and fear, and may all the affairs of the world be arranged for him.'

Part Two – Farāmarz Goes to the Islands of India and Sees the Marvels

Several words are spoken by the poet and the beginning of the story in which Farāmarz goes to the islands of India and sees marvels in the sea; accounts of this are given

The skilful narrator, intelligent, alert and very knowledgeable, has spoken the following words: 'Many years have passed for me and I have taken account of many things in the world. I had the wish to construct a little story about the history of the kings, so from every place I obtained something and caught all my wishes in my snare. Several epochs of former kings and accounts about well-famed men of those past times have been done justice to by the words of Ferdowsī of Ṭūs of pure lineage from beginning to end in his book. Among the things that one could not read in that book, about which he had not told a story to anyone, I did not rightly see any story about the speeches and actions of those ancient times except about the deeds of the famous proud Farāmarz son of Rostam, the honourable warrior. No stage remains on the face of the earth through which that lion-hearted man has not ridden his steed. No place remains in the sea, the mountains, the desert or the rivers where he has not alighted. Like the sun he traversed the earth's surface, sometimes seeking a feast and sometimes war and battle. He has seen much hardship and trouble in the world, getting his share of greatness, valour and treasure.'

When Farāmarz was finished with the province of Khargāh, with the battles in India and with the matter of the proud Mahārak of Sind, Keykhosrow of pure religion gave him those lands and the crown and the seal. The formidable lion had the wish to travel for a while around the earth, to observe all the bad and good things of the world and to traverse the earth several times. He led out twelve thousand warriors from Iran, who felt affection and friendship in their hearts for him, lions on the day of battle, proud men possessing what it takes to fight. From Qannowj he set off towards the West, taking an old sailor as his guide, so that he could show him the way across the sea, as well as look at the stars with insight. He drove his army on stage by stage, over mountains and across water, along main roads and off road.

He travelled over the sea by ship and sailed onwards, moving through the water with expedition for more than a month. He saw many amazing animals in the water, which were going after each other in a hurry. One had the body of a horse and the claws of a leopard; another one had a lion's head and a body like a crocodile; and a third one had the head of a frog and elephant's teeth, whilst his body was human but with a colour resembling indigo. Another one had a fish's body, a lion's face and its mouth open like a fierce dragon. Yet another one had the head of an ox and the body of a sheep, whilst its chest and shoulders had thick and long hair. He saw many amazing things of such a kind in the sea and was amazed about the workings of the heavens.

Farāmarz goes to the island of Farāsang and the king of that island fights Farāmarz; Farāmarz kills him and plunders that island

In this manner, Farāmarz sailed for more than three months. Beneath him was water and above him the sun and the moon. After that, an island appeared before him, which stretched for more than a hundred parasangs. It was called Farāsang by name, and on it lived a king with intellect and ambition, who possessed elephants, drums, treasures and soldiers. He held both the title of king and the crown and the court. When he was informed that the army of the champion of an enlightened mind was coming to his country, that renowned man lined up an army of warriors all suitable for battle. He led them to the seashore, in order to cause destruction to the enemy. His valiant warriors had bodies like black mountains and were all bellicose and eager to fight. In their hands they held swords and heavy maces made from whale ribs or elephant bones, whilst a group of them had grabbed hold of slings, which with their blows could lay low a mountain. In height they were like a mountain and their pace was fast as the wind; you would think they might be the offspring of demons. They were strong men with formidable bodies, going to war with elephants' tusks. Running in the manner of Āżargoshasp, they could pull warriors off the back of a horse, and when someone fell into their hands, their life thereafter would not last very long: with their teeth they would tear him apart like a mountain sheep, and they would eat him on the spot, totally raw.

When Farāmarz son of Rostam left the water, he was quickly taken up by their fight and anger. The entire army left the ships, so that black dust rose up to the sun. They lined up in search of fame and honour, and grabbed their maces and swords in their fists, whilst the drums roared and the trumpets blared, as the army leader spurred on his army from its place. They rained arrows down onto those fierce demons like rain from a dark cloud on the first day of spring. The island's army started to rage, and its roars reached the kernel of heaven. The rocks from the slings, the whale ribs and the bones turned the earth into a tight spot for the Iranians and darkened the sky, making the heads of the proud men weary. With a shower of rocks like hail, the slings rained down death onto the Iranians: when the rocks came down from the sky onto the shields, they pierced the shields just like sharp arrows, so that the shield-bearers started rotating on the battlefield from the molestation by the black rocks. Countless Iranians were wounded by the rocks from the slings in that battle. That large army endured hardship from those feisty, fierce demon-warriors.

When the army leader saw this, he took up his mace, spurred on his tall and speedy steed and pounded them with his heavy mace, like a smith's hammer on an anvil. Many of those demon-faced men were killed by the heavy mace and its severe blows. One fierce demon came towards him; it seemed as if his head rubbed the wheel of heaven. His dreadfulness would eat up the soul of an ill-tempered demon or beast. With a bone in his hand, of which the length was more than forty cubits, he went to contend with the champion of the world. He swung the bone at the champion, but the brave warrior lifted up his shield over his head and stretched out his fist like a male lion, grabbed him by his waistband, tore him from his saddle and dragged him from his place like a tall mountain. He threw him onto the ground like a huge rock, while the troops were looking on from both sides. He ordered his head to be cut off his body and to be thrown towards his renowned army.

Next, he took his lance and like the wind fell upon those evil-doing fierce demons. He looked where the king's position was, whether it was on the left or on the right hand side, and he galloped until he reached the presence of the king, while the world became invisible in the dust. He thrust his lance at his waistband and lifted him from his saddle like a ball. He rode in a gallop towards the Iranian army, threw that king down and ended his life. When the king without equal had been felled, his flock was left without a shepherd and was trodden underfoot. That country and its fields were subjected to plunder, whilst fathers sought a way out at the cost of their sons. The Iranians got hold of a lot of booty and captives, as well as ivory thrones, golden seats and golden crowns from the city. Everyone obtained a large portion out of that battle.

For two months they remained there in happiness, and at the end of those months the army embarked to leave there. Someone was appointed to command that land and then they stirred up the foam from the sea with their ships.

Farāmarz goes to the island of King Kahīlā and Kahīlā receives him; an account thereof

Like the wind they launched the ships and left, in haste accomplishing their journey to Kahīlā. Kahīlā was an island just like a paradise; you would think that Paradise itself grew tulips in it. There was so much freshness, goodness and pleasantness that it would make a dead man come alive. It surely measured two hundred parasangs, and anyone would say that there was no place like it on earth: with its many hosts of cypresses, palaces and gardens, with its plains and mountain-slopes full of hyacinths and tulips and with the many flower gardens and mansions it contained, it had a pureness of the kind of God's Paradise. On this island were many people and everything there is; the world in its beauty was filled with colour and scent.

There was a king who was famous and just, a young wise man with auspicious customs. When he was informed about the exalted army and about that son of a champion made for battle, he assembled all the great men of his army and arranged the men, in order to go and meet him with elephants of war that were decked with clarions and drums and that stirred up dust that turned the heavens ebony. They beat the cymbals and blew the trumpets, and then set off for the reception, whilst emitting shouts. They rode in a hurry to the seashore, as the famous warrior came up from the sea. When he had arrived close to the monarch, the king dismounted from his horse without delay, whilst the army leader, the hero full of honour, dismounted at the same moment, and they embraced each other. The monarch questioned him about the troubles of the long journey and about his battles. From there, he led him to his own palace and kept him there for two months as his guest.

Night and day, they were at the hunt and on the polo field, with moon-faced servants and musk-scented wine and with idols with fairy-like bodies and beautiful faces, because of which the moon would accept its heart from the sun. All day holding cups full of wine in their hands, they were sometimes alert and sometimes half-drunk. The good-hearted king, the monarch of that land of Kahīlā that was like a supreme paradise, had his loins girded night and day to be of service to the Iranians. All the many good deeds, the humanity, the good thoughts and the pleasantness that the exalted lion-hearted Farāmarz experienced from him made him from time to time become ashamed before him, so he praised him abundantly: 'May there be prosperity in your warp and woof!'

The episode of the black demon and his kidnapping of Kahīlā's daughter from a feast; Kahīlā is informed and becomes sorrowful

The customs of that region were that every year on New Year's Day,[14] when the plains and valleys became as if reborn through the wind of spring and the world was filled with greenery and tulips, the nobles of the country, both men and women, went all together to the plains. In this manner, they would spend spring amongst the roses, the hyacinths and the tulip gardens.

That king had a daughter, in beauty like an idol of Qandahar,[15] in height like a cypress and with a face like the moon. Along the length of her body a black musky plait hung down in braids just like a coat of mail, tress after tress of musk and amber. Her eyes like two narcissi were half-drunk and with her glance she could make the hearts of sorcerers abject. Behind her ruby lips were hidden two strings of pearls and the arches of her brows were joined to the moon. Her constitution was made up of goodness and of wisdom; one would say that it cultivated the soul. And on top of that goodness, the honourable girl was fully endowed with knowledge. She was wise, had glory and beauty, was bashful and had a smooth and sweet tongue and a soft voice. Her father felt affection for her in his heart, as he had no other child than her. In accordance with the customs, she had gone to the feast, and now she was sleeping among the roses and the jasmine.

There was a demon living in those lands in whose fist a hard stone could become like wax. In aspect, this demon had a height like a teak tree, two tusks like pearl and ivory, two eyes just like two pools of blood, two nostrils like two boats turned upside-down and two ears larger than two Gīlaki shields,[16] whilst fire shot out from his throat. His mouth was like a cave full of stones, in which his tongue hung like a camel's cheeks. His claws were like those of a rapacious wolf and his finger-tips seemed to be bearing long horns: nails had grown from his fingers longer than a boar's tusks. About that ugly beast with its dark face the island was talking all year long, because every day he would grab anyone he would see passing by on the road in the environs of that city and that plain, and he would eat them on the spot. It had gone on like this for him for months and years.

On that specific day, that dissentient demon was roaming around the plains in search of prey and he passed by that festival-ground where the king's daughter was lying asleep. When he saw the fairy-faced girl sleeping like that, he started running, and when he had arrived near her, he took that beautiful-faced girl in his arms, lifted her up from the ground and headed back along the road. The rose-cheeked slave-girls in her service, all beautiful-faced and heart-ravishing, went lamenting to the king and arrived crying like a spring cloud. They told the king the whole account, what plan that perverted demon had executed: he had come like a blustering elephant, huge and furious, burning the earth with his breath, and he had suddenly lifted up the fairy-faced girl and carried her off, causing ruin to their hearts. When the king heard this account, he became sorrowful; he lifted the crown from his head and threw it on the ground. A roar rose up from the king's palace and the world turned black for his faithful people. Slaves and servant girls with faces like the sun walked around with lamentations and ululations.

Farāmarz is informed about the deed of the black demon and Farāmarz goes and fights the black demon, kills him and fetches Kahīlā's daughter; an account thereof

The news reached the champion that the throne was empty of that moon with rosy cheeks. Everyone was lamenting with pain in their souls when they told the champion all about that malignant demon and his deed, and about that awful face and appearance of his. Having heard this, Farāmarz immediately came forth from his place like a fierce lion. He ordered his steed to be saddled and the people's hearts to be filled with vengeance for that demon, then clothed his body in battle-armour and set off to fight the black demon, with a lasso on his saddle-straps and a mace in his hand, and with a harness on his horse that was like a raging elephant. Full of hatred he mounted his swift and tall steed, with his mace lifted to his neck, his shield at his side and his quiver filled with arrows, his heart brimming with vengeance and his head with fight. His soldiers all said to the famous man that they would accompany him, but he did not accept this from his exalted men, saying, 'This business has come up just for me.' He launched himself onto the road and set off, hurrying fast towards the fight with the black demon.

When the lion had come close to the bush, he roared like a fierce dragon. When the black demon learned that a fight-seeking man had come to him, he rushed out of the bush, grabbed a rock large as a piece of mountain, which could cause a mountain to be distressed out of fear for it, and came up roaring in such a manner that a war-elephant could not have found safety from him. When he had arrived close to Farāmarz the warrior, he lifted the heavy rock above his head and threw it at the exalted champion, so that the earth's surface trembled under its weight. The powerful lion brought up his shield over his head, and when the demon hit the shield with the heavy rock, the iron shield was smashed to pieces by the blow. Another time he came up with his superiority, roared like a raging lion and drew up close to the champion. He wanted to grasp him in his claws, so that he might get his head under a stone, but the army leader held his royal bow in his fist, pulled poplar arrows out of his quiver and let his bow start raining arrows like a spring cloud onto that demonic creature. Whilst the demon was screaming and the lion roaring, the lion-hearted man became victorious over the black demon. He galloped around that dark-souled creature, launching the sting of death from his bow. The demon burned, as his body was being pierced with arrows which were up to their notches covered in his blood. While his body became like a sieve from the sharp arrow-points, the valleys and plains were turning into a pool of blood.

That bad-natured demon had a dark soul: with his claws he dug up a heavy rock and threw it at the body of the famous man, who vengefully fended it off from himself. When he had had enough of his arrows and arrowheads, he pulled out his glittering sword with a vengeance. With his head-turning sword in his hand, he spurred on his swift steed from its place, then brought down his sword and hit the demon on the head, so that his glittering sword broke into two halves. Now his sword was broken in that rocky place, he wrapped his fist around his life-robbing lance. As he pointed his lance straight at the other's chest, his horse stirred up the dust to heaven. He dealt the demon's body such a heavy blow that the lance inflicted a wound in his back. He threw him down abject on the battlefield and made the world free of fear of that demon: from the saddle of his huge horse he pulled his heavy mace, in fear of which a bedrock mountain would tear apart, and hit the demon's head with it, so that his back broke. He dismounted and tied up both his claws.

The news reached the king of the island that the surface of the earth had been emptied of that demon, that Farāmarz, that warrior disposed for war, had brought that fierce lion down into the dirt. A shout of happiness escaped from the monarch and the entire army started to churn like the sea. The man who had experienced grief experienced such joy that you would think he had never known fear and pain. He ordered a litter with a throne of turquoise to be placed on an elephant for the world-conquering hero of auspicious fate, and the warriors of the land, great men and nobles seeking excellence, beat drums and blew trumpets, whilst the world filled with the sound of Indian bells. In happiness they went to the champion, riding happily and with relieved hearts. When the monarch saw the face of that champion's son, his heart beat with pleasure in his chest. He dismounted from his horse and, having bowed his head to the ground, started praising him. The mother of the beautiful-faced girl also rubbed her cheeks on his feet. They sang his many praises and scattered jewels over the crown of his head.

The mother and father went to the bush to see their daughter of good glory. They worried that the black demon might have ruined their beautiful-faced daughter, but when they arrived and saw that moon-faced girl of good fortune sitting under a tree amongst roses, greenery and narcissi and completely surrounded by jasmine, they in their great joy sang the praises of that lion-hearted excellent champion. They took their daughter and brought her to the city, undefiled by that poison-stained demon.

Then the powerful champion told the great and wise nobles there to fetch a chariot and oxen from the city and take that demon to the parade-ground. When they had carried him off from there and thrown him onto the field, they first pulled out the two tusks by their roots. Next, he ordered a camel-driver to drive his camels in the lead of ten caravans and fetch firewood from the mountain to the field. He went, taking his herd with him, and everyone dragged a lot of firewood towards the parade-ground at the command of the great lion. They piled up the firewood into a tall mountain and then threw that evil-doer upon it and set fire to that dark-souled creature, letting the flames rise up to the high heavenly wheel. When the wind from the sky had flared up the fire, the earth, the black demon and the firewood burned. Thanks to the sword and the mace of the world champion and to the arrows and the lance of the young brave man, the islanders could rest from the inauspicious demon and sleep safely in their prosperous country. People great and small assembled in every place, whether they were boys, girls, men or women, and feeling at ease and safe in every corner, they gathered provisions and sat down with pleasure and in good cheer, without any news of trouble affecting their hearts.

Kahīlā's daughter falls in love with Farāmarz and tells her nurse; the nurse answers the daughter and goes to Farāmarz son of Rostam

Listen now to an account of what happened to the princess, for she had fallen in love with the famous hero during the time when that champion was noisily engaged in the fight against the wicked demon. That girl of good fortune had been watching how he was locked in a heavy fight with the demon, and because of his tall stature, his neck and his face, the heart of that beautiful-faced girl filled with love for him. She thought about how she could find a solution, of such a kind that it would not cause slander about her.

She had a nurse who was dear to her heart and who had seen many good and bad things in the world. The girl with a face like the sun said to her nurse, 'O dear good-natured mother, grant me a favour, for I have lost my heart. See my rose-coloured face dejected with sorrow and my soul withered with pain and sorrow; the blood from my eyelashes[17] has soaked my skirt, my stature like a tall tree is bent in two and my happiness has changed into grief.[18] Since the time when that great champion went up against that fierce, rugged demon and I saw his chest, face and shoulders, as well as his forearms and the blows of his mace, I tied my heart and soul to the love for him, and for many days I could not rest because of this sorrow. I do not want to seek help from anyone but you, who are like a dear mother. You must go to that pugnacious warrior and tell him, "The daughter of the great king of these lands sends you her blessings with liberality and glory. She says, O famous champion, 'If you with your enlightened mind will call me your servant, I will gird my loins for you like an idol of the sun, and maybe your heart will become cheerful by me. You must understand that I am your friend, a prisoner of your goodness and your actions. Also, because you have liberated me from that beast, you have vouchsafed my rest for me. Further, since you have carried off my heart, it would be proper if you now would take pity on me.'"'

Her nurse gave her the following answer: 'In terms of wisdom it is not suitable for a beautiful-faced moon possessing design and elegance, the daughter of a king, to display bad intentions and customs, act impatiently and be dishonoured in front of a sensible person. In this manner you will incite shame and by these means you will travel upon the road of disgrace. If your father heard these words, he would not rest for one minute from chastising you. You will bring danger upon your head and soul and ugly stories will be told about you in the world.'

When the fairy-faced girl heard her speech, her soul filled with pain out of fear for her. Her soul was downcast because of her words and bloody tears of sorrow flowed from her narcissus-eyes, pouring so much water from her eyelashes over her face, like clear pearls onto tulips and dog-roses. In lament she said, 'My bad fate caused me to reveal a speech of that kind to you, and then you poured so much calamity over my head that my bejewelled eyes started shedding blood. But even if fate points a sword or a javelin or scatters fire at my head, do not think that my heart and soul will ever be darkened because of my love for that lion-hearted man.'

When the nurse looked at her face and saw the bloody tears and that love of hers, she knew that that cypress with her sun-like chest had chosen love over wisdom. In apology she said to her, 'O beautiful-faced girl, God could not tear your love for him away from you. I am standing at your command and I will now seek a solution for your cure. I will make a plan in order to fulfil your desire and I will not take rest at night or during the long day. I will bring the king towards the moon and with my knowledge set this court alight.' The renowned girl became so happy that you would think she again had lost her mind.

In the dark night the nurse went quickly as the wind to the court of that warrior of auspicious lineage. With her wisdom she sought a way to him, for she knew how to convey her words correctly, and she sent a message to the army leader, which said: 'O lion-hearted great man of a good reputation, an envoy is standing before your door, an eloquent and intelligent free person. If you grant her access, she will come before you and praise your head and crown.' When the famous proud man heard this, he told the messenger, 'Bring her to me.' When the nurse came into the presence of the exalted man, she bent her stature in half and paid him her respects. Farāmarz called her to him, made much of her and let her sit in an elevated spot. He asked her, speaking upon this dark night, 'Wherefore have you gone through such trouble, O sweet-lipped woman?'

The nurse tells Farāmarz the secret of Kahīlā's daughter and Farāmarz falls in love; Farāmarz's answer to the nurse and they speak with each other

When the wise nurse began her speech, she spoke with goodness, just as she had prepared her cause, and said to him, 'O warrior, successful in all your undertakings, blessings from the sun and the moon are entirely upon you. The moon of the West and the lamp over the surface of the earth, that fairy-figured, moon-cheeked and musk-scented girl like a tall cypress of Kashmir and the sun of China, jasmine-breasted, sweet-lipped and tulip-faced, rose-bodied, rose-coloured and of a pomegranate appearance, who adorns the heart, is sought by the heart and ties her name to one's heart, who possesses wisdom, glory, beauty and bashfulness and who has a smooth and sweet speech and a soft voice, she has started running around out of her mind with her love for you and has been crying night and day out of love for you. She told me, "Go to that hero of a man and give him the message: 'O lion of superior force, from the moment when I saw you at the fight, sleep, rest and food have been far from me: the image of you has taken up a place in my eyes and my heart has conceived thoughts about only you. My heart has been tied by your bridle and my wisdom is in sedition by your intellect and authority. Who has through my eyes seen your neck, or your chest, forearms, upper arms and shoulders?! My heart is a target for your lance and my feet are muddied out of melancholy for your love. When that very first arrow left your thumb-stall, you could say that it sought my heart as its target. Your shout still echoes in my ears; the dust from your horse is for me like a crown. My soul has been felled by the love for you; show me the way to you right now.'"'

When the nurse's speech had reached his ears, the heart of the champion started to boil because of that good message and the smooth speech and because of those pleasant words containing glory and modesty. Patience was removed from the champion's heart and he became tortured by love because of that monologue. He then said to the nurse, 'O dear woman, provide a solution with your enlightened mind, so that you can take me tonight to that moon and by your quick actions produce a remedy. If I can secretly see her face tonight, I will make you wanting for nothing in the world.' The nurse replied to him, 'O lion of a man, you must make a pact with me that, as long as you have not asked for her hand from her father according to the customs commanded by God, you will not lay a hand on her in any such manner that does not suit our just Ruler.' For this pact he took her hand in his, swore an oath and made an agreement.

The nurse quickly got up and left his presence to give the good news to the moon-faced girl: 'That war-seeking warrior is pleased; that proud lion has come into your net. He will now come to you, so that he can brighten your darkened soul.' When the girl heard this, she became happy at heart and was freed from the fetters of grief and sorrow. She then said to her nurse, 'O dear woman, you must arrange things as well as you can.' The nurse left the presence of the moon on earth, fetched a robe of Chinese silk and adorned that heart-robbing girl from top to toe like the moon in the sky. A precious throne of gold inlaid with many jewels was set down, furs and silks were spread out in every place and musk and amber were scattered over the fire.

The nurse brings Farāmarz to Kahīlā's daughter and Farāmarz and she come together; the qualities of Kahīlā's daughter are described

When these tasks had been completed and things were arranged such as they should be, the nurse immediately went to the champion and said to him, 'O champion of the world, come and stride towards the heart-soothing girl with joy in your heart, O exalted warrior.' The army leader of enlightened mind went quickly with the nurse to that heart-ravishing girl, and when the exalted knight and robust warrior arrived at the great court, he saw an idol just like a sublime paradise which was praised by the sun, an image in front of whose cheeks the moon would lay its face upon the ground in confusion. Her glance was all coquetry and her eyes all sleepy, her lips hid a row of jewels and her heart was filled with haste. Her two braids were chains of curl after curl and her two cheeks had the appearance of flowers in a meadow.

When the quick-fisted noble came to her, the fairy-faced girl took him in a tight embrace. They joined together in such a manner as milk is mixed with wine. They sat on the throne that was decorated with jewels, now with wine and then with kisses and embraces. Although the whole matter had been arranged that he would become associated with the king of his beloved, his heart was troubled that he might be judged, as there was no ring on her finger. The exalted warrior was saying to himself, 'When will the long-lasting night come to an end? As soon as I see the face of the king, I will ask this heart-pleasing moon from him.'

Farāmarz goes with King Kahīlā to the hunting ground; an account of Farāmarz hunting and sitting at a feast of Kahīlā and Farāmarz telling his secret to Kahīlā's wise man

He spent that night in the arms of his sweetheart, and when the sun came up shining from its place, the battle-ready hero went to the court and came before the king according to custom. He then said to the king, 'O man of good disposition, I have conceived a wish to go hunting.' The monarch ordered the exalted warriors to bring panthers and falcons, and he installed his soldiers here and there on the hunting grounds in the mountains and desert. The warriors from the land of Iran rode out with the praiseworthy champion in their lead, and when they saw the onagers galloping across the plain, the agitation about the hunt entered their hearts. They all spurred on their steeds and threw themselves at the onagers and gazelles.

The formidable lion strung his bow and spurred on his tall steed to a gallop. He quickly laid an arrow on his bow, and when a brave onager rashly ran up, he shot it in its side and pierced it into two halves, bringing the swift onager to perdition. Another large onager came in front of him and the pugnacious army leader like a huge lion stretched out his fists, grabbed its neck and threw it on the ground, so that it cleft just like a mountain. Two other onagers appeared before him and the army leader of pure religion shot an arrow at the buttocks of the posterior male onager, so that it exited from the chest of the other one. He was galloping across the desert and mountain, but his steed did not become tired from running. At the foot of the mountain he saw a male lion that had brought down a male onager. The renowned man immediately shot an arrow at the waist of that fierce lion and with that arrow skewered the lion and the onager's backs together, so that they met a nasty end. Then that famous champion brought down forty-five mountain sheep, one after the other. Next, that skilful warrior saw that seven other onagers were coming towards him with a male lion chasing after them, now running high and then running low. As the fierce lion without delay shot down those seven with his diamond-tipped arrows, felling them each in a row, horsemen were watching him from every side. In this manner, until the sun turned golden he raised up the dust from those hunting grounds.

When he became sated with all that rushing about, he turned his reins towards the king of the island, and the army leader and the king of the island together went to rest without pain or sorrow. They sat down beneath a tall tree, and the servants were told to go and fetch the prey that that lion of a hero had brought down and was spread out across the mountain and the plain, so that the king could judge all the skills of the lion-slayer with wisdom. They went and grouped the carcasses together, throwing them all on top of each other as high as a mountain. The nobles and King Kahīlā were all speaking their praises of the lion of the pride. They ate a bit and then got up and got themselves ready to go to the palace of the king.

There was a famous man among the nobles of the city, who had his share of manliness and humanity, who was wise, eloquent and of good memory, young in aspect and old in thoughts, an exalted man with knowledge and ability, dear to the king and also benevolent. That exalted man of enlightened mind was all the time at the side of the lion-hearted champion, a whole-hearted friend to the heroic lion of a man and a confidant to his soul in every action. The army leader revealed his secret to him, saying, 'O good-hearted man to whom a good reputation is connected, I have a problem for your enlightened mind, which I will tell you, as you are dear to me. A wise man says: "Don't tell your secrets about anything that happens to you, great or small, to anyone but a wise man, and seek from him in every case a remedy for your pain, especially when he is a friend to you and your confidant in every good and bad thing." Listen now, O celebrated brave man: at the time when I had obtained a victory over that demon, I cast my two eyes at the bush and got acquainted with that daughter of the king. I saw her like the sun in the sky, and this very moment I am suffering out of love for her. Now, if you can offer help in this matter, you will provide me with an escape from this sadness and find a solution with the king by requesting that moon from him on my behalf. I will give you many treasures of every kind and I will not allow anyone to give you any trouble.' The wise man replied to him, 'O exalted man, everyone has a need for your affection: whether he is a king, a subject, or a soldier, you are the crown of place and time. Do not let any worry of this kind enter your heart. I will quickly arrange matters for your well-being.'

The wise man tells Kahīlā the truth about Farāmarz; Kahīlā's answer and Farāmarz's contentment

After that, he went to the king and kissed the ground before the throne. The king let him sit down by his throne and asked after the wellbeing of that celebrated great man, who answered him, 'Your throne is happy because of your fortune and because of your renowned glory. I am conveying a message to the king from that lion-hearted, noble war-seeker, who told me to go to the monarch and say: "O wise king of good disposition, Your Majesty, you have taken much trouble for me these days out of the goodness of your heart. I am abashed by that goodness from you and I convey many thanks to you. Now, O exalted king of kings, I have conceived a longing to be related to you. Give me that beautiful-faced girl, which I rescued from the claws of the demon with the strength of the Sovereign of the universe, in accordance with the customs of this country of yours, and renew for me your essence and your crown."'

Whilst the wise man was saying this, the monarch was listening, and out of happiness his heart in his chest came to rest. The king gave the wise man the following answer: 'O wise man endowed with ability, tell the exalted killer of enemies: "O glory of the army and the people! May the heart and soul of my daughter be true to you! May night and day pass according to your wishes and in happiness. This very moment I will tell her mother to prepare all affairs as are worthy of her."' The wise man went to the champion and recited the king's words to him. The champion's heart became like the pleasant spring and he gave orders for the arrangement of a feast. The knights of Iran with enlightened minds sat down to entertainment with the champion.

King Kahīlā gives his daughter to Farāmarz and Farāmarz holds a feast with Kahīlā; Farāmarz sets off from there with his wife and an account thereof

The famous king, for his part, gave the mother of his daughter of good glory the good news about her union with the lion, her marriage to the brave champion. The cheeks of the beautiful face of the girl's mother blossomed like roses, while she privately addressed many praises to God that her daughter was freed from her troubles. After that, she started making arrangements for the wedding, while her heart blossomed because of that pleasant happening. Two hundred silk robes were quickly brought, their warp and woof woven with gold and gems. The treasurer brought a throne, turquoise like the sky and with jewels shimmering like stars; a hundred and forty servants with golden necklaces; two hundred pretty slave boys with golden belts; a hundred and twenty cups containing musk and amber; a hundred and twenty ass-loads of pure gold; and more horses and camels than could be counted. He ordered them to be loaded up and sent them all to the champion, accompanied by a man of enlightened mind. The fairy-faced moon, that desirable idol tall as a cypress, was adorned with such beauty of a kind like a houri of Paradise that you would say she had acquired her disposition from the good spirit. They gave her a robe all decorated with gold, as well as bracelets and earrings, all inlaid with pearls and jewels, and thus dressed up that silver-breasted girl with the body of a wild rose.

In the evening, that beautiful-faced moon of enlightened mind came to the champion. An old and God-worshipping priest took the hand of the moon-cheeked girl and placed it in his hand, and they made a covenant according to the customs of religion, while the tongues of the nobles were full of praise. She was led forward and entrusted to the champion, and the warrior army leader took her to his quarters. Then, in happiness and goodness that good spouse pierced the unbored pearl. The young seeker of pleasure and cheerful lover obtained his desires from that moon in all tranquillity, and love was refreshed for both of them in such a manner that you would think love was raining from heaven.

When the sun threw out its lasso to the golden heavenly wheel and mounted its high throne, as the world tore its ambergris veil like golden rubies over the surface of the dark earth, the army leader ordered the men and women to gather from the streets and their dwellings, so that the world was all at once roaring with the sounds of the musicians, of pleasure and of drinking. For two weeks he provided entertainment of such a kind as no one in the world had ever experienced in a feast.

When Farāmarz had taken repose for a while in this city and had obtained his desire from that sun-faced girl, he made preparations to leave that place, so that he could see amazing things of every kind. The army leader ordered a good and beautiful litter to be constructed from fresh aloe-wood intended for the fairy-faced full moon, a litter made from aloe-wood from Qomār.[19] A dextrous carpenter put it together in such a way that it contained a place to sleep and to sit. Farāmarz had many ships built in that land by someone who knew the ways of the waters of the sea, and then he launched the ships into the water, dispatching them in a hurry. He let the fairy-faced girl take her place in the litter, made his preparations and drove his army on its way from there. The huge lion travelled over dry land, while the ships were launched according to his rules. The nobles of Kahīlā's city and the king accompanied him for three stages along the road.

When they had said good-bye and turned back, the exalted and proud army leader traversed the long road ahead with ease and quickly arrived at the coast. He himself and his proud men embarked and the captain raised the sails. The Keeper of the world, the Creator of life, was the support of the intelligent and alert army leader, who for a while did not encounter any challenges from the deep sea or from the wind's sharp breath, as he sailed happy with his heart-binding moon, without any worries about the journey or any trouble in his mind. In every direction there were many amazing things, which everyone pointed out to each other.

Farāmarz goes to the lands of the West and arrives at the island of the Dawāl-pāyān; Farāmarz fights the Dawāl-pāyān and he kills them

For two months he travelled in this manner over the water, quickly completing the route to the West. At the end of those months they approached land, without anyone from that select army having been harmed. The captain then spoke with the champion: 'O famous warrior of enlightened mind, there is an island on our course, over which land a ferocious lion would not go. It is full of a people of sword-brandishing warriors that would never congregate with us. They have no labour or agriculture, nor do they have any harvest; they know no good and they display bad behaviour. In those woods they obtain many fruits and foodstuffs of every kind, which are there for the purpose of cultivating the body. Those demon-faced people that live there, both high and low, are called Pā-dawāl,[20] O champion without equal. May no one in the world see their traces! Because they are very much war-seeking and pugnacious.'

As Farāmarz heard this, his heart constricted because of those malevolent and stone-hearted people. He replied to the captain, 'We must follow this course and launch an army against them. By the power of God, the Creator of life, I will clear the surface of the earth of them.' After he had said this, the captain steered the ship, and when they came close, Farāmarz called the heroes and ordered the sword-brandishing warriors to put on their coats of mail for battle. As the army leader came from the water onto the coast, his heart was racing because of those ugly-faced people. When those soldiers had arrived on the island, they arranged themselves to do battle, and a roar rose up from the Iranian army that brought the deep sea to boil. Those demon-faced people rushed forward and prepared a battlefield before them. There were more than fifty thousand demons that came to fight in the battle, and each one of them had in his fist a bone longer than a tree. They jumped up in the air and just like dust clouds were pushed by the wind towards the men, whom they hit on the head with those bones, so that their shoulders and chests were all in pieces. Many warriors from the land of Iran were killed or wounded on the battlefield.

The army leader spoke as follows to his knights, 'O famous leaders of war, use your spears in the battle, so that maybe you will bring them to destruction.' Roaring in the manner of raging elephants, the knights took their spears in their hands, and those javelins turned the battlefield into a reed-bed where neither sun nor moon was visible because of the spears. Every time one of those demon-faced people was pushed up a little way into the air by the blowing wind, a spear-thrower would strike him in the air with his javelin in the manner of a chicken on a spit. All their bodies were hit by those spears and they all were wounded by the points of the lances. Many of those evil-bodied people were killed and many were wounded, crying and lamenting.

When not many of them remained, Farāmarz led his army towards the woods, and the Iranians, who moved their hands from their spears to their swords, roaring, raging and shouting, killed any of them who were still alive and laid them low all together. The island was emptied of those evil-bodied people: they had jumped up high and into their graves. When they saw that none of them was left in that place, the army leader took the decision to leave.

Farāmarz arrives at the island of the Pīl-gūshān; the captain speaks with Farāmarz about their characteristics and Farāmarz's answer to the captain

Once again, he launched his ships into the water and sailed on in haste, quick as the wind. For three days and three nights Farāmarz, the proud champion, hurried the ships forward, and on the fourth day he arrived at the Pīl-gūshān and led his army onto their island. It was an island just like a paradise on earth, with many gardens, tillage and mansions on it. Here lived the people of the Pīl-gūshān, who exerted themselves severely in manliness. They were heroes with heights like tall trees, bodies like ebony and faces like ivory; from their heads to their feet hung ears just like shields;[21] their teeth were like those of male elephants; and their eyes were as deep as the Nile, from which a huge elephant would flee. Each one of them had weapons and tools of war, and for them fighting was more pleasant than feasting. Their army leader was a large, notorious, evil-thinking, arrogant and robust warrior. Their women were beautiful like the moon, with black tresses hanging from their cypress-tall heights, with purple faces, melancholy narcissus-eyes, eyebrows like bows and noses straight as pens. They were idols with statures like cypresses and faces like the sun, silver-breasted and musk-scented images.

When the world champion, the universe-conquering warrior, with his army and his drums and Indian bells, came close to that land, the captain said to him, 'O man of pure religion! We must pass by that country; we must not rest in those mountains and plains, for this is a formidable place. Maybe we will be protected by God, so that we can pass by this country with our hearts at ease; it is better if we do not look at these lands.' Farāmarz replied to him, 'Why such anxiety? Out of dread for whom does your fear arise in this degree?' The experienced old man then told him, 'O elephant-overthrowing, lion-grabbing warrior, the length of this island, like its width, comes up to more than four hundred miles. There are innumerable soldiers upon it, all seeking battle and full of strife. Their faces and eyes resemble those of demons, and all year long they are occupied with strife and uproar. An experienced man who had directed his undertakings to this place named them Pīl-gūshān. In height they are taller than a black mountain and with their teeth they can outclass a male dragon. Their spears are all made of iron and their maces make the earth tremble. Their steeds have bodies just like mountains and with their hooves cause distress to a mountain. They are braver than pugnacious lions and they run faster than the north wind. Such a people live separately from men and like demons and fairies they avoid men. Neither a bird in the sky will find a passage here, nor an ill-tempered tiger or a fierce lion. If you go with your army towards them, you will immediately regret your action. For each one of your renowned soldiers there surely must be ten thousand of them. Do not wash your proud head in blood like this, if you have no need for aggrandisement. Listen attentively to this advice of mine; you must not come to any harm there. A wise man would choose to remain far from a business that would cause pain to appear in one's heart.'

When the army leader had heard these words of him, he gave the old man the following answer: 'O pious old man of pure religion! If the Creator of the world is my friend, by the glory of God, the Ruler of the universe, I will remove their heads from their foundations in such a manner as a fierce lion will from a helpless onager, or a male falcon from a partridge with broken wings. Know that many days will remain in the world when they will speak in memory of us. God created me for the purpose of exertion; He did not create me for the purpose of increase and treasure. In order for me to obtain fame through my troubles, I will always perform my religion with justice and design. As long as I am alive, I will seek a good name and with valour achieve my desires by means of my fame. A wise man says: "At the end of the matter, when you must leave your life behind, go with a good name, for the body has died; he who seeks a good name will not fear death." As for those famous men and warriors of mine, those proud lions and valorous men of mine, no one will die before his time has come. Do not tire out your tongue over such matters. You, old sailor of pure intellect, must incline your ear to me in this world, for not one dry leaf will fall from a tree against the will and command of the Lord of fate.'

The Pīl-gūshān are informed of Farāmarz's arrival, they fight Farāmarz and Farāmarz kills the Pīl-gūshān

The raging lion of a hero came from the sea, with the warriors and brave heroes in his wake. The famous man had his tents and pavilions set up all over the valleys and plains and along the coast. When the king of the Pīl-gūshān was informed that the plains were full of horses and tents, he had his army mount and the trumpets and drums sounded. The earth became like ebony from the dust and the ground shook like the Sea of China out of fear for the army. The island was rocking from the force of their marching; you would think it might be drowned in the water. Their heroes, of the likes of the White Demon,[22] were hurrying like the sun on the turning wheel of heaven, and when they arrived to do battle against the Iranians they came prepared and ready to fight.

When the army leader saw the dust of the army, he said, 'Today we must not hide our courage. If the world-ruling pure God plans my destruction in this country and these lands, I certainly will not die in any other place and my life will not continue any longer.' No fear or dread entered his heart, as he ordered his army to split into two halves. One half he kept on the road towards the sea and the other half he assigned to face the enemy, so that the army of the bad-willing enemy could not come up via a secret route. He put himself forward to face the ranks in such a manner as suited his valour. The lion then said to the warriors of his army, 'O famous, valiant warriors! When the army comes close to us, we first must quickly seek to fight with our bows and arrows. When your quivers become emptied of arrows, you must reach with your hands of greatness for your spears. And when you have uprooted them from their places with your spears, you must turn your hands to your swords and maces, and with the maces and the swords of the finest steel you will bring these Pīl-gūshān to ruin.'

Having said this, he rose up quickly as a dust-cloud and made a move towards the malevolent enemy, in his hand an iron spear and his black horse[23] standing saddled-up. He quickly got up from the place where he had been sitting, jumping up in the manner of a raging wind, stuck the point of his spear from the air into the ground and used its height to jump like the wind into the saddle, with his coat of mail, his helmet and his tiger-skin cuirass, as well as his quiver and his sword at his waist. The heroes and nobles of the land of Iran all together started to praise him and then they all mounted their swift steeds, just as the lion of the pride was seated on his horse, all with their arrows in their hands and their bows strung, their hearts filled with hatred for those malevolent people.

As the army closed with the Pīl-gūshān, the dust of the battle rose up to the moon. Farāmarz the warrior-killing lion-grabber, with his bow strung and his quiver full of arrows, took his Chāchi bow in his fist and drew a poplar-wood arrow from his quiver. He laid it on his bow and drew it back, forming the shape of two new moons with his arrow. When he had pulled the notch right next to his ear, he raised it up to the sky and emitted a shout. As he held the arrowhead tightly in his grasp, he drew the colour from the faces of the moon and the sun, and as he released the knot of the notch from the string, he let the poplar arrow fly from the bow. It hit the waistband of a brave warrior and the arrowhead sharply passed through him, entered the side of another warrior and came out again at his other side. Like clouds in spring those famous men rained down arrows in that battle, and with every arrow that sprung from their thumb-stalls, the body of a celebrated man was wounded. Whether they were wounded or killed at that time, their souls in time would leave their bodies. Fifty thousand shield-bearing archers of the enemy were felled by arrows in that battle and killed upon that field of war, so that the surface of the earth turned into a sea of blood.

After they had brought the enemy to defeat with arrows, they then laid their hands on their spears. The soldiers with their spears charged up like a mountain, so that the Pīl-gūshān became terrified of them. The spears changed the battlefield into a reed-bed, and the blood the surface of the country into a wine-tavern. The army leader took a spear in his hand and entered the fight like a mad elephant. Wherever he launched his spear, he pressed the army into such a tight spot that when his spear struck the chest of one person, it made the back of another one bleed. With each charge he thrust them in ones and twos from their saddles with the point of his lance: he impaled them like birds on a spit and raised them above their company.

One Pīl-gūshi came quickly like a raging wind towards the champion and directed his lance straight at the champion's body, roaring as if he were a dragon. The fierce lion of a champion said to himself, 'The end of my life has now arrived.' When the other reached the lion of a man, he made an attack full of fighting spirit: he hit with his spear at Farāmarz's lightened breast and tore the entire coat of mail upon his breast. There was a cuirass underneath it, upon which the lance did not spark, so that his bright body did not suffer any damage. The army leader wielded his sword on the off-chance and hit the lance, which broke into small pieces. The male demon took up his heavy mace and emitted a shout towards the turning wheel of heaven, as he lifted it up and swung at the fierce lion. But the brave warrior lifted his shield over his head and, as the shield above the champion's head shattered into pieces, the army leader placed his hand on his battle-sword. The hero pulled his sharp sword from his belt and brought down the day of resurrection on the other's soul: he struck in such a manner that one half of the horse and the demon was still standing whilst the other half was lamenting.

When he had killed him, Farāmarz put on his Zāboli coat of mail and with his Kāboli sword came striding on the battlefield and once again engaged in battle. In that fight he did justice to his valour, so that fire fell down upon those Pīl-gūshān. With ease he grabbed one by his waistband and launched him into the ranks of battle, throwing him with such force onto the ground that his bones poured out of his body as his power was broken. He grabbed another one from behind by his shoulders and ears, lifted him up and threw him on the ground with a shout. Another one he killed with his feet, yet another with his fists, and a third one with a severe blow from his mace, heaping them up on that battlefield and polluting the ground with brains and with blood. The army was stupefied at his actions and everyone was singing the praises of that battle-seeking man.

Once more, he grabbed a spear like a black tree and became eager to fight. He looked out for the ruler of that army and the place where his banner and his crown were raised up, then galloped until he came close to him and, with that soul-robbing spear of his in his fist, quickly struck at the hump of his saddle, so that it exited on the other side of that saddle. He had skewered his underbelly to the saddle-hump, so that his soul was ignited by the point of the lance.

When that king of his flock had been killed, anyone who remained of the army went fleeing in a clamour, heading towards the woods, lamenting and shouting with darkened souls. Those lion-like men of war with their swords emptied the land of those Pīl-gūshān, after which, whether they were warriors or famous nobles, they girded their loins to plunder. They went to seek, and found, many beautiful-faced idols, and they carried off many jewels, gold, crowns and belts, as well as elephants and horses with golden saddles, and every kind of weapon and textile, as much as could be carried.

And after that, they set off on the sea, all with happy hearts and seeking pleasure. When another month had passed like this, they arrived near the lands of the West.

Farāmarz arrives on the island of the Brahmans, a description of them by the captain to Farāmarz and the Brahmans come to receive Farāmarz; an account thereof

In the distance, an island became visible and that man of pure intellect questioned the captain: 'What place is that', he asked, 'of such pleasantness that it will refresh a man's heart?' The wise man gave him the following answer: 'Do not turn in that direction for the purpose of increase. You should know that this is the dwelling of the Brahmans, who have opened their hearts to knowledge and who perform prayers. A group of all pure and God-worshipping men has settled there now like lowly people. Their whole business concerns knowledge, kindness, goodness, good deeds and honour; they are always talking about God, and in every place they assemble in groups. They take little food, only things that are suited for them, from plant roots and fruit trees. They take their measure of food once a month and they cultivate their souls with knowledge. They will inform you about things that are unachieved and have not yet occurred, about things great and small that will be and about everything you will ask; you will not find their tongues empty of answers.'

When the young man heard these words, he approved of what the old man said. He said to him, 'We must go there and stay a while with them. We will ask for their discourses and we will listen, whilst we will rest for a while in those marches. Perhaps we will gain profit from their counsel and enjoy their heart-binding talks.' When the captain had heard the speech of the army leader, he quickly sailed the ship to that land.

As the army approached dry land, the Brahmans received news of this and set off on the road. As the heroic champion arrived on the coast with everyone, young and old, who was with him, the Brahmans all came up to receive him, bowing down according to their custom. They bestowed many benedictions on his heart-kindling countenance and at length displayed their humility. One of them said, 'O sun-faced warrior, world-conqueror, exalted man full of affection, may the praises and blessings of God be upon you, may your warp and woof be of goodness and greatness. May equally your lands be prosperous for you and may all your enemies be your slaves. This island rejoices in your glory, O lion; no Brahman will become sated of your face. We will keep no munificent man hidden from you, for you are of an enlightened mind and a freeborn man. We content ourselves with our own poverty and step aside from the path of ceremonies, for a champion will not achieve contentment except through treasure, even if we go through much trouble. Further, it is allowable that you relinquish all that you know, for the knower of everyone's secrets is God.'

The army leader accepted their blessings and then spoke to that God-fearing man: 'Thanks to God, O experienced man, that after I have experienced much trouble and pain, my auspicious fate helped me so that I might see the face of a God-worshipping man. I thank you for your many provisions for me; no one should take any trouble on my behalf.' After that, he ordered his pavilion to be set up on the plain of that auspicious place, and the army leader sat down in it on his knees, with an open heart and his hands folded together.

Farāmarz's first question for the old Brahman and the Brahman's answer to Farāmarz son of Rostam

The Brahman came and sat down at his side, grasses covering his entire body and his eyes. Farāmarz spoke to ask of the old experienced man, 'O old man, joined with knowledge and intellect! What insight do you obtain from this life whilst you remain naked in your place night and day? Without food or sleep and without rest or desire, happy in your state of absence of desire, why do you put yourself through all this trouble? What do you hope for, living like this? The world is full of goodness and full of riches, all things are set in order.'

The Brahman gave him the following answer: 'O man with knowledge and eloquence! You must know that everyone who made his acquaintance with the world did not make a place to rest or stay in it. The world is just like a house for travellers; a wise man seeks to be cautious of this house. Any person who ties his heart to the world will be called sensible by foolish people: he collects treasures as well as riches and all his desires will be fulfilled, but suddenly death will perform a surprise attack on him and put a dark helmet on his head. It will haul him from his throne into the dark earth and bring his head and crown into his grave. His heart will remain tied to this world and he will not find any joy next to God. His soul will remain in that darkness and his spirit will all year long be in obscurity. Neither his body will remain there, nor his bed, his rest, comforts or food. Why would a wise man take trouble for those things?! For he will leave them behind here when he himself passes on. For death, a beggar and a crown-bearer will be equal on this passage. Since you must consider your body a nuisance, you must build up your storage with knowledge, because when you leave this transient world, it will be your assistant before God. Be light of load, so that you can fly and with ease travel the long road to your next dwelling.'

When the Brahman had given this account, the face of the champion blossomed like a rose.

Farāmarz's second question for the Brahman and the Brahman's answer to Farāmarz

Next, he said, 'O man of pure intellect! Guide me a bit towards knowledge. What in the world is good in terms of wisdom, with which a learned man can cultivate his soul? Also, what things are bad in the world, from which a wise man should flee?'

The Brahman replied to him, 'O intelligent man, if you want to get an answer, lend me your ear! A good thing is to worship God; acknowledge no other king than He. Know that from Him come the night and the day, the sun and the moon, greatness, victory and power. You must know that without the command of the pure God neither fire nor water, wind or earth would in their burning, blowing, growth or rain have power over their intentions, since they are at His command for eternity and ever more. When you know Him in the manner that He is, if you know how to worship Him, it is good. When I tell you to worship Him, I wash your soul of bad things. You must think of God and you must be fearful of His punishment in hell. You must not turn away your face from deeds that are pleasing to God, because that is bad for you. Be a protector of the religion and a seeker of religion and do not bear any hatred in your heart for a pious man.

'When you have become master of your desires, you must not thereafter torture the heart of anyone. Speak gentle words with good people and whilst you speak, seek the path of modesty and equity. Keep goodness in your heart and do not act severely. Do not make a union with a perverted demon, for harshness does not belong to God's justice; the Ruler of the world is not content with such actions. Whenever you do good to someone, do not talk a lot about your good deed, for your heart will be broken because of your speech and the door to goodness will be closed for you. Restrain your tongue from bad words, direct your heart and eyes towards sensibility.

'Do not flee from good speech and do not lament over disappointment. When your actions are not completed according to your wishes, take that road which is the order and the command of God, because the Creator of warm and cold has not made the world in accordance with your wishes. Always be happy, content and joyful with the good and bad things that the Ruler of the world gave you, and God will give you an increase of contentedness and He will grant your heart, when it contains thanks, a relationship with Him. Continually have praise and thanksgiving for Him and always be in dread. Also, when you obtain your desires from God and you achieve treasures, goodness and fame, bestow and enjoy what another person gives you himself: the Creator of the world will give a hundred in return for one thing.

'Be affectionate with your heart and munificent with your palms. Be free from suffering the sorrows of the world. Do not be happy with the disappointment of anyone, for he also knows a way towards you. Reflect on bad things and do not approve of evil, because you will become penitent when you are faced with wisdom. Do not tell a lie of any kind on any accord, for your honour will be darkened by a lie. Prefer rectitude in every deed and do not turn your tongue to twist your words. Stay forever far from jealousy and envy, and go openly around the world in liberty. A jealous-faced envious person causes heartbreak but is always bashful before good people. Be cautious around a hypocrite and calumniator; do not speak any words in front of him from your very foundation. Let your heart tend its ears for bad speech and take notice of wisdom in all your actions.

'Do not perform evil, even if it is with wisdom, against anyone who seeks to do evil against you. If he offers you his hand, show goodness, for goodness arises with God. If he displays evil and you also perform evil, you will throw a good man's profit into a pit. When you cannot distinguish between good and bad, intellect and wisdom will have to cry about that. Humanity is better than anything you seek, and humanity towards noble men is even greater. If you pardon a fault at a time of anger, you will not know any way to be more acceptable than that. However many words of this kind I will speak, my speech will never come to an end. Heed the advice of this old experienced man and do not fasten your heart to the deceit of the world. Since no one remains forever in this world, it is always better to be munificent in its midst.'

When the Brahman's speech had come to an end, the heart of the champion sighed from all the wisdom. He praised the Brahman abundantly and gave him his blessings before that gathering: 'May God be pleased with this wise man and may He give you a reward of good things. My soul has come to rest because of your speech and my heart is refreshed by the sight of you.' The army leader told his treasurer to bring many rubies, pearls and gems, and also robes and horses, as well as silver and gold, so that he could give them to his teacher. When they were brought, the wise men did not accept them from him and he said to him, 'O war-seeking noble! A Brahman has no need for these things, he does not come near money and jewels. If I had a wish for such things, I would fill the world with jewels. This whole mountainous country of ours would be here, whilst my heart would be full of hatred because of money. If wisdom was connected to money, one's heart would be wounded by desire and hope. Because of God my heart stays away from this, otherwise I would break my heart from my body.'

After that, he got up from where he was sitting and walked hand in hand with the army leader for a long time along the seashore and over the plains and mountains, until they became tired out from walking. One by one he showed him all the plains and valleys, full of red and yellow rubies, pearls and jewels. The champion became amazed at what he saw and sunk in thought he bit his lip with his teeth. From there he returned to the court and spoke with the priests and the soldiers. And when the famous man sat down at his court, he took the Brahman along with him, and the army leader let him sit on his platform and with goodness gave him many praises.

Farāmarz's third question for the Brahman and the Brahman's answer and his speech about ten demons

He again questioned the God-worshipper: 'O man with adroit knowledge! What thing is there further, by the actions of which one's intellect is afflicted and his soul gains a dark aspect?' He answered him, 'The actions and behaviour of a demon darken the soul and fill one's intellect with clamour.' 'Which is the impure demon,' he then asked, 'because of which one must undergo trouble and hardship?'

He gave the following answer: 'There are ten ugly demons, for which hell is their custom and constitution. The first of these is lust, which never rests from augmentation: of everything you give him, he needs more, and not for one moment is he sated with his possessions. Every day he is full of pain and hatred, sometimes over that and sometimes over this. He finds neither rest by day nor sleep at night; for months and years he is seeking after money. He does not get any ease from his own treasures and he cannot adorn anyone with them. He will not see the fruits of his efforts in this world and he will end his life in ignorance.

'The second malevolent demon is need, which seeks ways to obtain people's things. He goes about his affairs with thievery or deceit, in order to collect things from people. He displays neither forgiveness nor compassion: even if it was his own brother, he would disregard him and for the sake of one small grain of silver allow his head to be cut off without any fear or dread.

'The third demon is anger, with a fighting spirit, which provides men with bad reputations and evil intent. You would say he brings vengeance to the heavenly wheel like he places a saddle on his horse. He knows neither rest nor insight nor delay, but revengeful like a leopard he will incite haste. He is neither acquainted with beneficence nor will he reveal it. Like fire fanned by the wind he will never rest. Everything that appears before his hands he will break apart just like a raging madman. After his actions, he becomes remorseful and as he is reproached, he will start lamenting.

'The fourth, is the malevolent demon of hatred, which secretly divulges itself in the world. For months and years he is instigating man to create a place in his heart for sorrow and pain. Every day his heart is constricted with sorrow, and no one knows the secret of that stone-heartedness. Sometimes he disgraces this person with a bad name and sometimes he wishes ugliness upon that person. Not at any time is he civilised towards people and not for one moment is he pleased with his own actions. He has bad thoughts, bad actions and a bad character. For learned men hatred has no goodness.

'The next and fifth devil is ungratefulness.[24] Recognise self-willedness as worse than all of this, for he will not recognise goodness when you give him counsel; he will be like a madman on whom you place fetters. He will disbelieve that beneficence exists: what goodness could anyone who has a bad character perform? He doesn't know good from evil, hot from cold, ugliness from beauty or remedy from pain. Because of that self-willedness, at the end of the matter his life will fall into the trap of the enemy.

'You must know, my son, that the sixth demon is envy, whose liver is continually full of pain. For everything upon which his eye falls, he conceives hatred and anger within. He says to himself, "That thing which belongs to that man, why do I not have it? He is not worthy of it." Night and day he is in conflict in this manner, having constricted the world for his own heart. Because of this, he in the end will not see anyone in the world, openly or hidden, viler than himself. He is not content with the justice of his Lord. Anyone who has sought envy won't get any gain.

'The seventh demon with a bad reputation is a liar, which next to wisdom has no splendour. He first displays smoothness in his discourse, in such a manner that you would say he might be a relative of yours. He will flatter and give hope, as well as perform deceit and perfidy, in order to obtain what he desires from you. For a while he will keep you happy at heart and you will not be aware of the deeds of that heart-breaker. But when all his desires have been fulfilled by you, he will not call you by any name thereafter.

'Next, the eighth demon is a calumniator, whose whole understanding is bad religion. May there never at all be a slandering calumniator, for such a malevolent, dastardly, alone-standing man is so shameless in his speech that he will say: "No one in the world is like me." When he tells a story, he takes it from one point to such a point that whoever hears it dismisses it. His actions cause destruction to appear and his words cause people to be distressed. He has no purpose with his speeches and except injury nothing is brought into existence by him.

'Know that the ninth malevolent demon is sloth. Do not be slothful, even if you are perfect, because sloth is the foundation of disappointment and it encompasses sorrow, baseness and ignorance. What does a sluggish person do except eat and sleep?! His body is abject whilst his heart is in haste: he is always in despair about his expectations, his heart is dark and his eyes are white. He has fallen into a wretched state like dirt on the road, like an afflicted man without hands or feet.

'The tenth demon is ingratitude, for he follows the path of ungratefulness. There is nothing in the world that he will not seek after, both openly and secretly, but when he unexpectedly obtains what he wants and his actions are set right out of nothing, he will forget the Creator and make his two seeing eyes blind. He places fear in his heart about his money and he suddenly will be ungrateful towards God. He will remain all year in darkness, his soul in confusion and obscurity; no sign of knowledge will appear on him with which his soul could praise God.'

The army leader was pleased with his speech and was happy at heart because of his deeds and appearance.

Farāmarz's fourth question and the Brahman's answer and his speech about six angels

He again spoke, 'O old man, seeker of enlightenment, what thing is good amongst the people, which makes a heart refreshed and cheerful and which is acceptable to God?'

He answered as follows: 'It consists of six angels, which are created from God's light. Know that the first one of these is justice and equity, which makes a wise man happy. The key to the door of one's wishes is justice and nothing more. Never take one breath in injustice. To give a share of good and bad of oneself is better than anything you may seek from wisdom. If you are a distributor of justice, O seeker of fame, you will fulfil all your wishes. A way of escape from an impure demon will become apparent through good actions.

'Know that the second one, O skilful man, is modesty. Know it to be the door to goodness and the road to equity, because modesty is a divine gift. When you are without modesty, it is because of a lack of substance. When you have modesty and harmony, you also have propriety in your intentions. You will be honoured by a learned man and everyone will seek his way to you. The path to the pure God will lie before you and your heart and religion will be kept alight.

'Thirdly, kindness is better than anything that is. He who has a good disposition is undoubtedly a worshipper of the truth. Every month and year he is pleasant and cheerful; also, people are pleased at the sight of him. He feels affection for every person in his soul and he is their companion in everything good and bad. His hands do not remain empty for any wish and a life of goodness will show its face to him. Day and night he is well-wishing to people and his two lips are opened in good speech. He does not know sorrow, trouble, grief or pain, nor has he any fear, worries or cold sighs.

'The fourth you must recognise as charity and munificence, for a munificent person turns to God with thanksgiving. A munificent person generates excellence and also greatness, and because of him everything is pleasant, beneficent and better. All days are happy because of his deeds and he is pleasing to men of wisdom. A young wise man of a higher magnanimity will not hear a reproach from anyone in the world. In both worlds he will be cheerful and have a good name and he will obtain all his glory and wishes from God.

'The fifth good quality is patience, whether with oneself, an unknown enemy, or a friend, because patience is the summit of humanity; one must cry over impatient people. It will provide you a place in the heart of every person and it will make you loved by your friends. A wise and victorious person with authority and dignity, in good and bad actions or in haste and delay, will with his intellect, reflection, grace and insight bring the earth and his age under his command. Any wish he cultivates in his heart will never be confounded by his hopes.

'Sixthly, know nothing to be better than abstinence, for it will generate a good name for eternity. The tongue, the heart, the hand and the eye of a wise man will come to recognise bad conduct. He will not speak bad things and he also will not listen to bad things and he will never incline towards bad speech. The bad and good things of the world contain danger for him; he seeks neither money nor pearls or jewels. All day he is fearful of ugly behaviour and he hopes he will reach Paradise through the truth. In hope of absolution from God, he passes his entire life in dread. Such is it, O famous champion, what I have told you with enlightened mind.'

When the speech of the knowledgeable man had come to a conclusion and he had reached the end of all he had to say, the nobles of the army stood up and called God's blessings down on him.

Farāmarz goes to the lands of the West, he sees a mountain on his way and the captain gives an explanation; Farāmarz kills a bird, a description of that bird and an account thereof

When they had remained some time in that place, the army got going along the sea route. The Brahman came to say goodbye and Farāmarz took profit from his words. After they had rubbed their cheeks together, the famous hero set off in his ship. They sailed fast as the wind over the surface of the water, like fire over the earth, their hearts full of haste.

One evening, a mountain appeared before them, of which the height rose up for more than ten miles. When the day had been obscured by the dark night, the army leader came close to that mountain. As he raised up his head from amongst his men and suddenly looked at the side of the mountain, something appeared just like the sun, the likes of which he had never seen, shimmering like sunshine. The lion-grabbing leader ordered the old captain to quickly sail the ship towards that place, and posed him a question, asking, 'What is that thing in this dark night?'

The captain opened his lips to speak and gave him this answer: 'This is a bird; nothing on earth is as amazing as this. His length and width are two miles. Lions and elephants flee from his claws. When he takes flight towards the sky, the sky becomes hidden by his two wings. The heavens tremble in dread of his wings and those eyes of his are luminous like the sun. Out of fear of him, not one kind of bird or gazelle in this country or these regions dare pass by him, nor do men, tigers or brave elephants, fierce dragons or roaring lions, flying birds, demons or fairies. It would be best if we quickly moved away from him. He undoubtedly will come down from above like a mountain in a powerful assault upon anyone who passes by here. He would quickly lift him from the surface of the earth: in his claws he treats a mountain like straw. He would carry him from the lowlands to the dark clouds and tear him apart whilst still in the sky.'

That night, the army leader stayed in that place, and when the sun showed its shining crown, the huge bird took off in flight, so that the world turned black under the span of its wings. From up high it made for the ship, in order to lift it from the surface of the sea like foam. When Farāmarz saw the bird in that manner, he got excited and let out a shout. The brave warrior strung his bow and, as the bird came downwards from the sky, he placed an armour-piercing arrow with black feathers, which would make a mountain beg for mercy, on his bow and pulled back the knot, drawing back the open side of the arrow on the string. When the left and the right sides were aligned and the straight bow was bent, the curve of his bow became dejected with fear. After he had brought the thumb-stall next to his ear,[25] the arrow jumped like a fish from his thumb-stall: the poplar-wood arrow hit a wing of the bird and made the world a tight spot for the flying bird. The arrow pierced it through and kept on flying after it had made the bird's body powerless and deformed. High up, it turned upside-down and fell downwards, making the sea and the mountain tremble with its body mass, as it fell like a black mountain. The army was amazed at its appearance. The skilful hero came out of the ship like a raging elephant, with his sword in his hand, and he hacked at its stature with his sword until it was cut in pieces, so that that terrifying bird was rendered destitute. He picked out its beak, face and claws, as well as many bones and its breast and wings, and carried them back with him, then entrusted them to the treasurer, so that they could be counted.

Farāmarz builds a throne from the bones of the bird, paints the throne and sends it to King Keykhosrow together with the tribute of India

From those bones he built a throne, raising its top above the turning heaven. That throne had feet of crystal, and on it lions and camels had been painted. He further had painted pictures of birds and fishes on it, from the outside to the middle, and above them he depicted the heavenly bodies, including the images of the moon, Venus and the sun, whilst he inevitably made Jupiter, Mars and old Saturn appear on it. At the top, he painted the crown of the king of the world, the world-ruler Keykhosrow of pure religion, as well as his feasts and fights and his crown and his throne, upon which the monarch of good fortune was seated. Next to his throne stood Rostam and Zāl son of Sām, with all the champions of Iran. That foreseeing man had painted in such a manner that an adorned idol of China would remain stupefied about it. All the nails and dowels were made of pure silver and the throne was inlaid with rubies and bright pearls. Farāmarz sent it to the famous king, together with a hundred and twenty saddle-bags loaded with emeralds, turquoises, silver and gold, as well as horses, elephants and horse-armour, and also the lances and swords of the Indians and the entire tribute of India.

When that treasure with the throne inlaid with jewels had been brought to that king of the land, the monarch became very happy with that precious throne and sang its praises. He also blessed the warrior with his elephant body, Farāmarz the hero, abundantly in front of his gathering. The king decorated that throne with those treasures and silks woven with jewels, and with justice and magnificence he added every kind of royal brocade to it. Upon it he made four scenes appear, applying them with deliberation and according to his prudent insight, so that whether the famous king was seated upon it in the winter, summer, autumn or spring, it was in the month of Dey[26] just like in the season of spring, full of beautiful forms and marvellous colours, and in the month of Mehr[27] it was as delightful as a garden in which tulips grow during the vernal season, with its blossoms of such freshness that a blooming paradise would be jealous of it. That good-natured king even made the course of the stars appear on it. Every action that came to the king's mind, whether good or bad, was accomplished by him. The magnanimous king, that monarch of good repute, gave that throne the name Ṭāqdīs.[28] Each of the valiant kings who, one after another, mounted the golden throne of the land of Iran and sat with the glory of his kingship on that beautiful and splendid throne greatly augmented the beautiful things on it, to the measure of his own power. It happened in this manner until the time of ʿOmar,[29] who caused Persia to be turned upside down and who emptied that throne for another person and gave everyone a share in it, just like he did with the precious banner of the blacksmith, which had turned the face of Tūrān purple and which Fereydūn of auspicious fate had made when he had raised his head to heaven.[30]

Farāmarz arrives in a pleasant place and disembarks there to go hunting; a dragon appears and Farāmarz kills the dragon

Farāmarz of enlightened mind, for his part, when he had got rid of that bird, went on his way. Night and day they sailed the ships, all along praying to the Creator of the world. When they had sailed for a month by day and by night, they saw an island, marvellously beautiful, full of water and greenery and abundant in trees, a dwelling place for people of good fortune, containing birds, prey and predators without limit. The proud Farāmarz endowed with wisdom came up from the sea and quickly set off with his nobles in the direction of the woods. He told them to make music and drink wine on the edge of a river, so they sat down happily in the meadow there, with harps and lutes and with digestible wine.

Suddenly, a roar rose up from the plain, of such a kind that it reached higher than the wheel of heaven. Predators and prey alike started to flee and the entire army was trembling with fear. The army leader ordered several men to gallop and raise the dust up from the road, in order to see what that terrible roar was, who had made that kind of noise in those woods. They went and looked and then they returned, came before the army leader, and said, 'O lion-hearted commander, tear your heart away from entertainment and pleasure! Because a huge raging dragon has appeared, from which a war-elephant could not escape. He makes attacks on the woods from the mountains and has weakened this island with his noise. Prey and predators have been fleeing from him; he will undoubtedly cause harm to the army.'

Farāmarz, drunk with Zāboli wine, with his Kāboli sword lying beside him, a servant boy standing to attention at his side, his head filled with the sounds of the lutes and flutes and a bow with three arrows next to his hand, immediately got up from where he had been sitting. This proud, exalted conqueror of heroes laid his hand on that sharp sword and grabbed the bow and the poplar arrows in order to go to that sharp-clawed beast. The famous men clung to him, all emitting cries and laments. 'This is not a bird,' they said, 'it is a fierce dragon. It is not a lion, nor an elephant, which you can bring down with one blow, but it is a mountain of calamity. Do not consider this as a bird or a lion! If he from afar breathes his flaming breath at you, he will bend your erect stature. We must leave this fruitless region; it is improper for us to rest in this country.'

The lion spoke sharply to them, 'My dear brave nobles! If the Creator of the world wants to abandon me in the claws of the fierce dragon, how can my fate be turned away from me through reticence, since God guides it in this manner?!' Having said this, he set off from there roaring, whilst the hearts of his soldiers were beating with fear in their chests. As he approached the dragon, the black lizard quickly moved up from his place. He was like a mountain rolling from the black mountain; his tail was on the top of the mountain whilst his head was on the road. His size was the length of one mile, his belly was yellow and his body as dark as indigo. The plain and the mountains had been darkened by the smoke from his mouth and the world had become destitute from his heat and stench, whilst the earth's surface was burning with his vapours and the fields were frothing with his smoke. He could draw huge elephants from one mile away into his mouth and break them apart.

Farāmarz let out a raging cry that tore the dragon's ears, then went behind the fierce dragon's back and strung the snare of calamity on his bow. He drew back and launched a poplar arrow, which hit the sharp-clawed beast on the nape of his neck. The arrow exited at the other side and the beast fiercely moved from his place, agitated by the commander on his war-horse. The pugnacious lion of a man turned away from him and then laid on another arrow, which was aimed at his liver and took effect: the creature rolled roaring over the ground, tearing up the large mountain as he boiled with rage. Once again, the son of the elephant-bodied hero shot an arrow at the cursed beast and hit him in between his two eyes, so that the arrow pierced him through and his soul left his body. He fell down on the spot as he lost consciousness; you would say that no power remained in his body, whilst a river of blood was streaming out of him. After that, Farāmarz of enlightened mind went to the dragon with his sharp sword, in order to bring about the day of judgement on him. With the power of his heroic, good-fated sword he cut the dragon's body into many pieces.

The army and the nobles sang his praises and scattered jewels over that famous man. The world champion went from there with an enlightened mind to the water in a hurry, washed his head and body and bowed his face to the ground to give blessings to the Creator of life: 'You, Who are higher than any place or rank, gave me strength against that wicked creature. I give thanks to You, since You are the Ruler and You are my assistant in my troubles and hardships.' Next, he and the champions of the Iranian army went off to feast.

For three months he stayed in that pleasant country, night and day with harps or at the hunt. He saw many amazing things in that place and led the army further from there, where he saw entire mountains of ruby and crystal, which brought commotion into everyone's heart. The warriors with their golden belts carried off many red and yellow rubies and other gems, before they with contented hearts returned happily to their ships and embarked as quickly as the wind.

Farāmarz arrives in the West, in the country of the Zangīs; they fight and Farāmarz kills the Zangīs

As they approached the region of the West, news about them reached the king of the Zangīs,[31] who arranged his army for battle. His army consisted of more Zangīs than could be counted: the sight of his endeavouring soldiers like a range of mountains would deject the eye. In height they were like mountains, in face like demons, and a dragon would turn weak by the stratagems of their fists. They had no weapons of war to lay their hands on, nor any horses, coats of mail, maces or arrows, but they held bones in their fists with which they could defeat a mountain in a fight, whilst they at a time of valour would not flee from a sword, a lance, a mace or a dagger. Raging, they went to the battlefield and came bravely to fight against the Iranians.

When Farāmarz saw their actions in that manner, the famous hero lined up his army, and he fought and battled against those Zangīs, inflicting destruction upon their malevolent souls. A dust-cloud rose up from the field of war which robbed the colour from the face of the sun. The army leader spoke to his leaders as follows: 'You need neither swords nor heavy maces, but you must seek to fight with bows and arrows and nothing more, for God will be our assistant and the solver of our problems.' Howls and shouts were emitted by the army and a cloud rose up from the battlefield, which cloud rained down a shower of death that hit nothing but bodies, shoulders and helmets. Many leaders of the Zangīs were thrown upside-down, but they did not turn their heads away from the battle against the Iranians. They charged towards the Iranian army, coming full of vengeance and eager to fight, so the army leader ordered his men to draw their sharp swords and to stir up the battle with their fighting spirit. They drew their swords and heavy maces, and the large armies mingled with each other. Amongst the aspect of the Zangīs and the dust of the army, the swords on the battlefield appeared like lightning flashing from a black cloud, as they kept coming down upon their heads, shoulders and crowns. Many renowned Iranians and Zangīs sacrificed their heads in search of fame and honour.

For three days and three nights the battle went on in such a manner, with the swords and the bones scattering heads. On the fourth day, a fierce wind rose up and brought a dust-cloud of fate to the plain. It blew in the faces of the Zangī soldiers, so the Iranians performed a charge. The army leader made an attack with his sword and defeated everyone at whom he hit out. His troops, all grouped together in this manner, went towards their enemy like a range of mountains and with their swords killed many from that renowned army on the battlefield, which was like a diamond sea turned into a mine of rubies, as the heads of the corpses were crushed under the hooves. Farāmarz, the army leader of enlightened mind, running in every direction with a sword in his fist, with each blow hacked off ten heads from their shoulders and with his shouts filled the entire world with noise. Those brave soldiers had had enough and started fleeing high and low, running like mountain sheep from the claws of a wolf, so that that large army became dispersed. The entire country of the Zangīs was subjected to plunder and the world was made into a tight spot for the Zangī hearts: their heads, hands and feet all over the plain were eaten by falcons, vultures and eagles. When that entire country and tillage had been pillaged, the Iranians sought their way from there to another kingdom.

Several verses in praise of Sultan Neẕām al-Dowle and his vizier[32]

As the sun left the constellation of Pisces and filled the whole world with hope, he entered the constellation of Aries and settled happily on his throne and put on his majestic crown, filling the world with scents and colours with his glory, so that the earth turned luminous from the many colours of the flowers. All the plains and fields were like the gardens of Paradise; sorrow had left the world entirely. When nature opened her bag of pleasure, the air was perfumed with amber by her disposition, and when the gentle breeze spread itself out, he could revive any creature that had died: you would say he might be Jesus son of Mary,[33] or that the flowers were just like virgins and he a salve that caused their eyes to scatter jewels and made their hearts produce mournful sighs.

In these times, any person who has wisdom drinks ruby-red wine as sweet as sugar in memory of the eminent sun of glory, the heaven of munificence, the minister of happy disposition, the world of greatness, the administrator of riches,[34] the exalted wisdom and the power of the turning heavenly abode, Abū Bakr, the Jesus of exceedingly prosperous breath, the exalted Moses with his hand of pure religion.[35] His palm is a mine of generosity and a knower of liberality; his breath is precious benevolence and a knower of happiness. On the ground, grace acts as his door, at the side of which the world has become so fortunate, whilst heaven has its belt girded round its waist night and day as the porter to his office. By these means fate has decorated my nature with royal jewels, in order for it to see with eyes of wisdom how life passes for a man. May he be remembered amongst great men in such a manner that his name never will be concealed. He must be accompanied by much fortune and be remembered in this age. To this deed I have consigned my wisdom and for this wish I have pursued my desire. I have completed this remembrance and I have exalted his head beyond heaven.

I have laid the foundations of a royal palace, but not of wood, brick or reeds. Do not consider its reward to come from the course of the instruments of power, but know that it has an exalted meaning. You will not see water or earth inside it, but it contains a field with a wall of a pure soul; it is not made of stone that can be shaken by the wind, nor is it made of soil that can be flushed away by water. In the name of the exalted World-ruler of sublime essence, Who has wisdom, beauty and glory, may a memory of the good name of this book remain for a long time in the world; as long as there is good and bad in the world, wisdom will consider it acceptable. Now, in order for the exalted minister, the lord of victory, intentions and glory, to accept this servitude from his servant with the insight of his greatness and nobility, I will lay my saddle on the green horse of heaven and make the sun my bed and the moon my pillow. May the world below and above be his foundation, and may it be his assistant and mercenary at times of victory and conquest! God will be his protector in every action, the heavens his servant and fortune will be smiling upon him.

Farāmarz goes to Qīrwān and the king of Qīrwān rides out to meet Farāmarz and brings him to his own city; the events of the king and Farāmarz

When Farāmarz, the army leader with glory and intellect, the young world-conqueror with glory and pleasure, was finished with the lands of the West, he travelled with the famous men of the land of Iran from that place towards Qīrwān and for six months followed a route over dry land.[36] When he arrived in the borderlands of that country, he sent his blessings to the king of the country and informed him of each of his actions, showing him all his good fortune and saying, 'If you come now, as wisdom ordains, then fate will not let anything bad happen to you. Agree to pay tribute to the land of Iran, and you will know that you will not have to strive against us in battle.'

When the ruler of Qīrwān was informed that the champion was coming to his country, his face lit up with happiness and he immediately went from his palace to the street. He ordered the exalted men of the city, nobles who had status and excellence, to gird their loins in order to receive him in accordance with the customs and the ways of the kings. They travelled in a gallop for two weeks along the road towards the champion, the army-protecting warrior, with the copper drums tied to the elephants and the earth calling for help against the horseshoes. When the king got the champion in his sight, he dismounted and walked forwards on the road. The army leader also dismounted from his steed, as did his exalted men in one body. The king of Qīrwān happily embraced the champion, asked him about Rostam and about Zāl son of Sām, and then he had all that was needed in terms of forage and supplies brought for the army leader, the famous warrior, so much that the eyes of the Iranians were stupefied by it: the world entirely became like a Chinese bazaar with all the carpets, foodstuffs, clothes and accoutrements, so that the tongues of the champions were full of praise. For two months they stayed outside the city, everyone having his share in happiness and cheerfulness, sometimes with the ball and polo stick, at other times at the hunt, at yet other times at a feast with harps and digestible wine.

After that, one day a star rose when the right time had come to go to the city. The renowned king took Farāmarz from that place to the city, towards his illustrious crown, tiara and court, and when they had arrived at his palace, he sat him on the throne and showered him with coins. Then both the ruler and his subjects girded their loins like servants and night and day displayed their worship for him to anyone who was a stranger or a relative. All the many good things that the king performed made the champion's face turn yellow with shame, so that he all the time was embarrassed before him and augmented his profuse thanks to him. In this manner, they spent one year, during which they considered all the mountain-slopes as their gardens, whilst the king during his good deeds and that generosity of his did not let the slightest lamentation enter his actions. What is more agreeable than a friendship with someone who has a large share in knowledge?

The army leader held conversations with the renowned king, and one day he asked him, 'O good-hearted, well-spoken king, my face is flushed with embarrassment, because of these many benevolences and this generosity that emerges from the essence of man and that you have shown me these days. I pass on thanks to you from the part of my king. I am now hoping that you will tell me your wishes, whichever ones you harbour, so that I can see whether it lies within my and my army's power to fulfil them for Your Majesty. I will strive with my life for that cause, so that I may examine the king's wishes.'

The king of Qīrwān quickly rose to his feet and thanked him profusely, as was proper. He said to him, 'O lion with glory and fame, I rejoice in your fortune, as do my kingship and my design and fate, as well as my country, my lands, my crown and my throne. But there is a wish in my heart; although it is painful for us, since the champion requests it of me, I will tell it to the famous man this very moment. I have found a beautiful book of such a kind that I hurried to quickly read, for many stories rooted in knowledge are recounted in that ancient book.

'The warrior Garshāsp son of Atrat, whose nature was made up of culture and knowledge, wrote in it: "In the time when Ẓaḥḥāk the tyrant sent us to these regions and we conquered this country by sword and subjected the world with our daggers,[37] in that time I wrote this book in Persian, and it would be appropriate if you listened to me. I have seen from the revolutions of the sun and the moon, when I looked at my own horoscope, that when one thousand and five hundred years have passed after me, a young man from my own lineage will come, a wise and exalted warrior with fame and with power, who will not be anguished by a lion or a fierce dragon and who will not be afraid of hardship or a day of calamity. With his valour he will subject the world, and he will accomplish many good things. He will descend from us through five generations, and when he comes to this region and this country, three great deeds will be performed by his hands, about which brave and robust men will be amazed.

'"In this country five wild animals will appear, which will cause evil to fall upon the world. There are two lions, two wolves and one dragon, which will bring calamity to the universe and because of which five sharp-clawed beasts the world will be dark and narrow for the great men. The lands of the West will be entirely ruined and all of Qīrwān will be afflicted by them, but when that famous hero arrives here, he will make those homelands safe with his mace. By his hand the beasts will be destroyed, and he will not feel any fear or dread in his heart. Halfway up in the mountains, on the right hand side, stands a monument from us in the form of a tall obelisk. As a means of remuneration for that young son, I have placed a treasure underneath it. When this business has been completed by his hands and he has acquired fame through his warriorship and valour, this treasure of ours will be his reward; let it also be a lustre from Ormozd."[38]

'Now, in this book, O champion, a portrait of a handsome young man has been painted, which is the face of him who will tear the skins of the dragon and lions. Since the thoughts in my heart for a long time have been about that elegant face, O exalted leader, when I look at your face and at your stature, I believe with my enlightened mind that that auspiciously starred warrior is you, that you are that master of the mace and the fight.'

The celebrated warrior said to him in reply, 'Bring that good book to me.' It was fetched and everyone who saw the book conceived affection for that handsome figure, which you would say was Farāmarz the lion-slayer, dressed in his coat of mail, ready for battle. The warrior of champion stock was happy about it and directed many praises at his forefather. Next, he requested of the king and the priests, 'You must now indicate to me the place where the dens of the wild animals are,[39] for even if they were elephants, I would lay them low.'

One of their renowned men then said, 'If the famous pugnacious warrior gallops along the road from here for three days, he will see a high and black mountain-range. When the sun starts turning on the heavenly wheel, it first illuminates the top of those mountains: a world-traveller says that this tall mountain range, the height of which is dreaded by the heavens, surrounds the entire world and it contains no other thing than poison.[40] When you have arrived at the foot of that mountain range, a dry river-bed will come up before you, of which the width is more than three parasangs and the length cannot be encompassed by any thought. It is the dwelling of the malicious large dragon, which has brought calamity to the entire world. You will find him with a body like a mountain and the hairs on his head dragging over the ground like ropes. His length is more than two miles and with his breath he can draw in both a lion and a huge elephant. His mouth is like a cave filled with smoke and heat, so that the sun in the sky is terrified of him, and he has horns like ebony trees, because of which a bedrock mountain would fall into pieces. His two eyes are like two pools of blood, from his palate the heat of hell is emitted and there are scales like shields on his body, much harder than steel or iron. When he moves from his place with his body like a mountain and his tongue hanging out of his mouth, neither a bird dares pass by in the sky nor any lion or large elephant on the ground. When the sun starts shining on the heavenly wheel, it becomes terrified of the fumes from his heat, whilst the ground starts to tremble under his weight and the heart of the mountain is torn apart by his heat. Whether it is a sea, a mountain or a plain, he can pass through every place with ease. When reports are made of his movements, the world becomes empty of predators and prey: no animal remains on our plains, neither prey nor predators, birds, oxen or asses, and the ones you see inside the city we dare not let go out of the city. It is in this manner that we suffer trouble and calamity. Any person who brings us relief is admitted.

'And on the other side, at a three days' distance, there is a forest just like a banqueting hall, which will spread out before you over more than sixty parasangs and in which live a pure people of pure religion. You would say it is a paradise with its colours and scents and with the animals of prey and birds of every kind inside it. In that region, two types of creatures have appeared that are fiercer than that dragon. On one side of the forest there are two raging lions, which are each other's mates in destruction. They are like two mountains, both roaring like clouds, so that they could tear the hearts of elephants and tigers. And on the other side there are two robust wolves, each one greater than a large beast. All of the region in its entirety, whether on the plains or mountains or in the river full of water, is in ruin because of them. This is no place for me to speak about these four. What can I say, when speaking is not the same as seeing? The surface of a land with such colours and scents has been put to ruin by them. This is an occasion for mercy for this country, which will be executed in the name of valour and law. It certainly is the command of the pure God that those lands, which are in fear and dread, are made safe by your sword and your mace and that this darkness is lit up by your glory.'

The episode in which the Iranians give Farāmarz advice about fighting the dragon, the lions and the wolves and try to dissuade him

When the exalted demon-binder heard these painful words from that wretched man, he immediately stood up from where he was seated, laid his hand on his breast about this terrible business and spoke as follows: 'This matter is my business, in the same way that those beasts are my prey. With the strength of the just Creator of the world and by the glory of the victorious king of kings, when I have tightened the girth of the saddle on my black horse, I will wash my fists in the blood of wild animals.'

When he had said this, each one of his pugnacious warriors cringed at his speech. They secretly said to each other, 'Each time this lion-hearted belligerent warrior brings about bad things to his soldiers, for he at every moment enters the mouths of malicious creatures. He does not worry about lions or fierce dragons, nor does a raging elephant escape from him. The heart of a wolf cringes at his sword and the body of a tiger trembles before his mace. In this manner he has taken three fights upon himself. It would be appropriate for us to be amazed at him: previously, that hero with his sharp claws sought out many fights against lions, demons and leopards, in which he was victorious and which made him famous, whilst the evil eye remained far from his sight. But for three fights of such a terrifying nature as no experienced man ever has seen or will see in the mountains or on the plains, in water or on dry land, a wise man would not wager his reputation. Of course, neither his youth, warriorship, glory and honour nor his pedigree, greatness, fame and essence would remain for him as long as he would keep his body at rest when he was frightened of the day of hardship. But his heart jumps up from its place in every fight and his mind is thinking about battle every day. However, not all days are such that he should seek a championship for himself in the world. What shall we do? What is the best advice in this matter? Which way of speaking shall we take with this young man? May we not become distressed because of these fights and our hearts and eyes be lamenting. Although the young man is skilful, he must not feel secure about his life, for however many times he is victorious in battle, there will be a day when his head is laid under a gravestone. When going to battle, one must first contemplate the saying: "a jar cannot at once be filled by barley". Anyone who considers going to battle must not leave the road to turn back.'

In the end, the Iranians in one voice started to praise the champion, then as one body opened their mouths to give advice and to plead with the noble demon-binder: 'May the evil eye stay far from your glory. May every night and day, every month and year be a feast for you. From the time when you left your fortunate father, as well as the court of our victorious king, until the present, twice five plus four years have passed and not for one moment have you sat quietly, all year round seeking war and battle. You sought out every fight for the sake of your high reputation, sometimes with your bow and sometimes with your lasso. The Ruler of the world granted you victory; may He enlighten your heart in every action. The dissident heaven became obedient to you and the fights against brave men occurred according to your wish.

'Having trembled badly during those fights and having lamented night and day on your behalf, we have agreed that our pain and sorrow has come to an end, and we will not experience any more affliction and torture. At a time of happiness and cultivation of the soul, you will bring sorrow to the hearts of your friends when you gird yourself for these serious fights that you accepted from the king of Qīrwān, against the lions, wolves and dragon that have put this land and these times in affliction. Just as the sun as part of the seven exalted orbits keeps its distance from this fight and battle, do not do this, O champion, abstain from this, for this is a bad business, even worse than bad. If you would fight against a human, you would increase your reputation, but do not darken the days for your friends and do not torment your body with these fights! Why do you hold your youth, warriorship, strength and glory in contempt, O celebrated man?! Because we have heard a lot about, or even have seen, the fights by Garshāsp and the brave Sām or the battles by Tahamtan, the hero like a male lion, whether against demons or lions or against elephants or wolves, whether against dragons or feisty warriors, we approved of them because of their good reputations. But no one in the world has seen three such fights, or heard about them from mace-bearers of the past. No wise man of high repute and with sharp wits has ever on his own accord stepped into the mouth of a fierce lion, and he would equally never allow himself to enter the mouth of a dragon.

'You are made neither of stone nor of iron, steel or brass: tell us how you will oppose these beasts?! We are not alone in this affair. You must accept this lesson from these righteous men. If you are harmed far from here or if even one hair on your body is fettered, what apologies can we make to Rostam?! How can we look the white-haired Zāl in the face?! What will we say to the king of the world?! Nobles and lowborn men will make reproaches. Not one of us will remain alive in his place; we do not see any sense in these fights.'

Farāmarz gives an answer to the Iranians and he makes preparations to fight the dragon

When the brave man heard their speech, he raged like a fire fanned by the wind. His heart filled with pain and quarrel because of them and a frown of anger appeared on his brow. To counter their dejection, he said to his nobles, 'Why are you so demoralised about me? With this friendliness, advice and counsel you will not hold me back from an elevated reputation! Because however keen a young warrior and knight is, he will become famous by means of his trials. If you feel affection for me in your bodies, you will not break my heart over this fight and battle. Since they request us to perform these fights, I will not turn my face away from this fight because of some counsel. I will not withhold my body from hardship, nor from a fight against lions or from a mace or sword. I will single-handedly perform the fights all by myself and I will bring the heads of these wild animals under a stone. I do not want a large army to help me and my black horse against the lions and the wolves. You may lay down your heads in repose and give your hearts entirely over to hunting and entertainment. You will see a fight from a real man who raises up the dust from the forest and the mountain. With the strength of God, the pure Ruler of the world, I will bring down the heads of the wolves and the lions into the soil. As my assistant, the pure God is enough; I do not seek support from anyone but Him. I will turn a while around that big dragon: if he can find an escape from my sharp sword, I will not gird my loins with valour and I will hide behind a curtain like a woman.'

Having said this, he instructed the king to fetch a steel-worker. When he had been brought, the formidable lion ordered a soul-robbing sword longer than thirty cubits. That brave lion further had half a hide brought, with which he could string his bow: the proud young man endowed with vigour and lustre twisted a string from the ox-hide, stretched it and knotted it to the notches, thus stringing his heavy bow. The quick-fisted exalted man also ordered ten arrows of poplar wood, each with arrow-points of ten *setīr*,[41] which were laid before the brave warrior. The raging lion requested his coat of mail and his tiger-skin cuirass and immediately put them on, then laid horse-armour on his black steed and hung his royal bow on the saddle-straps. As he filled his quiver with the arrows, the heart of the mountain turned upside-down out of fear for him; when he took a four-forked sword in his hand, the wide world got into a tight spot because of him; and when he laid his cow-headed mace on his saddle, the vigour of fate was stung by him. With his sword of glittering steel in his waistband, like an inverted dragon hanging from the height of a mountain, he happily mounted his black steed and rode like the wind towards his fight against the dragon.

When the warriors of the land of Iran saw the weapons and the exalted knight armed in such a manner, they all held up their hands to the sky, their laments reaching beyond the heavenly wheel. When the army leader had said goodbye to his army, he hurried like a dust-cloud towards the fight with the dragon. The entire army and the king of Qīrwān accompanied that champion, but when the large lion neared the dragon, he spoke to the brave nobles as follows: 'You must stay here and you must not go any further. Ask God to assist and support me, and maybe I will grab hold of the dragon with my fist. My heart certainly will have resigned itself to death when my sword rains down on its head like hail, and I will not return from the fight until I have lived up to my reputation and fulfilled my desires with this. A brave man who seeks fame and honour when he faces the battle with valour will undoubtedly not fear a fierce dragon, nor a wolf or a ferocious lion when they oppose him. No great deal of this will be registered when you keep pain and sorrow about dying in your heart.'

Farāmarz goes to fight the dragon and he kills the dragon, he gives thanks to God and the Iranians praise Farāmarz son of Rostam

Having said this, he spurred on his black horse, straightened his shoulders and raised his royal fist. When he came close to the place of the fight, he roared like a lion of prey, and when that roar reached the ears of the dragon, it raised a clamour like a ferocious lion. The fierce dragon shook itself and its poison was scattered in the air. The mountain and the plain trembled out of fear of it and the entire sky darkened with its smoke. When the contumacious black horse saw it, he neighed, raged and snorted. He was frightened and would not go towards the dragon, whilst he turned the expanse of the sky dark with dust. The champion knight angrily struck him, so that he would go closer to the battle, but the horse sharply turned away from the huge dragon, because he did not dare go near it. The army leader became upset with his steed, when he could not bring himself to go towards the dragon, so he dismounted in anger and let him go, then went on foot towards the dragon.

He saw the entire world filled with smoke and heat, with the sun turned black from its smoke. The brave warrior took refuge in God and then engaged in the fight like a brave lion. From his quiver he pulled his Chāchi bow, placed an arrow with a heavy steel point on it and laid it on his thumb-stall, taking the grip of the bow in his hand. He crooked the arch of the bow, whilst an exclamation of rancour rose from the notch. When he had brought the notch close to his ear, he let the poplar arrow fly from the thumb-stall and hit the middle of the dragon's tongue and mouth, so that a stream of blood rose up from its liver. He shot another arrow at the middle of its head, which went one cubit into its brain. When the dragon came close to him, the raging lion sought an escape from it and hit it again, between its two eyes, increasing the pain and anger for the dragon. Next, he drew the four-forked sword from his waist and advanced towards it at a run. When he had come close enough, he stabbed it on the head, whilst the world turned dark with the vapours of its smoke. Its mouth was opened like a gaping cave, so the heroic army leader gripped his four-forked sword and thrust it into its throat, so that blood spurted up from there, streaming like a river. The sword caused its mouth to remain open, scattering poison towards the turning wheel of heaven. As the sword hardened inside its mouth, the young proud man of wakeful fortune produced his scimitar as sharp as diamond, his head full of fighting spirit and his heart in turmoil, then he pounded the sword with both his hands onto its head, not sparing his arms with his blows. When he had had enough of thrashing his sword, he pulled his heavy mace from his waistband, raised it up and struck down on the dragon's head, breaking it into pieces. No one had ever seen superiority of such a kind. Now the beast was killed, the fumes and the poison caused his coat of mail, which had had such a large share of the smoke and heat, to fall from the raging lion's body, as did his mail cap, his helmet and his tiger-skin cuirass. He left that place and with his bare body ran to a clear stream, where he fell trembling onto the warm ground, his tongue all cracked from the heat.

As soon as the champion of enlightened mind had dismounted from his horse in anger and vexation, his steed had gone running back to the place where the warriors were standing, who saw him with his poplar saddle upside-down and his leopard-skin saddle-cover completely torn. A roar of lament rose up from the Iranians, and the soldiers cried bloody tears onto their chests, for they believed that, when that quick-fisted hero had come into confrontation with the dragon, the dragon had during the fight unexpectedly brought him to destruction. As the lamenting of the nobles continued and the heart of every person was wounded in pain for him, one of the renowned men of the city, who had a share in valour and sagacity, said, 'O famous and valiant men, listen to me from beginning to end: lessen your lamentations for a while and raise up your heads from the foot of this mountain, whilst I shall go towards the champion and see him with his enlightened mind. If the young man has been killed far from here and the head of the fate of us all has been turned, I will come and inform you of that black humoured ignoble deed. But if our victorious God now has taken pity upon this country and the hero like a great lion has with his sword brought down the dragon from its height, I will come and give the good news about his actions, about the fight, the battle and his deeds.' The nobles were pleased with this speech, and because of his insight they all at once stopped lamenting. The brave young man tied his belt tightly, mounted and raised up the dust from the road.

In the meantime, the exalted ambitious man spent a long time in the water. When his body was clean, he left the water and hurried towards a place to pray to the Ruler, the pure God, where he wallowed for a long time on the dark soil. He said, 'O pure Omnipotent! You gave me a share of good fortune. It is to You that I am thankful, not to myself or to my valour, my sword or the strength of my body.' He displayed his humility in this manner at length, and after that he stood up from there as fast as smoke.

Whilst the sun turned yellow in the west, he hurriedly went from the plain towards the army, going at a run like a madman, having subjected the heart of the mountain with his mace. When the brave horseman, who in his nobility had come there to get news, saw the champion from afar, he directed a shout at the Iranian army, crying out, 'O, honourable wise men, proud knights and priests! I have good news for you about the raging lion, who has returned victorious and happy from the fight. Do not retain any fear or sorrow in your hearts and do not keep your souls abject with sorrow.' When the warriors heard his cries, they one by one laid their faces on the ground, and then, still giving thanks, they took to the road. When he came within sight of the king and the army, they praised God for that famous champion of good counsel. Everyone, whether a soldier, vizier or king, scattered jewels over him. When they had exhausted their praises, the brave men all raised up their heads, and the women, children and men, young and old, sat down to entertainment in Qīrwān. Their tongues were night and day filled with praise for that son of a champion of pure religion. They had no memory of fear or sorrow in their hearts, and not one person in that country remained melancholy.

Farāmarz speaks with the Iranians and they give an answer; Farāmarz's fight against the lions, his killing of the lions and an account thereof

When they had passed some time eating and drinking happily, the famous hero, the warrior of auspicious stock, spoke with the famous men of war: 'It is not agreeable for the Creator of the world that we set ourselves to repose and give our hearts and souls completely over to entertainment, whilst other people remain in sorrow, turmoil and pain, with grief and cold sighs. They are prisoners in the claws of the wolves and the lions. A valorous man does not find this acceptable. We must go to that region for a while, to block the way for the lions and for the wolves. We will empty those lands of them, and after that, we can settle down in loftiness.'

His nobles all prepared an answer in which they sang his praises anew: 'O famous warrior of good fortune! Our Omnipotent God is your protector. May you profit from all good things and may your fame be spread around the world. Go upon that road as is to your liking, O great man; your command to pick up your mace is permissible. You are the champion of the entire world; because of you, honour became visible in the universe; and because of you, protector of the Persian kings and support of the nobles, the royal crown is illuminated. You, who put the body of the dragon under the ground: the heart of the mountain will be torn apart by your mace, and with your sword the plain will become like a sea and the length of the world will be equal to its width. How can the lions and the raging wolves prepare themselves against your arrows, when you put a string upon your bow? We have all been rescued by you from bad things; with our lives we stand entirely at your service. You have made a name for yourself in Qīrwān, which will not be hidden for as long as the universe exists. All the regions and countries are at your service, because the souls of many people are alive because of you. May the Ruler of the world be your guardian; may wisdom be your assistant in good and bad things; may the eyes of malevolent people be far from you; may the eyes and heart of your enemy be blinded.' When they had finished and their praises were exhausted, the warriors sat down to entertainment.

When the dawn raised its lance behind the moon and made the world all over resplendent, as it sat down upon its azure throne and spread yellow rubies over the earth, the army leader Farāmarz, tested in battle, lifted his leg over his royal saddle and ordered his entire army to gird their loins for the fight against the lions. He rode towards the forest with his army, the army leader in front of his soldiers. As he drove on his soldiers, who with their heads held high were striding and galloping with panthers and falcons, they let smoke rise from that road towards the forest, all their activities consisting of feasting and hunting. In this manner, they covered three day-marches. When the army arrived near the forest, the famous lion-catcher ordered the pavilion of the leader of good fortune to be erected on the meadows there by the river, next to blossom-strewing trees.

The lion-like army leader went towards the forest, accompanied by several brave warriors, and when the people there were informed of him, they headed from the forest towards him. The nobles and the warriors of that region went up to that famous man, and when they saw the face of the world champion a roar of pain rose up from the great men. Everyone lamented in fear and pain and every person described the pain in his heart caused by those ugly creatures, both the lions and the wolves, those huge enemies so full of destruction. They said to the eminent brave man, 'O elephant-sized noble brave lion! Deliver us, for we are desperate. We are prisoners in the claws of the beasts. In this country, O battle-ready leader, many proud great men have tied their belts around their waists and many pugnacious celebrated men have gone and exerted themselves a great deal, but eventually they were weakened by them and in their helplessness had to forsake the fight and turn away from them in disappointment.

'But now, God our Ruler has shown His love for these lands, for He has allowed a lion-hearted noble warrior like you, a brave and valiant knight, to pass through this country and this region, so that the matter will be settled by your hands. In this region, the plains and mountains were such that the ground there was by nature without fear. They were full of gardens and castles and filled with cattle and tillage, the rivers were full of water and plants, and both on the plains and prairies and in the sea there was prey. These forests and meadows were a paradise. But they have been completely ruined by the claws of the wild beasts. We cannot see the bright face of the sun. The world has been completely emptied of animals, both on the mountain-tops and in the plains and valleys. Now, O exalted defeater of enemies, army leader and son of the elephant-bodied hero, have mercy on the souls of these poor people, these innocent, suffering people, so that God the victorious Ruler, as a reward for this goodness, may entirely grant you an eternal life and give you happiness in the other life. Anyone who has the ability to do good things must not withhold that from anyone, especially when he is from the stock of a world champion, exalted with excellence and strength. When he knows that goodness is better than anything that exists, he will be pursuing goodness in every action, for anyone who has sown a seed of goodness will not leave here before he has reaped its fruit. A wise and well-spoken man has said: "Do good, then throw yourself into the river Jeyḥūn." '[42]

The army leader was distressed by that pain and grief of those people who were dejected in their sorrow. Pain over that business welled up in his heart, and he immediately made preparations for the fight. He asked for a brave steed that was like a lion at a time of battle, and they placed a leopard-skin saddle on it, which they tied tightly for the fight. It was brought together with a cuirass, a coat of mail and a helmet, which the warrior proven in battle put on. And when the army-protecting warrior had put horse armour on the black steed, he moved on from his place and, with his helmet and coat of mail and wearing a frown on his forehead in anger, mounted in the saddle.

Holding his cow-headed mace in his hand and his waist tied with his golden belt, the brave warrior rode towards the forest, and when he had come close, he roared a terrifying roar in the manner of a lion, so that his shout tore the heart of the mountain apart. When the lions in the forest opened their ears, their hearts started to boil because of that yell and they came roaring out of the forest, levelling the valleys, plains and prairies into one lot. As soon as they saw the raging elephant upon his horse, they went running in the manner of Āżargoshasp and in anger headed towards him. The warrior-killing, war-seeking army leader put a string on his bow, placed a poplar-wood arrow, with a point that would turn stone into water, on the bow and shot it at the female lion, so that the lioness became sated with the fight: it passed through her chest to her back and she fell down on the spot because of the severe wound. When the other sharp-toothed beast saw that his mate was lying on the dark earth as a result of that wound, he went towards the mounted champion and stirred up a dust-cloud from the fighting ground, so that the surface of the earth became dark with that dust and the eyes of the raging lion were clouded over by it. When he had come close to the lion of a champion, he wanted to bring the young man down, but the young exalted man with his alert mind pulled his soul-robbing sword from his waist and, as the lion came up next to him, struck him on the head and in one blow cut his body in two halves.

When those two terrifying lions had been felled, the young man went towards a stream, opened the royal belt on his waist and removed the cuirass and the coat of mail from his chest. He washed his head and body in order to pray and sought a place to do worship. He came and wallowed on the ground for a long time, saying, 'O powerful God! You are the protector of Your servants from all evil. You provided me with valour and strength and You granted me power, warriorship, glory and strength such as I desired from the courses of the moon and the sun, and if You had not, I would not see anyone more abject than myself in the entire world. Because of Your justice, one atom can become the sun, and because of Your glory, a tiny fragment can turn into heaven. Also, a mountain will start to tremble because of Your anger or will crumble under one breeze of Your power. I can see great and small, good fortune, loftiness and lowliness, bravery, sorrow, grief and trouble, fear and pain, goodness and greatness, both for women and for men, all there is, because of Your justice. Except You, no one has a hand in this.' After that, he put on his battle armour and followed the route towards his own army.

All the famous men had both their eyes fixed on the road, to see when the battle-seeking hero would return in victory from his fight against the fierce lions, having separated their heads from their bodies with his sword. When they saw him coming in a hurry from afar, a roar of happiness rose up from the warriors. Praising him, they went towards him and congratulated him in great measure. The brave warrior dismounted from his horse and told two men to hurry just like lions to the field of the fight, pull out the two fangs which were like boars' tusks from those black beasts with bodies like mountains and bring them to his noble self. They went and saw two creatures like big mountains of a very terrifying nature. They pulled out the teeth long like pillars and larger than a camel's thigh, and brought them, so that everyone who saw them showered his praise over that champion. The nobles of the country and the king of Qīrwān all together showed their amazement about him, and everyone was saying, 'This lion of a man can bring down the top of a bedrock mountain. May the evil eye be far from this lion-like man; may he forever remain victorious and happy! May the world never be empty of such a hero! For the times of goodness have been renewed because of him, who is a son from the stock of Tahamtan and who is a brave and enemy-overthrowing hero. About this young brave man there is a saying: "From a lion no child descends but a lion." What comes from fire except heat and flames that burn the world when it makes haste? In his swiftness, Farāmarz is like fire; he is a world-conqueror and a bold and powerful hero.'

Farāmarz's fight against the wolves and his killing of the wolves

The next day, when the monarch of the sky brought the dawn down from the heavens and, as he showed his face from the fourth sphere,[43] adorned the entire world with sunlight, the army leader put his coat of mail on his body and knotted together the mail that was made of steel. His heart was prepared for the fight and the strife, his belt was knotted and his quiver filled with arrows. With the strength of the Ruler of the world, his Guide, he mounted his black horse and went roaring and raging toward the fight against the wolves, his huge steed galloping beneath him. When he had arrived, he loudly roared once, with a noise that made the trees shed their leaves, then he continued until he came close to the wolves and a pleasant meadow appeared before him.

When the wolves heard his shout, they set off from the forest towards him. These wolves, which like demons of Māzandarān were braying and digging up the earth with their teeth, could break the heart of the mountain with their roars and would not turn their heads away from a fierce dragon. The horns on their heads resembled ivory,[44] and their bodies, just like those of elephants, were all the colour of teak. As they came to fight the intrepid Farāmarz, they came roaring in the manner of demons. When they had arrived close to the army leader, the young mounted warrior prepared his bow and poplar arrows, placed an arrow with a point of the finest steel on the bow and shot it at the body and chest of the male wolf. The beast was finished off by the arrow-wound: he fell down and with a roar gave up the ghost on the spot. His mate came like the wind, stirring up the dark dirt from the battleground, and made an attack on Farāmarz the hero. The wolf threw herself upon the feet of his steed, the horn on her head being just like a large stake. She thrust the horn into the black horse's underbelly and in one thrust tore his stomach straight apart. The steed fell to the ground in pain, so the lion-like hero jumped off his back and reached out with his hand to draw his mace, his heart beating as the wolf approached. The warrior lifted it up, hit her on the head and laid her low, breaking her head, shoulders and neck into pieces.

When he had overthrown the wolves, the splendid hero left there in a hurry towards his men. On foot he arrived at a source of water, his face purple and his heart satisfied. With good thoughts and right judgement he drank the water and washed his face, head and body, then displayed his humility before the Ruler of the world and added blessings as were appropriate for Him, saying, 'You, Who are higher than any place or position, You were my assistant against those beasts.' In this manner he kept on speaking about the amazing things he had seen, of that kind of beasts that no one in both worlds had seen, and when he had completed his praises of the Creator of the world, he turned away from the field of strife and hurried quickly towards his own army, striding and seeking prey as he went.

On the other side, where the famous army was standing, having become sorrowful about the mounted champion, every person was saying, 'It has lasted a long time and the world-champion, our battle-seeking leader, still has not returned from the battlefield; no one knows what is going on. May the evil eye of fate not have caused any harm to that famous man. From so many fights and on the verge of the day resurrection that came up before him at times of conflict, he every time returned victorious, so that he through his glory became necessary for the world. But now, since he does not return from the battlefield, we must gallop and raise up the dust from the road, in order to go and see what the situation is. May we not have to cry about our fates!' So, the warriors went, all of the same sentiment, roaring, full of pain and lamenting.

When they had travelled up for one mile in a gallop, that warrior of pure religion appeared, on foot and with his heavy armour on his body, sweat running from his body like a rivulet. Cheering, the nobles fetched him his horse, when they saw his footsteps in the dirt of the road, and they sung his praise and they scattered jewels all over him. The champion then said to the warriors, 'You men of enlightened mind should turn towards that plain of the fight and take a look at those fierce wolves, for never have brave and pugnacious robust men seen two large wolves of such a kind, nor will they have heard how the measure of their days was filled by the sword and scimitar.' The warriors went and saw the wolves, which were hardly wolves, but more like feisty dragons. Young and old were praising that force of the brave warrior's arms. They pulled out their fangs at the root, their speech all full of praise.

They returned to their army camp, feeling safe from trouble, torment and anguish. The story was spread in the country amongst the noble conquerors of countries, how the world-ruling brave warrior had with his sword entirely emptied the face of the earth of the wolves, of the dragon and of the lions. The nobles of every region went with praise towards him, in order to scatter coins over him, and they brought every thing that would be of use.

In that pleasant country the king and the champion, together with the famous auspicious warriors, spent some time with music and drink, all drunk with entertainment and their heads full of noise. Sometimes they were hunting in the reed beds, and at other times they attended a wine-drinking session. In this manner, another six months went by, either by the river or in the mountains and on the plains. And after that, Farāmarz of enlightened mind with the king and his soldiers, both young and old, hurried from there to the city, having all accomplished their desires and wishes.

An account of Farāmarz retrieving Garshāsp's treasure and a description of his letter

When they had sat at the court for one week, the army leader spoke to the king as follows: 'That treasure of Garshāsp the warrior-knight, which you mentioned to me several times, where is it? Show it to me now; it is proper that these people get to see it.' The great king got up from where he was seated, together with his monarch-obeying famous men, and Farāmarz the hero and the Iranian army, too, went from the city to the place where halfway in the land stood an obelisk, in the same manner as the book had indicated. The tall obelisk was made of stone and plaster, and its height came to twenty cubits.

He went up and knocked it down from its foundation, so that a dark hole appeared there. They saw a statue in the dark pit, at which the brave lion took a look: it was a man of turquoise on a golden horse, with in his hand a life-taking sword. He was seated on that golden horse in such a manner that you would say he was that very moment engaged in a fight. The army leader Farāmarz, that brave warrior, ordered someone to go down, in order to see what there was in the deep pit and how they could find their way there.

But when the man set foot in that place, the sword turned as quick as the wind and suddenly brought down the day of resurrection upon him, as the sharp sword that very same moment hit his neck. The world champion stood in amazement and spoke the name of God many times under his breath. With his heart fully downcast by pain for the young man, he had the earth all around the pit dug up and then saw the whole trick and contraption of the pit, which they broke, so that they could see the way clearly.

The heroic champion entered that place, accompanied by several of his renowned men, and he saw a delightfully decorated dwelling, adorned with turquoises and rubies. In it, he saw many jars of gold, in which a man on a horse could become lost and which were full of clear pearls and silver and gold strung together on chains. From end to end he saw many rubies, turquoises and other gems, such as tourmalines and emeralds, scattered about in every place, all mixed with each other.

There was a tablet of ruby like sunlight, beautiful and clear as a drop of water, on which some sound advice in good, wholesome and fruitful words had been written. The lion found the following message written on it: 'O brave champion full of honour, world-conqueror and exalted descendant of mine, protector of the Persian kings and leader of your people! May our blessings upon you be plentiful and may goodness always be your warp and woof. Since you arrived here with your enlightened mind, this country of Qīrwān because of your glory again became a paradise with colours and scents. Because of your grandeur, O pugnacious lion, all darkness will be polished off it, and it will once again turn its face towards beauty. Take this precious treasure as your reward for yourself, for the many troubles you had to endure.

'But take heed of my counsel from beginning to end: consider the actions of the world as futile. Since no one will stay in the world forever, you must not tie your heart to it, O heroic champion. Enjoy all that you have and give away part of it; do not darken the day of fortune for yourself. Do not make your heart downcast about life, turn your head to goodness and never feel sorrowful, because if you strive and gather a lot, you will also have to let it go and leave it behind. I too, my son, enjoyed glory and pleasure. My heart and brain were wise, as were my eyes and ears. I had greatness, a reputation, excellence, good fortune and the world championship with a crown and a throne, and no place on the face of the earth remained where my elephant had not set foot. With my sword, my arrows and my heavy mace I have broken many vast armies. Time and again I have separated the heads from the bodies of many elephants and lions and of many dragons. With my sword

I have cleft the heart of a mountain and I obtained from the world all the wishes in my heart. My share in life was more than a thousand years. I have taken many countries and cities, both in the days of Ẓaḥḥāk of Arabian stock and in the times of Fereydūn of religion and justice. My actions were right and my days, at ease. And after that, having illuminated the world, when I said that I wanted to take some rest and wanted to take up my cup in repose, death suddenly plotted an attack and let its arrowhead pass through my helmet and headgear. I was brought from my throne down onto the dark earth and my head was unavoidably laid in my grave. We have left you behind until the next world, may you remember us amongst the great men.

'You are a memory of me in the world, so may God be satisfied with you. Since you have learned, O famous champion, that the world will not remain forever, do not put your body through any trouble on behalf of the world and never give your heart over to wickedness. Do not set yourself on fire in search of money or treasure, as we cannot expect to live from one night to the following day, so we will come to regret the goods we have gathered when we thereafter are scattered in the ground. Strive towards those things on the world, O famous man, which will cause God to be satisfied with you.'

When the army leader had read the counsel of his forefather, tears were running from his eyes over his face. He emitted a cold sigh straight from his heart as he let the yellow water flow from his eyes, then for a long time remembered the deeds of his ancestor, after which he opened the door to the treasures. He distributed much of it to every person, so that everyone was happy and joyful because of him.

For one year and six months he remained in that region, and when the soldiers became heart-sick, they mounted. After he had found his way out of that country and that region, he twisted his reins towards the East.

Farāmarz goes towards the East and the ships of the Iranians become dispersed from each other; Farāmarz arrives at the island of the Asp-sarān and a description thereof

He hurried and marched on until he reached the sea. He saw a deep ocean without limit, which joined the Sea of China. You would think that the land could be drowned by it: it would take a ship one year to cross it. The world-champion warrior ordered forty ships to be built and to be launched onto that deep sea. The man of pure religion travelled for six months over that deep sea, passing by China and Māchīn through the water, and after that, as he entered the seventh month, a fierce wind suddenly rose, of such a kind that the sailor could not remember in those parts. All the ships became dispersed, as destruction was brought down upon the sea and the ships. The soldiers and the army leader became separated from each other, so that the hearts and souls of them all were afflicted, as they were all together dispersed by that wind and were moaning with the pain of separation.

Farāmarz the army leader, together with his spouse and the old captain and with a wounded heart, fell upon a place just like paradise, an island full of people and full of tillage, where all the woods were filled with fruit-bearing trees and all the mountains and plains full of tulip gardens. They headed towards that island, lamenting about their pain and about the turmoil. When the ship landed from the sea on the coast, many people became visible there, with heads just like horses but in body human. The heart of the champion was sorrowed because of them. Thirty or forty of those horse-faced people[45] went towards that lion-hearted man: they gave the champion their benedictions, but the young man did not know their language. His heart filled with sadness because he knew neither their speech nor their business, so he lamented a lot, sighed plaintively and prayed to God, asking from the Creator of life, the Giver of daily bread, to restore goodness and glory to him.

Farāmarz meets a merchant who gives Farāmarz an account of Sīmorgh

God with His victorious justice took mercy on him and opened a closed door for him. When the Ruler of the world shuts a door, He will open for you a hundred doors in secret. Never despair of God, but entrust your upright heart to Him, for He is of a victorious destiny and He is victorious, and He won't relinquish you from His embrace on a day of hardship. At that moment, a merchant endowed with wisdom suddenly appeared. He came towards the world-conquering warrior and rubbed his face on the ground before him. The famous man set him at ease and treated him kindly, as he asked him, 'O man of pure actions! How have you happened upon this place; how did you find your way to this region? Tell me all your adventures and refresh my wounded heart a bit.'

The man then told him in reply, 'O lion-like exalted warrior, you must know that I was a merchant and earned my wealth with a caravan. For the sake of augmentation, profit and increase I arranged to go to the Ethiopians, but suddenly a nasty wind appeared and all my possessions and men disappeared. All of a sudden I found myself without means on a piece of driftwood heading for Mount Qāf. From there, I walked a lot over dry land, without anyone to help me on that road. The land was full of hardship, suffering and avarice and the road was long, full of terror and without water. Without delay I came to the Western sea, and after that I arrived in the land of the Franks,[46] from where I embarked in another ship, seeking a way for my soul and a remedy for my heart. When I had travelled a while over the water, our destiny fell asleep and the ship lost its way, whilst there was no one on our route to help us. Suddenly the ship twisted under the wind of calamity and entered the mouth of a dragon. A wise old man of ancient times has said, when he loosened the feet of his speech from their shackles: "In all your actions you must give thanks, for it can be worse than bad what happens to you." The ship sank because of the raging wind, but I remained on one plank, with sorrow in my heart.

'In the sea, I saw a tall tree, its greatness passing beyond all width and length. You would think that the world would be hidden under the shadow of that tree's branches: its top was reaching out into heaven and its branches were scratching the face of the sun. A Brahman with a wise heart has said that there Canopus shines over Yemen. I always carried along a rope with a length of ten lassos, twisted from strands of raw silk, without thinking that one day it would be of use to me in the world. When my raft came under the tree, I at once threw up the rope from the raft, threw its noose over a branch and twisted it, so that it was tied tightly to the branch. Quick as the wind I gripped it with my hands and happily climbed up to the top of the branch, then sat down and looked at the surface of the water, my heart racing about that deep sea. How well the wise insightful man spoke: "In every business, choose God."

'I sat on that branch for three days, and on the fourth, when the world-illuminating sun rose and brightened the world, and made the earth all over like a flower bed, I saw a bird like a huge mountain, like a dark cloud driven on by a strong wind. The world, over the length and width of the earth, turned black under its wingspan. It came down to settle upon that tree and set its sharp claws on that branch. I looked, O famous man, at its foot, at the largeness of its height, its talons and its width: it was such that if thirty or forty people sat upon it, it would not be harmed. I thought a lot about it, how I could escape with my life from there, and I went and sat myself on the back of that foot. The bird rose up from that place in flight and went flying towards the dark clouds, filling the world with a roaring like lions with its wings. It went so high towards the exalted heavenly wheel that, when I looked at the surface of the earth, the world was a ball before my eyes, or you could say that it seemed even smaller than a ball.

'My eyes became tired during this flight, and place and time turned dark before me. Then, from high up it headed towards the earth and like a ship continued along its route, quickly flying to this place where you see me, O warrior, protector of the army! From the sky to the surface of the earth there still remained more than thirty cubits, O exalted man! I threw myself down them, for I knew no other solution than that. I fell upon the ground and was wounded, but God the pure Ruler had mercy on me and restored my dead body back to life. I stood up from the ground fast as the wind and, giving thanks, I sought my way and cleared my heart of its past anguish. I had arrived in this land lamenting woefully, in such a manner as you see, with my bad fate. It has been two years, O king greater than I, that I have been a prisoner amongst these people, lamenting, unhappy and mournful, melancholy, bewildered and afflicted like this. I have no road out, no friend and no one to guide me; my heart is full of pain and my liver full of blood. Maybe God, my pure Sovereign, will grant me an escape from this hardship.'

Farāmarz the hero stood in amazement about him and was surprised at what he had said. Then he said to him, 'Keep your heart happy and consider all your past sufferings as nothing. Many soldiers and leaders of mine, who each are a token in the world, have also been lost at sea from me like on the day of resurrection, because of the waves and because of a sharp wind. I have accepted from the pure Creator of life that, if I by the glory of the Creator of the world will see the faces of my champions, those praised warriors and young men of mine, the face of my resplendent fortune will shine upon me. If the Keeper of the world grants me His assistance and I find a passage across this deep sea, that same fortune will return to me and protect me just like my own friends, and maybe I can restore your peace of mind to you.'

When he had heard this, that man praised him abundantly and laid his head on the ground. After that, the heroic champion said to him, 'O wise man of enlightened mind! Go to those people and talk to a group of them, because I have become sick with worry. You must pose them a few questions; perhaps they know of some kind of solution for us, how we can conduct a search for my army and maybe drive the worries from our hearts.'

The merchant hurried away from that famous man and went to the people of that region, and then questioned those miserable horse-faced people. Having explained to them the whole situation of the army, he extracted a secret that had been hidden and obtained the following answer from that calamitous group: 'At ten days' distance from here, a tall mountain rises up before you, of which the top cannot be seen; no one has ever heard of such a mountain. By the decree of God, the Commander, its foot stands on the world's foundations and its head is in heaven. On it lives a bird with insight and wishes, which a world-wise man calls Sīmorgh by name. Perhaps your problems can be solved by him, for he is a guide to lost men. You must go to the bird and tell him these adventures, for he is very wise and sagacious of heart; every learned man obtains profit from him.' When he had heard this from them, he immediately returned to the champion of the world and repeated to him their words about the mountain and about Sīmorgh and the hidden secret.

The army leader sank into thought about these words and remembered an ancient story of how the white-haired warrior and world-champion Zāl had received several feathers from Sīmorgh: on a day when his abject fate had brought hardship, pain and sorrow upon him, at a time of strife when treasures or soldiers were of no use to him against fate, he should place a piece of that feather in the fire, so that he might release him from his destiny. The white-haired Zāl had given two pieces from one of Sīmorgh's feathers to this famous man, saying, 'One day when your situation is too difficult, place it with aloe in the fire and wait and see how that world-illuminating bird comes to you with his affectionate heart. He will bring about all that you wish for, and he will make the unmanageable wheel of heaven obedient before you.'

Farāmarz places the feather of Sīmorgh on the fire, Sīmorgh comes and an account of him with Farāmarz; the bird gives three stones to Farāmarz and a description of them

Then the noble, sharp-witted man cut a piece of that feather with the tip of his arrow, set it alight with aloe and burnt it. Suddenly the face of the sky lit up, and when Sīmorgh saw the fire and the dark smoke from the sky, he quickly came towards Farāmarz. He sat down upon the ground and paid his respects, whilst Farāmarz stood amazed about him. When the bird saw his dejected face and his wretched heart, he asked of him, 'O strong hero! What cruelty has been done to you by the world, what has happened that you have become afflicted in this manner? Tell me now what is the matter, so that I can turn your sorrow into happiness, because I feel affection for the brave Zāl, as well as for the elephant-bodied Rostam, that huge lion. Anyone else who is of their lineage is for me like my own relative.'

Farāmarz gave him his benedictions and praised him extensively. He recounted the whole situation of the army to him and also spoke about the waves of the sea and the strong wind, saying, 'My soldiers have been dispersed from me, so it is fitting that I suffer grief because of this pain.' Sīmorgh replied to him, 'There is no need to fear that there is a poison in a place where there is no antidote. Do not keep your heart in turmoil because of this business, but go quickly to the island of Maranj! For I will fulfil all your wishes there and return all your soldiers to you. You must not worry, O champion of the army, for not one of those men has perished.'

When he heard Sīmorgh speak in this manner, his heart fluttered in his chest like a dove, and he congratulated the bird of enlightened mind. After that, the army leader, the heroic champion, launched his ship on the water and hurried with an elevated spirit towards that island. He went sailing together with the merchant, with the bird of fortunate soul above them.

When he arrived at the island of Maranj, his pain, sorrow and anguish were removed from him. He left the water and went to the woods, quickly strutting through that auspicious region. There was a place more pleasant than the new spring, a river's edge full of tulips and roses, upon which a castle with a royal portico had been erected with goodness and glory. It was a beautiful castle, suitable for a champion and exalted like a pleasant paradise, because it was Dastān's castle and portico and it was a place for worshipping great men. In times of valour, when Dastān son of Sām had obtained his rest and pleasure in the care of Sīmorgh, Zāl was raised in that castle and received all he needed there. Because the noble bird had been his teacher, he was a monarch with good intentions and justice. Everyone who talked about that castle called it the castle of the white-haired Zāl. In that castle, the warrior with his sun-like glory, together with his moon-faced, silver-chested sweetheart, ate, slept and rested happily; you would think no recollection of sorrow was left in his heart.

After that, the sovereign bird flew to and fro through the sky. He went to every forest, mountain and sea and saw the scattered soldiers in every direction: in every corner a group had landed abjectly, all their bodies full of pain and their hearts mournful, all dishevelled, bewildered, broken-hearted and lamenting, and with their hearts darkened by their pain and sorrow. He returned to the champion and reported, 'Your soldiers are joined to pain and sorrow, but although they are distressed and destitute, not one of them has been destroyed.'

Farāmarz said, 'O lord of glory, provide a solution, so that we can travel refreshed from here to my famous men and reach those wise and good friends of mine.' Sīmorgh replied to him, 'I will seek to fulfil your wishes and set your heart at rest.' He then produced three iridescent stones, which were shining like the sun with their various colours and which he gave to him, whilst he said, 'O pugnacious warrior, keep these always with you. They will be of use to you when you are at sea, they will come to your aid at a day of hardship. Now listen to their properties, so that you will see their mark everywhere in the world. One is such that, when the wind is fierce and the raging heaven makes you dull, you must tie this stone to the tip of your lance – but do not talk to anyone about this in any way – so that the wind will immediately become quiet, and thereafter you will not remember its fierceness. The other one is such that, when the wind does not appear, when there is no passing through the windless sea, you must cast it into the water, and then you will see a roaring wind rising up from the face of the earth, which sets the ship in motion in such a manner that a champion will be astonished.' Farāmarz became joyful and happy about this and his past troubles left his memory. There was another stone with the colour of crystal, the sight of which caused turmoil to the heart: there were a hundred colours mixed together and in it an image of the moon was reproduced. He gave it to him and told him, 'Keep this one, for this stone will be of the best use to you. In the sea or on dry land, in any place where you are, you can make an augury for yourself with it. In a place where you do not know the way but where you unavoidably must go, throw it in water and watch with amazement, for it will turn its head away from the wind in the right direction and show you the way according to your wishes, lifting the sadness and worries from your heart.'

The face of that noble man lit up, you would say that it reached the high wheel of heaven. He blessed Sīmorgh abundantly: 'May you always go under a good star. You are the educator of the white-haired Zāl; you are entirely the crown of us all; you are the guide of lost people; you are better than all the wise men joined together.' Sīmorgh replied to him, 'O famous man! I am a lesser servant of God. I have a long-standing duty towards you, towards Zāl and Rostam the exalted warrior. You must give me information about every business, good or bad, O wise man, so that I immediately can come to your side in such a manner that I can be of service to you. At the command of God, the Creator of life, I will set your affairs right if they consist of a fight or a dispute.' He pulled out a feather from his breast, gave it to that commander of the troops and said to him, 'This is a souvenir of me and also a memory of my name for you. Any time you want me to come to you, you must place it on the fire with incense made of aloe.' The famous hero praised him and embraced him to say goodbye. He kissed his face and his enlightened breast, and then left there in search of his army.

Farāmarz reaches the ships of his Iranian men and arrives in the land of the East, at its islands; an account of the marvels there

He embarked in his ship and set off across the water, his soul occupied with the army and his heart palpitating. He carried those stones with him and tested them amongst the people, in every place where he deemed it wise, putting the stones into practice according to their uses. For one month he travelled around the sea and passed by every forest and mountain. After all that time, and despite the sea full of waves and the strong wind, not one man of that large army was harmed in any way, so no sorrow or pain was left inside that ambitious man. Seeing that all his soldiers were happy, the champion of pure birth became joyous at heart. When he had assembled his entire army, he went on his way and hurried along the route to the East. He travelled for six months over the water, with expedition in his heart because of the troubles of the voyage.

Suddenly they arrived at a country, an island with a select people on it, all of pure religion and all of pure intellect, worshippers of the one God. When they were informed about the champion, they hurried from their land to meet him and brought a lot of food to him, all that was needed for his use. The champion treated them very well and he rested there with an enlightened mind.

The next day, as the monarch of the stars raised his shining lance to the turning heaven, when the lion looked around that place with his famous brave nobles, he saw a mountain close by, of which you would say that heaven had drawn it up. Upon that mountain plants like humans had grown, with two feet in the air and their heads in the ground. In a similar manner, species that resembled animals had grown as plants upwards from their heads: whether birds, cattle or sheep, they had all grown in front of the tall mountain. They carried off a lot of them to serve as food of such a kind that cultivates the body. Everyone who ate from them became robust, happy at heart and flushed of face.

Farāmarz sees the tomb of King Hūshang; a description of his testament

From that place, he went to the top of the mountain with a company of famous men from Iran. He saw a fortress constructed from marble, in which you would think the moon had his dwelling, and with a width of more than five miles. Upon it a letter was inscribed as grand as the Nile, in which place the world-ruler King Hūshang had written a lot of good advice: ‘The world is a transient place full of pain and suffering. No one is happy in this lodge. It is an inn, to which two doors are open and which one must enter full of affliction. When you enter by one door, a man leaves through the other door like a traveller, accompanied by neither his son nor another relative. He will see no one from the world next to himself, except what he has performed in the world in terms of good and bad things, openly and secretly. Turn to goodness and perform goodness. Tear away your heart from any love for this fickle world. Do not harbour any hopes that this world may be eternal and do not tie your heart to its black and white, for just when you have said that you want to sit restfully, death lowly makes a surprise attack on you, suddenly lifts you up from your rest and entrusts you to the dark earth. As far as you can, do not perform anything but goodness, for this seed you will reap in the other world. The Creator of the world is eternal and nothing more. He is the Commander of both worlds.

'There was no king in the world like me, no one was as famous and powerful as me. I went through a lot of trouble to perform my deeds in the world and I made many hidden secrets manifest. Demons and fairies were at my command. I possessed magnificence and heroism. When the world was set right because of my actions and all matters happened according to my desires, my heart said it wanted to take some rest and in tranquillity raise a cup to my authority, my kingship, my designs and my treasures, after I had gone through so much trouble. But suddenly God's command came upon me and stirred me like a fierce wind from my place. By necessity, I could not take one more step, nor could I breathe one more sigh after the other. Neither my treasure nor my reasoning was of use, nor my army, for which the demons had been in terror. He threw me from my throne onto the dark earth and felt neither bashfulness before me, nor fear or dread. Neither grief remained for us, nor sorrow, nor did our kingship, country or region. It was as if I was not in the world for more than a moment and I never saw any delights in the world. It is right that everyone who reads this inscription knows that the world is a transient dwelling. When you have gone and the world is finished for you, it will undoubtedly appear to you like a dream.'

When the brave warrior had read this message, he became sated with the workings and the burdens of the world. After that, he went onwards into the tall castle and towards the tomb of the demon-binding king. On the tomb he saw a tablet made of ruby, on which an inscription was written in black: 'For anyone who arrives at this place and comes to ask from my tomb I do not have anything more in my power than this counsel, which is a memory of me and nothing else. A wise and noble-born man of good fortune will know that this good counsel comes from the crown and the throne. First, O wise, noble-minded man, you must always keep your face turned towards goodness, for goodness is your assistant in both worlds, such as it is indispensable. Further, you must guard your tongue against bad speech, O leader with wisdom! Next, without any doubt, do not postpone the deeds of today until tomorrow, not even out of wisdom. When you are sluggish, O man of insight, you will come to regret it at the end of the matter. When you have tested an honest person of an upright intellect, you must not test him again, for you will regret that trial and you will in return be tormented by his behaviour. Do not treat an ignorant man with severity if you do not want to obtain thorns in your fist from him. Nothing but a bad action comes from an ignorant man. Why should wisdom place its hope in demons? Weigh all the words that you speak with knowledge, so that you will not obtain any trouble from your speech, for there is no use for speech that has not been weighed and all suffering of the heart rises up from lowly speech. Also, do not tell your secrets to women, since no woman ever is insightful. Never set your heart on that thing of which the result will suddenly make you ashamed. O son, do not underestimate your lowly enemy, for at the end of the matter you will experience trouble from him. Because, although a snake may be small, it will in the end undoubtedly turn into a fierce dragon. Do not give a hypocrite access to your presence, for everything he produces is lies. When he has told you about someone else's faults, he will also tell about yours to someone who wishes evil upon you. Never consider yourself safe from a two-faced man, neither at a time for feasting nor at a time of fighting. Be sincere with everyone with whom you consort. Be wise with esteem and with honour. When God helps you to obtain your justice, give thanks to the Creator of the world and to no one else. Remain far from harming noble-born men; even if you are a noble man, be a friend of the law. Everything that comes to you in the world, whether good or bad, openly or hidden, you must consider it all as good and see it as good, for good has been created by the Creator of life and nothing bad comes from the deeds of the Ruler of the world. Heed this counsel, if you possess wisdom. Speech gives no access behind this curtain; you have no business with the good or bad of Him.'

When the brave warrior had read this, he wept. He closed the door of the tomb and descended. With an enlightened heart that had become happy with that counsel, he came down and made preparations to leave. He quickly set off on the route to the land of Farghān and travelled for nine months over dry land in that direction, all the way happy and hunting, whilst the entire army had become pleased with him. Every day they reached a different place to stop and pleased their hearts with a different deed. They arrived at the sea, built ships according to the rules and raised the sails.

Farāmarz arrives in the kingdom of the East and an account of his fight there against the Farghānis; the Farghānis are put to rout, speak with their king and an account thereof

In two months he sailed to the East, where he saw those lands of beauty and glory. There was a king who ruled that region, who was of noble birth as well as possessing power and who had an army beyond measure, all pugnacious and all full of trickery. When the champion neared that region, his heart once again became set on war: as he approached a beautiful country, in those majestic environs he came to a place of battle. When the king heard that an army of soldiers was coming from abroad, he at once became agitated. That king was called Farghān, and he was unsteady, quick-tempered, evil and self-willed. He ordered all the soldiers he had to mount, beat the drums and led them out of the city. The warriors were brave like lions and leopards, all renowned and all quick-fisted. Clad in iron and large as Mount Bīstūn, they all had washed their fists in blood. The dust of the horsemen, which rose up to the clouds, made the ground as dark as a lion's mouth, while the world turned black, the sky was obscured and the faces of the moon and the sun were equally darkened. The neighing of the horses and the shouts of the warriors filled the sky with roars and the ground with turmoil. In this manner, he drove his army on for three parasangs, all the while scattering the dust of war, and when he had reached his destination, they dismounted, having arrived in the vicinity of a river like the Tigris. Farāmarz, the army leader and defeater of armies, marched onwards with his large, enemy-overthrowing army, and when he had arrived close to them, he had his soldiers dismount opposite them.

Night fell and made the world like the mouth of a water-monster, giving the sky the colour of black musk. Both armies sent out a patrol of warriors, in whose bodies the blood was boiling. The guard of Iran was Keyānūsh, in a fight against whom a lion would be powerless. He rode with a thousand renowned men, exalted and sword-wielding heroes, whilst the patrol of the enemy on that dark night consisted of three thousand brawling brave men. Unawares on that dark night, the proud men suddenly collided with each other and a clamour of struggle and fight arose, with the soldiers roaring and the horses neighing. They all wielded their maces, javelins and swords:

you would think they might set the reeds on fire. There were four parasangs between the armies, and neither army was aware of the battle, while those companies fought with each other in such a manner that the plain became black with the dust of the soldiers. A cloud became enveloped by a dark cloud from which maces rained down on helmets and cuirasses. In the dark night swords glittered like lightning flashing from the heart of a cloud. The entire night, the companies were engaged in battle and many of the celebrated men perished.

In this manner, until the sun raised up his head and moved to the heights like a golden shield, not one man rested from doing battle with the tip of his lance and showers of arrows. More than a thousand Farghānis were killed in that battle. The brave exalted Keyānūsh, with his fast-running steed beneath him, like a dragon with a lance in his hand, and with the dust from his horse twirling through the sky, with his stature of a mountain he performed such an attack that those soldiers were stupefied by that assault. He felled many of their renowned men, and the enemy was confounded by the battle: by the time just two hundred men remained, those who were still living sought their salvation in flight, and as they fled from that fierce army, they dropped all their weapons and belongings. They went in disappointment and having lost their reputations and their senses; there was neither vigour in the men nor strength in the horses.

Each one said in pain to Farghān, 'The sun turned dark-blue in our eyes. You must regard that famous valorous champion, who has come to this region like a fierce lion, with lofty insight, good thoughts, advice and counsel and agree to pay him a lot of tribute and taxes, for we have no power against him in battle. Perhaps he will be turned by gentle words. No one should consider a dragon's mouth as contemptible. This fight that we experienced tonight was not a fight that we found agreeable. There was a champion with a thousand men from that huge army, all men of war. We did our best, but although there were three thousand of us, we were like animals of prey against them who were like lions. In this manner they destroyed us and returned to the champion of their army, their army leader who was not aware that they had emptied the country of us. So now, before it becomes clear to what evil this will lead, when their commander starts seeking war, you must avert calamity from yourself with goodness, for goodness is much better than bad actions. Even if their thoughts had been about victory, not one of these warriors' hearts would light up about this battle. May this court not be stained by defeat because of a malevolent man who has lost his way!'

When Farghān had heard these words of them, he flared up against that gathering of renowned men. Such a speech did not please him, and his eyes and face filled with anger and vengeance. He shouted out at those noble men, 'The brave men have become afraid!' He continued, 'About whom are you speaking such words that your speech does not come to an end? Your hearts have been filled with fear for a fight and your livers have been split in two because of them, a group of confounded men without worth or fame, running night and day with no idea of their purpose, who have been scattered, tramping dispersed like carrion and like wolves in every direction around the world. No one should speak in this manner any words of this kind to the leader of his people. No reputation of manliness will appear from a warrior who at a time of honour and battle makes the skills of the enemy visible, so it is not proper that one remains motionless because of what he says.'

Farāmarz's fight against King Farghān and King Farghān is put to rout; his soldiers ask for protection, which Farāmarz grants them

Having said this, he immediately mounted and in vengeance laid his hand on his sword. He had his soldiers mount and the trumpets and drums sounded. The ground turned ebony from the horses' hooves, as the war-mongering and vengeance-seeking horsemen approached the Iranian army. The Iranian mounted patrol flew like the raging wind to the champion and told him that the enemy's army was coming and the world had been entirely made black by the soldiers. When the champion heard this, he arose as quickly as a vapour drift and, undressed, he quickly set off towards that fight. Fast as the wind he mounted his horse and he vehemently swore an oath: 'By the life and head of the king of the land of Iran, by his crown and throne and by his sword and seal, without my coat of mail, armour or tiger-skin cuirass, I will go to battle with my heavy mace and I will put many of them to ruin with the strength of God the Omnipotent.' He spurred on his grey horse and rode off raging like a thunder cloud. When he had come close, he roared in the manner of a lion and pulled out his heavy mace, fanning a fire upon that battlefield.

He fell upon the army of the malignant man in the manner of a flood coming from the sky. He laid his hands on his mace and his sword, and from the back of his horse laid low many men. By means of his mace he turned the ground into a river of blood, with his sword he turned the heads of the commanders upside-down and because of his lance the face of the sun turned red from the abundance of blood that he scattered up into the sky.

His lasso, just like a fierce dragon, did not allow the warriors any escape from its mouth, his arrows cleft the heart of the bedrock mountain and the feet of the turning heavenly wheel were tied by fear for him. When he galloped from a declivity onto a height, the heart of the mountain melted out of fear, and when he rushed through the dust over the plain, the mountain of steel turned into a sea of water. In this manner, he kept on galloping to and fro and from left to right in every place, in whatever way he wanted. With his sword on the day of the battle he prepared from his enemies a banquet for the wild animals of the world. By means of the scimitar of that brave lion of a man and because of the club and the mace of that raging lion not one of those war-seeking warriors of Farghān remained alive on that battlefield, when at last the army of the world champion joined the champion in the struggle.

When Farghān saw how intense the battle was, he knew that his fate and fortune had changed. The world tuned black in colour before his eyes and he saw no chance for tricks or delay. The earth had become assimilated with the blood flowing from his soldiers and the banner of the leader of those famous men was upside-down. He pulled his reins and quickly fled, since there was nothing left to seek from the battle, such as it was. Fleeing on his own and with his heart in two pieces, full of sorrow and fear about the warriors of Iran, he went into his city and closed the gate tightly, his heart full of terror about those events.

Farāmarz ordered sharp swords to be drawn and fighting spirit to be placed in the hearts, and many of the people who had remained in that place or were in the villages close to that battlefield were killed or wounded. Not one of the nobles was there left. When he had brought down destruction to the land of Farghān, everyone from the country who was wise came lamenting to the army leader and, crying about the bad situation, they asked for protection against the injustice of their foolish king. They said to the famous champion, 'Following the path of injustice he went seeking war, although no one else wished for this evil. Now, since the victorious God gave you valour, strength and glory, keep tyranny far from these innocent people and be mindful of this heavenly wheel which is not eternal. After your victory on the day of the battle, it would be proper if you applied forgiveness, O munificent man! Spare us and make the hearts of benevolent people sorrowful about their anguished fate. By God, Who created life and the world and Who created earth, heaven and time, may we be freed from this king, may he be cursed by fate.' The army leader pardoned them completely and the raging wolf provided protection for the lambs.

Farāmarz goes to the city of Farghān for a reception; an account thereof

When the famous king was finished with fighting, as a result of the power of that army full of glory, he came on foot to the city with such a disposition and with such dejection that he got rid of his animosity. The people loosened their tongues before the king: 'Remember the reproach of your own behaviour!', and he became regretful of his own actions and secretly left the gathering. Unseen, he wretchedly went into his quarters with a glittering dagger in his fist, and that foolish man without friends or support thrust it into the hollow under his ribs, thus killing himself. Because of his bad nature and his short temper, he had ruined both himself and his people.

When the nobles and the men of high birth received the news about the action of that king without religion or justice, they stood up and made arrangements to receive a guest. They quickly opened the gates of the city of Farghān, and everyone who possessed wisdom went outside to receive the champion, hurrying like a raging wind as they went. When they had arrived, they paid the exalted warrior their respects, and he entered the city. He rested in the city of Farghān for three months, sometimes with wine and sometimes with a polo-ball or at the hunt. At the end of that time, he chose a famous man, noble, exalted and with authority. His name and lineage came from Jeypāl,[47] and he was young, wise and strong. Farāmarz made him king over that land of Farghān, concluded a covenant with him and made an agreement that every year he would give three ox-hides completely filled with red gold, by way of tribute and taxes.

After that, that lion-like man made preparations to go, and his army brought up the dust from the road. He turned his horse towards a long journey, at the end of which they arrived close to Mount Qāf. On those plains there were many people who in their conduct and in their faces were like the shining moon: although from top to toe their bodies were full of hair, all their heads and torsos were wholly like the face of the moon. They ran more swiftly than the raging wind and they fled from people like arrows out of a bow, as they did from the celebrated men of the Iranian army, who were galloping over the road on their Arabian horses, so fast that when a bird took off in flight it could not go in pursuit of their horses. They galloped a lot with their lassos and bows and they performed many tricks and ruses in order to catch one of them and take him to the tall champion. A black smoke-cloud rose up from the plain, but they did not get any result from their galloping. They all remained empty-handed and turned back, riding full of sorrow, pain and anguish. The world-champion warrior laughed and then told his nobles and warriors, 'No experienced man will ever capture these people in the crook of his lasso. You have given yourselves and your steeds much trouble, but they are not feisty mountain sheep or robust onagers. I have heard that great men with knowledge and success gave these people a name, calling them "innocent" and knowing them as demon-people.'

Having said this, he took to the long road and descended towards the sea. On one side there was the sea and on the other the mountains. The demons were afraid of those mountains and of the sea. For two months he remained on the edge of the deep sea and from every corner summoned skilled men, who during those two months built many ships, after which they raised the sails on the sea. The ships quickly sailed onwards over the sea, with the wind blowing none too strongly over it. With goodness and with glory he came up from that deep sea to a vast plateau, where he had the throne brought out next to the tulip fields and sat down beside the river at a drinking party. He drank, slept and rested well, his heart cheerful after all the troubles and the long journey.

Happy the man whom fortune lends a hand, someone who can sit happily in any place.[48] He will obtain half his food in the eternal world, which he will enjoy and also share with everyone.

Farāmarz arrives at Kalān-kūh and fights the sorcerers, and the sorcerers flee into the fortress; an account thereof

When the brave warrior had rested for a while, he left that place in the manner of a lion and with expedition headed towards the land of China, resting neither night nor day as he travelled along the road. There was a mountain upon that difficult route which good fortune had named 'Kalān-kūh'.[49] When the mounted warrior effortlessly neared Kalān-kūh, he looked up at it and saw a fortress that reached up beyond heaven, and where the sun's halo encircled its gate Saturn was its watchman, the moon its chamberlain and both Mercury and Mars were its masters of ceremonies. When the army leader saw that mountain-top, he bit his lip with his teeth, sunk in thought. He had heard from Zāl and Sām the knight that in the region of China there was a mountain range in which there was a mountain that from the surface of the earth reached beyond the elevated heavenly wheel and that the guide called Kalān-kūh, a mountain full of detriment in a terrifying place. On it had gathered many demons, a fight against which would turn a mountain fearful. There were thousands upon thousands of demons and sorcerers, which an engineer could not count. Each one of them was a soldier, and they were braver than pugnacious elephants. One demon-sorcerer was their army leader, their king and commander in everything good and bad: the entire colony was at his command and the country of China was in dread of them. In the times of King Fereydūn the hero, the army leader Garshāsp endowed with power might have seized the crown from those sorcerers, but no other person had followed the traces of that champion. When this famous hero arrived there, he secretly thought, 'O God! With Your power You will make this place be revealed; You are the key to closed doors.' And after that, he let his army dismount and had his famous pavilion set up.

News was brought to the king of the sorcerers that a large army of men had come. He gathered his army and came down from the mountain to the plain: the ground was stupefied by the damage the demons inflicted. As they neared that prairie, the clouds above the mountain-range froze and an earthquake befell the plain, so that its soul escaped from its body. With all the shouts of the demons, the darkness of the dust and the clamour from the drums and the battle-horses you would think that the world was filled with thunder-claps or that the day had become hidden in the darkness of night.

When Farāmarz saw their business in this manner, he flared up and drew up the ranks for battle. He prayed a lot to the Creator of the world, as he scattered the dust of vengeance to the moon. He ordered the trumpets and the drums of war to be sounded and made a charge to engage in battle. The brave horsemen with glory and stature drew their swords, javelins and maces, whilst the dust of the army darkened the sun and the swords made the world look like a sea of water. As the swords, maces and arrows were clashing, the ground in its entirety turned into a pool of blood, so that the world completely seemed like a sea: the water-monsters within it were the maces and the swords, the fishes were the lances and the dragons the lassos, whilst arrows were flying over it like birds in the sky and the horsemen were like boats driven on by that famous man through the blood that streamed in every direction. And like the sea, an attack stirred up a wave that turned the cheeks of the moon red at its highest point. Farāmarz, the proud champion, with his large army in a very short time killed many of that countless army of sorcerers during the battle, until the hour when the dark night drew close and the warriors as one body returned from the fight. The famous Farāmarz of enlightened heart sent out a patrol into the plains and valleys.

The next day, when the sun showed his face and spread his benevolence over the dark earth, the two armies clashed together again; it was as if they were setting reeds on fire. As the shimmering of the sharp swords became visible, the earth went fleeing in terror. Three litigious feisty demon-warriors from amongst those shouting and clamouring sorcerers, each one in body like a black mountain and with armour and helmets of iron and steel, came roaring out of the army, you would say they were running with fire inside them. Twice forty of the Iranian warriors were killed, so that the day for the fighting men was changed. A lamentation arose from the Iranian army, as the world turned black for the Iranians, and the brave men turned away from the battlefield and all abandoned their positions.

The news reached the brave champion that the lions had fled from the demons' attack. The army leader knitted his brow, as his head was filled with anger and his heart was sorrowful, and he at once spurred on his horse with iron hooves and grabbed his lance. He made an attack on those feisty demons, and it was as if the ground tore in the fight. He hit one of them in the waist with his lance, so that half of it came out of his back and he fell, whilst he at the very same moment gave up the ghost. Farāmarz turned his head in vengeance towards the other two, took his cow-headed mace in his hand and laid the other demon low upon the ground. He came upon the third one in a hurry, with a shimmering sword in his hand, and sliced him from his head to between his two legs, so that the demon was cut in two halves whilst he remained standing in his place. The next moment, the demon contorted and fell, as he emitted a howl.

There was a terrible demon with such strength and power that you would say the world was in turmoil because of him, and as he came roaring towards the champion, you might think that the world tore out of terror for him. The raging demon engaged with the lion, but the brave and exalted young hero made an attack upon the unfortunate demon that was precisely as the action of a heroic man should be: he hit him on the head with his ox-headed mace, so that it was just as if a mountain had fallen on its face, which is what Farāmarz the lion believed, when the head of that malevolent creature fell from high up down below.

Amongst the sorcerers there was one like a dragon of such a kind that no one could find an escape from him. He roared and made an attack on the champion, stirring up the dust from the field of war and sticking out his tongue like a black snake, so that the world was ruined by his poisonous fumes. The pugnacious hero was afraid of him, but the vengeance-seeking warrior took out his bow and rode up towards the dragon with his arrows in such a manner as a leopard rushes towards a mountain sheep. From his Chāchi bow he rained down arrows, so that a pool was formed on the ground by his arrows. When the valiant warrior had reached the dragon, he made a fierce attack on him and struck him on the head with his life-robbing sword, cutting him into two halves from his head to his waist.

Having put that demon sorcerer to ruin, he performed an attack on that army of sorcerers. And when the Iranians saw such superiority from that lion-like warrior of a man, they all drew their sharp swords in vengeance and brought down the time of reckoning upon the demons. They killed so many of those sorcerers that blood was flowing all over the mountainside and the desert. Such a smoke cloud blew up from that battlefield that no one could see the mountain, the desert or the prairie. That army without boundaries was put to rout and none of those sorcerers remained upon the plain, as in their flight they ran into caves and up the mountain out of fear of the sword of the brave lion. The army leader was galloping like a fierce lion, with under him his steed with a body like a mountain, and in this manner brought destruction upon those feisty demons, until he reached the foot of the fortress. The fighters closed the gate of the fortress and rained down heavy stones from that mountain. Farāmarz returned from that place and led his army to the wide plain. As night fell, he rested on that battlefield and sent out a patrol onto the road in each direction.

When the day became light, he had the army mount and with fierceness led them towards the fight against the sorcerers. He arrived at the place of the battle, sunk in thought about how they could bring that fortress to destruction. He rode a lot around the fortress, seeking a solution, but he did not see any solution in it that might show its face. He said, 'O God, our Ruler, give me access to those malevolent creatures.' He prayed a lot and then returned to his camp, having become sorrowful about the demons with their evil intentions. He left sunk in thought and rode on full of sorrow, all the while without hope and joined with pain.

Farāmarz dreams of Rostam; an account thereof

He had a dream in which his father said to him, 'You will be victorious, my son! For tonight your affairs will be performed according to your wish; that unmanageable wheel of heaven will be obedient to you. Get up in the dark night and go towards the fortress, where you will see how the Omnipotent shows you a way into the fortress. The king of the fortress will be killed by your hand. But you must go alone; you must not breathe one word about this business. Your lasso and your arrows will be your assistants, and nothing else; may you have no one as your protector except God.' Farāmarz immediately awoke from his sleep, taken aback in astonishment at his father's speech. That very moment he leapt onto the back of his steed and rode off with his sword and his lasso.

A horseman appears and he shows Farāmarz the way into the fortress; Farāmarz fights the sorcerers and the black demon and he kills them

When he had arrived at a gallop at the foot of the fortress, a horseman suddenly appeared before him. He dismounted, took his hand in his own hand and went up to the fortress from below. He led him up to the ramparts of the fortress and showed him the way to enter the fortress. After that, when he had pulled away from the champion, he at once disappeared from his sight. Farāmarz knew that that guide had come to him in that dark night at the command of the Ruler of both worlds, that he had come to show him a stratagem against this evil. After that guide had been hidden by God from the eyes of the hero of pure mind, he immediately laid a noose in his heroic lasso, not drawing one breath in that dark night. He threw it up and let it fall around a parapet, then climbed up the ramparts like the sun. More than a thousand sorcerers and demons were all guarding that mountain. When they saw that famous champion, with his sword and mace tied to his waist, they started to fight with stones and with swords, scattering up the dust of battle. When the army leader saw the sorcerers in that manner, he stretched out his hand and drew his sword from his waistband, then roared like a fierce lion and scattered heads around like falling leaves.

Several demons fled from the famous man and went towards their evil-natured king. Farāmarz immediately went after them, rushing in the manner of a raging tiger. He knew that it was an ill-advised place, so he said a prayer to God, his guide. There was a dark and very terrifying cave, a place entirely of hardship and of fear and dread, where a dwelling had been hacked out in the bedrock, of a largeness that made the world seem small. Raging, Farāmarz entered that dark cave, and when he came close to the malignant demon, he rubbed his eyes and then looked and saw a mountain inside that dark cave: the length of that demon was more than a hundred cubits and his body was just like Mount Bīstūn. His face was dark and his eyes were white; you would think that the world would become restless out of fear for him. His whole body was full of hair like a sheep and his body was yellow and black in the manner of a stallion. His mouth was like a cave with pitch inside and his tongue was like a snake inside a cave. Also, his nails were like a boar's tusks and his two fangs were just like tall trees.

When the dark-souled demon became aware of the noise of the footsteps of the famous champion, he suddenly jumped up from his place and like a raging elephant started to fight with the famous man. He emitted a cry that would make a fierce lion powerless, came forward from his place like a huge mountain and threw a rock at the champion, but that agile man raised his shield above his head and was not defeated by that rock. The ambitious man took his sword in his hand and rushed at him like Āżargoshasp. He stabbed at the black demon's waist and on the spot cut him in two halves. Such a roar rose up from that dark cave that it was as if that mountain would tear apart.

Every demon and sorcerer that was inside the fortress was informed about what had happened to that demon, and they headed towards the dwelling of the king, all pugnacious and filled with anger and vengeance. The fierce lion came out of the cave and started to fight the army of sorcerers. That battle-ready warrior sought to fight on his own, single-handedly and without his army, and with his sword and mace and with stones and with his fist he killed such an amount of both sorcerers and demons that the blood of those malevolent sorcerers started flowing down that mountain like a bloody inundation. In this manner, until day broke, that lion of a man caused destruction amongst the demons and the sorcerers.

The army goes to Farāmarz and Farāmarz fights together with his own army against the sorcerers; Farāmarz obtains a victory and goes on his way from there

When the sun rose towards the top of the turquoise sky and shone glittering from the fourth heaven, Farāmarz's warriors got up and got themselves ready in accordance with the customs of the army. Joyful and with enlightened minds they went to the court of the world champion, but they did not see their army leader at his court, and the world turned black for those renowned men. They started to jump about like insensate men, running to every corner, searching for a sign. Disbanded they went towards the fortress in search of the world champion, and as they went they heard a clamour from that mountain, a roaring of the people in the fortress. Amongst that noise, the heroic and proud men also heard Farāmarz's roar and, as they recognised his voice, the soldiers at once became aware of his secret. Amazed, everyone said, 'No lion has courage of the kind of this bold man, who in his manliness has gone on his own into the fortress and has shaken up the fortress, the castle and its people.'

They then went towards the fortress, the road to the fort being full of blood and filled with corpses, and they set fire to the fortress's court and set to fight with arrows and swords. When that famous army entered the castle and saw their champion engaged in that fight, everyone prayed to the Creator of the world on behalf of the champion of the land. Next, the proud, pugnacious heroes drew their swords and hatchets and killed so many on that mountainside that a deep sea of blood appeared. Because of all the blood that went flowing down the mountain, the sun started to flee from the turning heavenly wheel. In this manner, until the sun with its victorious destiny carried its goods and chattels towards the west, not one body of those fame-seeking fierce demons with sorcerer's power was spared. They were all killed, wounded or mournful; it was as if none of them was to be seen. Neither any youngster nor any old man was left alive, and the women and children also were taken prisoner. They put the entire fortress to plunder and searched the plain, mountain and valley: many jewels, silver, silks and treasures, which the demons had gathered with effort, came from the mountain into the hands of the Iranians, who became exhausted from dragging it all out.

After that, now that the champion had finished with the malevolent demons and with the sorcerers, he took off towards the land of China, riding with a joyous heart and eager for the journey. When they had been galloping along the road for six months, the soldiers had become worn out from so much travelling. They arrived on a plain like Paradise, full of flower-beds, gardens and neat tillage, and in that pleasant place on earth no person was visible on the land. All over the plain were gazelles and animals of prey, at which the world champion showed his amazement.

Farāmarz goes to the hunting grounds, loses his way and prays to God; a gazelle shows him the way and Farāmarz kills a wolf

It happened that one day that elephant-bodied man went to the hunting grounds without his army. He let his bay horse gallop a lot over that plain and desert and caught many gazelles and onagers. When night fell, he and his entourage on that wide plain set off back to the army camp. As the night darkened, the champion with his following saw a fire on the mountain ridge: he thought that his army had lit that fire on the watchtower to serve as a signal, so he gave his swift-paced steed his head and went off at a gallop with the few warriors. He rode on in this manner until the clear day, when the night tore her black silk and the king of the stars lit up his torch of yellow gold from behind the azure blue curtain. The army leader had travelled thirty parasangs and had become enraged like fire because of the fire. Confounded, he sat on the back of his saddle, full of anger about his warriors and his heart full of strife. As the day grew long, stomachs turned hungry and the breaths of the renowned men were filled with sighs.

When the sun became hidden in the dark-blue veil and the colour of the night appeared, the world became like the face of Ahrīman and the turning heaven opened its mouth like a black dragon, the ground filled with terror for the dark-coloured night, as the noise of bells was coming from every direction. The bodies of the steeds were tired and battered and the souls of the horsemen were disturbed with anguish. They dismounted at the foot of the mountain and rested a while on that dark earth. Once again, that brilliant fire became visible from afar, from the pit. The warriors and their leader mounted their horses and rode like Āżargoshasp. The distant fire burned in such a manner in the night that you would think it was very close by. In this manner, they rode for twenty parasangs, not knowing what that bright fire was.

When the sun lit his flame on the heavenly wheel and pierced the eye of the night with the point of his lance, whilst the world became like a sea of ruby and the dark night became nourishment for the sun, the famous man spoke as follows to his entourage: 'O pugnacious famous men! Having lost our way in this terrible forsaken place, tired and afflicted as we are, we have use neither for valour nor for maces or swords, and there is neither any road of hope nor a path of escape. With our valour we have entered the trap of calamity and set foot in the mouth of a dragon. We must all raise up our hands to appeal to God, we must lament, shout and wail, and perhaps the pure Ruler will be our guide, set us free from this plain which is a place for beasts and restore our peace and quiet, so that we can once more fulfil our wishes. If not, we are in the jaws of a crocodile and have fallen from valour into a whirlpool of disgrace.'

They all together dismounted from their horses and rested a while on that hot sand. The young man started to pray: 'O, You Who are higher than intellect, insight and the soul, on this dry plain without help You know that I will not direct my petition to anyone else. You are the guide for those who have lost their way; You are God, the pure and highest Ruler. O, if you are satisfied with the troubles of this servant, I will trust that you have remitted me, I will allow my soul to leave my dark body and I will throw my body onto the ground. And if not, O God, look with forgiveness upon this lamenting poor man! Give me an escape from these tight fetters, just as I am upon this exhausted plain.'

After saying this, he mounted onto the back of his bay horse with the glory of the Lord of Venus and the sun. That very moment, a dark dust-cloud rose up from the plain and turned the sky dark blue: it was a fast-running, agile gazelle chased by a vigorous wolf. They left that dark dust at such a speed that I do not know how they ran. The gazelle came running in fear for its life and threw itself at the champion. The army leader pulled a poplar-wood arrow from his quiver, took his royal bow in his fist, laid the arrow on it and shot at the chest of the prey-seeking wolf. The arrow passed through its chest into its liver, and the seditious wolf came to an end: it fell down and that same moment gave up the ghost. The warrior of a commander's stock then said, 'This gazelle, which was miserable about its misfortune but escaped with its life from the claws of the terrible wolf, came to us for protection as if it was guided by God.' Now that the wolf had been killed, the gazelle left in safety and ran swiftly towards a meadow. As it ran, they quickly went after it, galloping with their bows strung.

They arrived at a place of such a delight that no man's eye had ever seen. It was a meadow like a pleasant paradise, you would say that the Garden of Eden grew its tulips in it. It was full of streams of water and fruit-bearing trees and full of shade and colours and pictures. They started to praise God, the forgiving Lord and fulfiller of wishes, for He had delivered His servants from that difficult journey and shown His benevolence. When they arrived there, the night had darkened and the hearts of the renowned men were tired out from their sorrows. For three nights and three days the army leader with his entourage as one body had galloped in hunger over that obscure plain, both through the lows and the valleys and over the mountainsides. There was much fruit in that meadow, of a pureness and goodness no one had ever touched. The army leader as well as his famous men at once dismounted from their steeds, ate the fruit and relaxed, and when they were rested and felt secure, they slept beside a stream of water, thinking about the heavenly wheel with its dark soul.

Farāmarz falls in love with the daughter of Farṭūrtūsh, king of the fairies; Farāmarz talks with the army and their answer

When the sun mounted his turquoise throne, so that the world became like a sea with ruby water and the night, out of fear for the sun's sword in battle, tore her black veil down to her navel, the army leader went to the stream at dawn to wash the dust of the road off his body. He saw a moon-faced girl like a Judas tree sitting next to the water stream, in height just like a tall tree, her black musky tresses curling on endlessly and with a face more pleasant than a paradisiacal garden; you would say that that moon had obtained her nature from the life-giving spirit. Both her eyebrows arched like Chāchi bows, and there were many darts within that bow surrounding her glance.[50] When she launched an arrow with her glance, the body of her lover completely lost its heart, and when Farāmarz the hero saw the fairy, he bit his lip between his teeth in amazement about her. He said to her, 'O moon with beauty and glory, what are you looking for, all by yourself by this stream? Are you Sorūsh, moon-faced girl, or a fairy? For you nourish hearts as if they were souls.' She gave the following answer: 'You do not know which wish has entered your heart because of this speech.[51] I am the daughter of King Farṭūrtūsh, the world-ruler with glory and with intellect and insight, who is king over all the fairies: from the constellation of Aries to Pisces, they belong to him.' Having said this, she disappeared into the stream, whilst the heart of the champion was palpitating out of affliction over her. His heart was filled with love for that moon-faced girl, and he became thoughtful and seeking a solution with his heart.

Imbued with pain he hurried away from the stream and returned full of sorrow to his friends. He said, 'O celebrated men of enlightened mind, a fairy has carried off my heart, senses and soul from me. She has thrown me from bravery into a game, and through her games she has captured me in the snares of affliction. She has lit the fire of love in my soul, so that even if I pass away, I will not be finished with this speech. I will exert myself, I will gallop around the world, so that perhaps this hidden girl will be revealed. Whether I catch this wish in my net or obtain humiliation, I will not worry about demons or fierce dragons, or about arrows, swords, maces or calamity.'

When the warriors heard his speech, their hearts withered because of his cause. No one knew the name of Farṭūrtūsh, and every person's heart started to boil with sorrow. Everyone spoke to him in reply, 'O famous, pugnacious warrior! For three days and three nights we have been separated from our base-camp during our peregrinations. The soldiers are not aware of our actions or of these darkened days of our affliction. Undoubtedly they are full of pain and have wounded souls from not seeing their champion, so we now must go to the army and we must not delay in this matter. When you see the army with your enlightened mind, young and old will become happy with you. And after that, you may travel upon whichever road is to your liking, since you are the commander of us and of your army.' After he had listened to the speech of his leader-obeying men, they mounted onto their saddles and took their swords in their hands, then sought the way towards their own army, searching confounded with their hearts ruined by grief.

Meanwhile, the soldiers of the world champion, night and day powerless from pain and sorrow, had been running all day across the plains and mountains, looking for the army leader and his following. Wherever they sought, they got little result, so they galloped back to their stopping-place and camp. In despair they had to stay there, although it was dishonourable for them to be without an army leader.

The story of Farāmarz's fight with the black demon, Farāmarz capturing him alive and Sīyāh-dīw talking with Farāmarz

The army leader, for his part, arrived at a mountain so high that its top was invisible: from its protuberance it had stuck its head into the clouds, and not even a flying eagle had seen its top. As the night spread her musk-like veil in the world across the golden tents, that lion-hearted man dismounted before the mountain, having become distressed with love for the fairy-faced girl. Sometimes he suffered with love for his beloved, sometimes he cried plaintively on behalf of his army. Suddenly a roar arose from that mountain, and to his right a fire flared up, which fire burned so ardently that you would think it wanted to burn the plains and valleys. The army leader looked up at that mountain and at that fierce and copious fire, and then he said, 'That fiercely burning fire, which is tyrannising the turning wheel of heaven, must be the same one that my eyes saw from afar and that drew us away from our army in this direction.'

As he was saying this, suddenly a roar rose up: 'O champion! Are you the man who says, "I have such valour that I can tear out a huge mountain by its root; I am a famous lion-hearted man amongst great men and I am galloping around the world in manliness; I have taken Kalān-kūh with my sword and in that manner defeated the army"? If you are a man of war, O champion, you must stand firm like bold men do, for you will now experience wounds from a sword and from arrows; I will thrash you in the course of our fight. Now try and hold out with your valour when I come to face you to do business. I am a pugnacious lion, called Sīyah-dīw,[52] and I will this very minute be successful in my business with you.'

When the army leader heard this, he quickly jumped up and as fast as smoke put on his coat of mail. He placed the horse-armour on his steed, tied his twisted lasso to his saddle-straps, laid down his heavy mace on his saddle and mounted his horse like a mountain in rage. He roared, 'O dissentient demon, your adversary is coming now, so get ready for business! With my sword I will turn this plain into a sea and I will turn your stature of a mountain into a vast plain. I will twist you in such a manner, O creature of evil stock, that you thereafter will have no memory of Kalān-kūh! Just like the demons of that country and plain, you must be laid low in your life and soul.' Because of that speech, even before it was finished, the demon roared with ferocity in that dark night and, beneath him a horse swift as a cloud, rode towards the roaring lion. He undoubtedly was a terrifying mountain, beneath which you would say the ground was moving. With his helmet of steel and his cuirass of iron he had covered his body from head to toe.

When he reached the brave warrior, the two bold warriors like roaring lions fell upon each other in that dark night; you would say that they mixed together. They raged about with blows of their hatchets and were pounding each other's heads with their swords. When the brave warrior had exerted himself for a while, he drew towards the left like a fierce lion, pulled a sword of sublime essence from his waistband and smashed it down onto the huge demon's crown. The glittering sword touching the helmet of the pugnacious horseman in the dark night made it seem as if the sun was scattering sparks of sandarac onto ebony. In this manner, until the sun lit its golden lamp over the surface of the plain and the mountain-slopes, they kept on making attacks on each other, and neither one turned his head or chest away from evil. Eventually, the brave warrior moved from his place and braced himself with some vehemence: fast as a dust-cloud he moved towards his right and, holding his lance, aimed the point straight at the demon. He struck at the waistband of that bad-natured creature, and it was as if both the mountain and its side tore apart. He lifted him from his place like a black mountain and threw him down abjectly onto the battlefield.

He tied both his hands tightly behind his back and said to him, 'O demon of upturned fate! Why did you go through all that boldness, design and boasting, when you had to bow your head in foolishness. I will not cut off your head, because it would cause me dishonour, since I can grab five hundred like you in my fist.' He then pierced both his ears with his sword, placed two heavy iron hoops in them and said, 'Now be my guide towards my army, if you want your head to remain in its place.' Sīyah-dīw answered, 'O hero without equal, lord of the mace with wisdom and stature! No one has with his valour gained the upper hand over me, not even a fierce lion has gathered the dust off my horse. Many are the famous, experienced horsemen who are afraid of me in battle. No one had power against my sword and mace, and heaven kept its head averted from my fights. My belief was such that there was no one in the land who at the time of battle could let the wind scatter dust over my horse without being turned to dust on the day of the fight. But opposed with so much valour and the power of your stature, I became weak in your fists. I have rings in my ears for your valour and I am equally a servant to your glory and warriorship. I will show you the way to every place you tell me to, and not for one moment will I turn away from your command. But in this mountain I have many treasures and crowns, as well as earrings. There are slaves, servants and vassals, and also horses, accoutrements and carpets to sit on, which I have gathered over a long period and carried up to this bedrock mountain. Wait, so that I can bring them all to you, and your ill-wishers may be filled with pain.'

As the army leader considered his speech to this effect and saw the heart of the bad-natured demon in servitude, he became thoughtful and said, 'You are a sorcerer with deceit, cunning, evil and a bad nature. With this sweet talk and smooth tongue your head will effortlessly be cut off by me.' Sīyah-dīw jumped up and swore an oath by the white day and the dark-blue night, by valour and warriorship, by the throne and the crown, by the sword and the mace and by the sun and the moon, saying, 'I speak words from the path of justice; do not treat me badly because of my speech.' Farāmarz knew that he spoke the truth, that his oath was joined to manliness and further that he had done justice on his own accord, so that he should not conceive any bad memory of him. Whether you see a demon or a man, when there is a core of manliness in him, you must accept his words and not treat him badly, especially when he presents justice in his words. The young proud commander untied his fetters and set him free.

Sīyah-dīw brings the treasure to Farāmarz and an account thereof; Farāmarz reaches his own army

Sīyah-dīw went off running in a hurry, and he quickly ran up the mountain in a stride. He brought so many crowns and thrones, pearls and jewels, slaves and servants, silver and gold, as well as horses, camels and sheep, and oxen that roam around mountains and valleys, that anyone who saw it would bite the tips of his fingers with his teeth in astonishment. The army leader stood amazed about that and he secretly called upon the Creator of the world. He asked of him, 'These riches, on account of which you have arranged your land, tell me how you assembled them all, these sheep, horses and herds?'

Sīyah-dīw answered, 'O world champion, from the age of Ẓaḥḥāk until the present time I have had my dwelling on this mountain and in this plain, and the world was for me like a ball in my hand. On this mountaintop every night I burn a fire with which I gladden the hearts of people who have lost their way. Everyone who has seen from close by or from afar how the fire drew up its flames towards heaven remains unaware of my trickery, or of my sword and lance, or of my intentions. They come to me unsuspectingly, whether they are an army or a caravan, and all at once I cause them to writhe and I completely make their hearts and eyes lamenting and lifeless. I take all their cattle and all their goods, not allowing one hair to be damaged, and I place them on the mountain. Do not consider this mountain of little worth! For today or after hundreds of years, those who pass by will see this mountain and find money and treasures on this mountain, and they will be troubled to carry it all down. I myself have no measure of my money and treasures, or of the jewels and rubies of which there are many here.'

Farāmarz was taken aback in amazement about that and took counsel from his speech, how this demon had displayed so much greed and had drawn so many people into his lair. He ordered him to load up all those things and to gather together the treasures and the flocks. He headed towards his own army, with Sīyah-dīw going in the lead seeking the way.

As the sun raised his banner in the east and the colour of the land turned purple, the army leader arrived at his army camp and saw each of the commanders of his army. They all laid their heads on the ground before the victorious world-ruler, because they saw him happy and sound of body and they did not have to wash their cheeks with blood.

Farāmarz sits with his army at a feast and the soldiers speak with Farāmarz; his reply, and Sīyah-dīw reveals the secret about Farṭūrtūsh to Farāmarz son of Rostam

The army leader sat on his golden throne and the warriors sat down with their loins girded, all refreshed in face, happy at heart and freed from their past sorrows. That champion organised a banquet, about which you might say that heaven would scatter its soul. The wine in the cups laughed in happiness and with its reflection filled the sky with a rainbow. Fairy-faced servants, with bunches of flowers in their hands and goblets of wine in their palms, were all half drunk, and their cheeks, tulip-coloured from the liquor mixed with rosewater, looked like wine that had dripped onto narcissus leaves. Silk sighed in a low plaintive tone, its whisper making intelligent men drunk.

When the proud man had become intoxicated with wine, with love in his heart for that sweetheart, patience chose to distance itself from his heart and soul, and he was all the time biting his lip with his teeth. He did not drink with gusto from the cup out of which he was drinking, and with every breath he emitted a cold sigh. The nobles of the army, one by one, such as Keyānūsh the counsellor and the pugnacious Tokhwār, as well as Shīrūy and the famous hero Ashkash, all spoke with each other in a gathering: 'Our lion-hearted famous and exalted leader with knowledge and full of honour did not return in the same state as when he left here. We do not know what has happened to him. We do not see the colour of cheerfulness on his cheeks, and all the time he is sighing cold sighs.' Those renowned men that had accompanied him and all shared the secret about his beloved, as one body opened their mouths to tell everything about the famous champion: about the business in the desert and with the gazelle and the wolf, as well as about the fire and the deeds of the robust demon and about that meadow and the stream of water, how the famous champion went to the source of the stream where the fairy was standing like Jupiter in heaven and how the champion was enamoured with that moon-faced girl; that demon surely had enchanted him. When the warriors heard their speech, their affairs became darkened by worries. They drank some more wine, then retired from that feast when the colour of the night turned black.

The world pulled a dark veil over its head and the colour of the sun became invisible in the darkness. After the warriors had retired according to their customs, the army leader called Sīyah-dīw to him and asked him about King Farṭūrtūsh, that insightful king with intellect and understanding: 'If you have no information, search for it, but if you do know a solution, tell me.' The demon said to him, 'O noble-born man, exalted warrior on the day of battle! No one in the world speaks his name and no one dares disturb his peace, for he is king over all the fairies, he is an army leader with justice and command. Both Gorgsārān and Māzandarān, from border to border, stand under his command. That famous monarch is also the ruler of this land here, in which region we are dwelling now, and so on, all the way to the gateway of the East; everyone keeps his loins girded for him and the world has been brought under his submission. He has more soldiers than there are grains of sand in the desert. From here where we are a traveller would have to gallop for one month to reach him. If you give the command, I will gird my loins as a servant to go with a thousand horsemen from here and deliver your mandate to that king, and perhaps I can fulfil your wishes there. Dictate a letter with affection and justice, in such a manner as behoves men of munificence. In the letter you must speak words without fight and utter all that you have to say in a festive manner, for he is a monarch with purpose and intellect, who is great and has submitted the world under his command. Tame his heart with sweet words and gentle speech deriving from affection and modesty.'

When the army leader heard this from him, he became happy and was freed from the fear about his sweetheart. He slept and rested completely until daybreak, when the face of the earth became shimmering from the sun and the sunlight spread a shawl of gold and pure ruby over the earth's surface. The army leader sat on his throne and his famous men, proud knights and nobles, came before him, their hearts in thought and their feet in the mud from worry about that famous man. That champion knew their intentions and he spoke to them as follows: 'O commanders! News of my situation will certainly in passing have reached the ears of the nobles, of the wish that I hold in my heart, so it would be proper if you were to seek a solution for me. Although this wish is but little, we will strive as long as there is a vein in our bodies and souls. We have passed by demons, sorcerers and dragons, by deep seas and fortresses and by calamities, we have crossed through each land, hot or cold, and we have experienced fear and pain, but thanks to the victorious World ruler no disaster has befallen us, and of these valorous renowned men not even one of the lesser people was lost. However much an army leader may be illustrious and more elevated in manliness than his illustrious men, one business remains for us, with the fairies: we should search in this region, for this is another purpose that has arisen these days, by the victory of the Ruler, the Creator, and that will become for us a story of such a kind that no-one who hears this story will remember anything about us except our manliness, so that we will remain happy of heart and of good fortune. After everyone has gained a name in the world, it will never become hidden in the universe.'

All the champions raised up their heads, and they all together at once prepared an answer for him: 'We approve of your wish and your command; your purpose is entirely our intention. Even if the mountain or the sea becomes filled with swords, or if swords pour down from a raincloud, because you wished it, O champion, your soul will not regret your great men.' The army leader was refreshed by their speech and the desires in his heart became without measure.

Farāmarz writes a letter to Farṭūrtūsh, the king of the fairies, and has it delivered by Sīyah-dīw; an account of the letter reaching Farṭūrtūsh and his becoming thoughtful

He ordered a writer to come to him, had him sit on a throne next to himself and dictated a letter to Farṭūrtūsh with insight and intellect and full of affection. Like a fish coming up from a sea of musk, he passed over the surface of the dry paper, joining a cloud like tar to the paper and raining royal jewels from it. First, as he placed his head upon the ground, he started praising the Creator of the world: 'The Lord of visible things and of hidden secrets, the Lord without assistant, companion or partner, in six days set up the nine circles of heaven and gave the world a place in them. Proof of Him are the particles of the sun and the moon, by which the years and months are counted. Look at the demons, the animals, humans and fairies, and from the sun to the atoms: they are all servants and they are searching as well as running in their servitude. His kingship is current upon the world, for He is the Creator, He is the King. And the king of kings, the world-ruling, intelligent and clear-minded Farṭūrtūsh, is worthy of His blessings, for he has both a good offspring and a pure religion. Also, he is the highest of the monarchs of the world, exalted and a leader of great men. He is the lord of the treasures, the crown and the belt, a lord with elegance and with intellect and glory. From us, too, many blessings upon him, which blessings are interwoven with our affection for him.

'I have arrived with good intentions in these lands where the leader of the country is that famous monarch, with my army, my trumpets and drums and my soldiers, and with my nobles with golden belts. After I had been granted a share in this life by the turnings of the dissentient wheel of heaven to become amazed several times at this world and to see many things open and hidden, we have come to your country and have taken rest for some time in these lands. We have heard from every person all kinds of things about your deeds, your speech and your culture, about your manliness, your aspect and your magic, and that you have a large share in knowledge. Such a wish has risen up in my soul, upon which my mandate is eternally fixed, that I might make your acquaintance and become enlightened by seeing you. I am the praiseworthy offspring of champions, exalted heroes on the face of the earth; I am a world conqueror and the son of a world champion, the army leader Farāmarz of enlightened mind. Whilst Dastān is my grandfather and Rostam my father, the proud and famous world ruler, my eminent forefather is the knight Sām, who robbed prey from the claws of lions, in such a manner that the reputation he gained with the blows of his sharp sword will remain until the day of resurrection. Now I am a memory of him in the world, honourable in battle in every circumstance.

'I have heard that in your private quarters, in the women's inner chambers, there is a moon-faced girl named Ārezū,[53] and in my heart the ardent wish has arisen that I could also make a family bond with you and with goodness take much counsel about improvement. Give to me with good principles that moon, that jasmine-scented picture of my heart's desire. Within these words lies no fight, nor is there dishonour for you in a connection with us. What did that wise man of pure intellect say when he opened his lips for an elegant speech? "The world is delightful when one is related, but a heart is sorrowful around strangers." Do you not see, when someone of good fortune connects himself to the branches of a tree and when a branch raises up its head and comes to fruit, that it will produce a fruit that is sweeter than what you have been given?! In a similar manner, look at how flowing water, when it connects with other water, with its force will turn into a deep river and how the world in its length and width will be his. The water will become a sea with ships upon it,[54] and men will dive in it to seek a name.'

When he had finished dictating his speech, he appointed Sīyah-dīw as a guide and sent him off with a thousand brave horsemen from his sword-drawing warriors. Taking presents and decked horses, as well as money, treasures and riches, the demon travelled a long distance, galloping his bay horse for one month along the road. Sīyah-dīw, endowed with passion and power, arrived in the environs of King Farṭūrtūsh's court and sent someone ahead to tell that victorious king that a messenger from the famous man was coming to the pure-minded king Farṭūr. When the monarch heard this, he sent out an exalted hero to meet him: he was a renowned warrior, named Changū, who had gained trust and esteem with the king and who set off together with some noble men of power and rode along the road to receive them. When the exalted horsemen of pre-excellence reached Sīyah-dīw the warrior, he dismounted from his horse and at length inquired after his wellbeing. Next, he dispatched a horseman like a lion to inform the king that this lion-like man with nobility was Sīyah-dīw, the proud lion-killer, who you would say was a mountain of fire on his saddle.

When the monarch heard this, he arranged matters on behalf of that company of intrepid knights. Sīyah-dīw, like a mountain, arrived together with the company of Iranian warriors, and when that exalted man entered the palace, he conveyed his blessings and displayed his reverence. He had those presents and decked horses, as well as those treasures, money and riches, brought, handed them over and delivered the letter, making much mention of the Creator of the world. He praised Farāmarz the warrior, his valour, his breeding and his power, and he gave the king of the fairies an account of those deeds that he had performed and what he had achieved in India and in China, to which the king of kings listened and about which he was amazed.

After that, Farṭūrtūsh gave orders that his servants with intellect and understanding should set in order a grand villa and furnish it on behalf of the hero Sīyah-dīw. When the court had been cleared of the warriors, he came and sat upon his throne and had that heart-pleasing letter brought, from which he opened the seal and unfastened the ties. When his young secretary had read the letter, young and old showed their amazement at that fine speech and those sweet words which that lion-hearted noble had presented. The ambitious monarch became thoughtful about him seeking love and a family bond with him. On the one hand he became happy about a connection with him, but on the other hand it filled him with lamentation, as he thought, 'We must not get involved with man, at all. Men are prisoners of anger, vengeance and oppression. Even if in the beginning they display goodness, they eventually break their covenants and promises. They are not committed to one intention and jump up from their places with every contumacious wind. Instead of goodness they perform evil and into every uprightness they introduce crookedness. If I oppose myself to this speech and do not allow my daughter to become his wife, the heart of the champion will be filled with pain and he will turn away from the wine-goblet to his bow and arrow. Against my will I will have to strike out against him and after that, I do not know what will be. A war will come about in the world and the lives of many commanders will come to an end. After that, who knows except God who will return victorious from the battle?! A wise insightful man has said: "Everyone who makes the seed of vengeance appear will quickly become suffering from his actions, and the strength of his kingship will be ruined. He will suffer trouble and hardship in the world, and at the last judgement his fate will be equally bad." Therefore, in order to settle this matter with justice, we shall display all our affection in our answer. For the world is treacherous and full of pain and suffering, whilst this transient world will not remain forever. May our command and our good deeds, counsel and covenants all be better.'[55] Since his endless thoughts were making him melancholy, he raised up his head and faced the assembly.

Farṭūrtūsh speaks with his nobles and consults with them and the nobles give him an answer

He then addressed his renowned men, the nobles of the country who were in his presence, saying, 'O exalted men with intellect and insight, wise men with knowledge and guidance! You must know that from a province of the land of Iran a young, proud man of pure religion, who is a son of the world-champion Rostam and a descendant of Sām and of Narīmān, who is a nobleman, knowledgeable and of a good lineage, a wise man endowed with virtue, modesty and justice, has arrived in our borderlands and has become informed about our wisdom and our worth. He has the intention to become related to us: who can withstand his insights?! Sīyah-dīw, the wind of whose sword makes water congeal like blood in a stream, whom no one has managed to defeat from the age of Ẓaḥḥāk to the present time, of whom no one in the world has seen his back in flight, out of fear for whom no animal of prey or predator rests, now stands before Farāmarz, just like all servants, at his command like a submitted man. He has been sent here on this business because he has intellect and judgement and is of excellent worth. I have become full of thought about this dilemma, for how can a fairy take up with a human?! Since we are not of the same essence as each other, may we not be tainted by calamity because of this matter! What do you say and what is the best course in this? How do you regard this well-intentioned man?'

The following answer came from each noble in that gathering who was a commander: 'O Your Majesty with knowledge and guidance, you are a guide for wisdom with your knowledge, but since you make a request of us, we will say something that may be of use. First, you must invite the young man to come to you, to a hunt and to music, wine and a feast with a banquet. You will observe and learn whether he agrees with you and whether he appears glorious to your heart, with regard to his aspect and his speech and how he eats and sits. We will test him in every examination. Also, the priests will ask him several questions about learned things before our gathering. If this famous, proud and alert champion of enlightened mind, with an upright disposition and an intelligent heart, a pillar in manliness and riding with knowledge, then fulfils his promise, and affection, intellect and wisdom are cultivating his soul with knowledge, in view of all his warriorship, strength and glory, his great offspring, modesty and cultivation, it will be appropriate if you decide on a family connection with him, and you will be rejoicing to be his relative.

'Further, when the exalted lion sets off and bravely rides to our country, he will not come along the road upon which the demon came when he travelled with his brave famous men. Because when Sīyah-dīw returns from here, the mountains and the plains will be cold and full of snow, now that autumn is coming, and the month of Dey,[56] when the blood coagulates in our veins, souls and feet. In the winter and the cold neither a demon nor a brave man will dare travel along that road, so he must resort to a roundabout road, which will be a more pleasant way to travel. On this road, if[57] you thus give the command, as you are the king and we all are slaves before you – since you want to examine his manliness, munificence, glory and wisdom in all good and bad situations, test him properly and augment his trials with demons, sorcerers and warriors, with trickery and demonstrations of learned people – we will tell them to conjure up wild animals before the army for seven stages of road: lions, wolves and a dragon, and also the calamities of both cold and heat, as well as a dragon-like, demonic and ghoulish sorcerer, who causes pain and trouble, as well as fear and terror, and further a demon-rhinoceros without fear and dread, which will cause a bird to fall from the clouds to the ground, will appear on the path of that lion of a man and raise up the dust from the world with their fights. Now, if this lion-like man of a warrior, the proud young man with power, with his glory and his manliness and with his strength and skill, passes through these seven stages, he will undoubtedly be deserving of praise and you can praise him for his valour. At that moment you must not be ungrateful, but you must think well and not pass an ill-considered judgement. Follow the road that he shows you, for he will make your wishes come true.'

When the king heard this, he deemed it suitable; all their words seemed profitable to him. He organised a royal banquet and decorated his palace and the grand court, then sent someone to call Sīyah-dīw, whom he had sit beside his throne with golden decorations. A golden carpet was laid down and the warriors sat down by the king's throne. It was a castle as delightful as Paradise, with musk and ingots of gold all over the ground. The doors, ceilings and walls were covered in paintings and the curtains inside it were decorated with jewels, with pearls, rubies, Arabian shells, precious stones, yellow rubies and emeralds inlaid in gold. Its ground was covered with brocade and all kinds of silks, in such a manner that the sun and Mercury were displayed on them. Slaves with faces like the sun were lined up in rows behind the monarch, all their lips full of drink and their heads bowed, standing in front in utmost service, with wine in their hands, their eyes half-drunk and holding bunches of wild roses and tulips in their fists. Much amber and Tartar musk was scattered over everyone in the gathering, so that the entire castle smelt of that musk, whilst the building was resounding from the musicians. The singer's voice ran through the sky, as he joined the high notes with the bass notes. The songs and the voices, the music and the clamour made Sorūsh fall down from behind his curtain; you would say that Venus was playing music with Jupiter at that feast. In this manner, until the sky became dark in appearance, they drank from their cups in thought of Farāmarz. Their words were all about his aspect and about his manliness and his deeds.

Sīyāh-dīw speaks with the king and gives a description of the lineage and the valour of Farāmarz son of Rostam; an account thereof

Since everyone was speaking about the champion, that king of warriors and famous men, the loquacious Sīyah-dīw opened his mouth and recounted Farāmarz's deeds. First, he spoke about the lineage and origins of that famous champion and summed up for them his ancestors one by one. He went from Rostam to Narīmān the warrior, made mention of Kūrang and Aṡraṭ, and so on recounted their lineage back to Jamshīd,[58] including Sām the warrior, Narīmān the lion and Garshāsp the hero, the brave champion. He also traced his lineage via his mother, the daughter of Keyqobād, the king of kings with glory, wisdom and justice, back to Fereydūn, who drew the world in blood with his sword.

'In the manner in which I spoke about his lineage just now, I can say even more about his skills. However many words of this kind I speak about his wisdom, glory and splendour, his greatness, generosity and authority, my speech will never come to an end. It has now been more than thirteen years that this honourable man with his guide has been ambitiously travelling around the world, sometimes seeking fame and sometimes following his desires. Many wolves, lions, leopards and crocodiles have been laid low by his mace on the day of battle. There are many pugnacious demons and fierce dragons that have not found an escape from his sharp sword. Whether there were foundations of fortresses or mountains and plains, the hooves of his horse have flattened them. Many mounted warriors in battle and many lion-hearted celebrated soldiers have averted their faces from a fight against him and abandoned their hopes and wishes before him.

'His father, that world-champion army leader, the protector of Iran and the support of heroes, since the times of the king of the world Keyqobād had his loins girded in valour and justice. All the lands of the Turks, Māchīn and China, and so on until Egypt and the land of the Berbers he has completely trampled under the hooves of his steed and among the populations there he has stirred up destruction and turmoil. In the battle against the demons of Māzandarān he scattered the dust to the heavens with his sword, as he single-handedly all by himself sought to fight and from the beginning did not seek any assistance from anyone. Not one sorcerer, demon or fierce dragon found an escape from his sword. Not one person remained in the world who could gain victory in a fight against him.

'Also, his grandfather Sām son of Narīmān, who was exalted, insightful and powerful, during the time of King Fereydūn's reign had his belt girded around his waist in valour. That hero subjugated both Gorgsārān and Māzandarān with his heavy mace. One thousand one hundred and sixty raging demons, which each were like ferocious elephants and which were the nobles of Gorgsārān and were proud, fierce and feisty creatures, were captured in his lasso and all were humiliated under his yoke. Whether against a dragon or against a fierce demon, whether against a lion or elephant or against an intrepid wolf, the lion-like man was the same in the fight; who could scatter the dust of battle over him?! In these lands where you now reside the traces of his horse's feet and of his mace are manifold. In the country of China he with his sword blackened the surface of the earth with Ẓaḥḥāk's relatives. There are also stories in this region about Narīmān, who was the father of Sām the knight. And no one in the world was like Garshāsp himself: who could try him in battle? If I talk about the deeds of that famous man, there are so many that they cannot be counted. The crown-bearer certainly will have heard about the actions and the valour of that man full of honour, how that brave man operated with his sword of oppression against Menharās and also against the dragon.[59]

'Now, this young man of such lineage, young, wise and praiseworthy, with a face just like the moon, the tallness of a cypress, a body like a huge elephant, the gait of a partridge and two arms resembling an elephant's thighs, who will make the river Nile boil with his voice: his skills, considering his lineage, about which I told all, will before you, O king of the people, certainly not be more than one out of a hundred, and there is no one living in the world who is as famous as he.' When Farṭūrtūsh had heard these words, the justice of his intellect entered his heart and the wish became manifest in that king to see the face of that ambitious man for a while.

When the load of the night started bending the back of the sun and the sun's face was covered by a veil, a cloud of smoke and dust rose up from the world in which everything that had been visible was hidden, and everyone retired with their hearts in good health.

And when the sun washed the face of the bright day and picked up a golden shimmering sword with which it enveloped the world in gold, Sīyahdīw came before the king, together with the brave men of the Iranian army, and he spoke as follows to king Farṭūrtūsh: 'O insightful king with intellect and understanding! My sojourn in these marches has lasted long and the heart of my leader will be filled with concern about us. You must now write a letter of reply, with goodness and elegance like a houri of Paradise. You must also act out of greatness, justice and wisdom, in such a manner as suits courtesy.'

The king gave him this answer: 'O good-hearted famous commander, stay with us for one more day, until I have drawn up a letter of reply. Stride with happiness to your palace and do not mention leaving any more today, until we have taken counsel about a family bond with him and have cleared hostility from our hearts.' After Sīyah-dīw had heard this speech, he left, hurrying with the famous men to his mansion, where the brave men sat down with him and refreshed their downcast faces with wine.

Farṭūrtūsh writes a letter of reply to Farāmarz, sends presents and gives a robe of honour to Sīyah-dīw, who returns; an account thereof

The next day, when the sun had raised his banner and the purple face of the heavenly wheel became like camphor, the king of the fairies mounted his throne, his heart far from worries and cleared of sorrow. The king dictated a good letter addressed to Farāmarz, the protector of the army. The writer put his hand to the letter, having cut the end of his pen and closed its lip, then swiftly letting it run on foot and giving it a crown of amber. From this crown it rained precious pearls, each of its pearls entirely filled with praise. First, he made mention of the Creator of the world: 'From Him comes all rectitude and justice. He also brought heaven into existence and further created things clear and hidden. No one is king over the world except Him, and one must seek protection both from Him and with Him. From the sun and the dust-particles to the elephants and the ants, from the black earth to Saturn and the sun, they as one body are worshipping Him and they are all augmenting their servitude. Apart from Him, I do not know a lord in the world worthy of being worshipped in private. May His blessings be upon the army leader of the land of Iran, the commander Farāmarz, the exalted son of the elephant-bodied hero, worthy of every assembly and gathering, who has glory and stature, as well as a name and a lineage, who is noble-born and a warrior with splendour and justice, a lord with strength and prosperity, the protector of the world with his valour.

'This heart-pleasing letter came to us by the hand of Sīyah-dīw, the tall warrior, who was all politeness with justice and intellect, displaying happiness at the court like a paradise, decked out as he was in a paradisiacal manner and adorned with pure speech. I became happy at heart because of your intellect and because of that elegant, heart-adorning speech of yours. It is just like that son of a champion said: the path of a good man should not be hidden, for the world will become joyful from a family bond, which is the same for subjects and nobles. Son of the world champion full of honour, exalted and a famous slayer of lions, if you have plans to become related to us, as well as the eminence to match our superior rank, may these plans not become stale and may these words forever be supreme for us.

'I now have a wish, O champion, that you turn your horse to the road towards us with all the champions of Iran, who are a flock for their army leader: he should come to these famous lands of ours and see our worth and our value. We will also become pleased with this visit and we will speak a bit and also listen. He will stay for some time happily as our guest and know this house as his own home. With sweet words we will provide him with entertainment and we will not deviate from our promise or his plan. May you not become distressed at reading anything great or small about you in this letter. We have withheld ourselves from a more elevated speech. Sīyah-dīw further knows everything there is.'

When the letter had been written, a seed of goodness with love and loyalty had been planted in the epistle. To accompany the letter, he arranged so many gold coins and royal presents of every kind that, if you would count them, there would be more than a caravan could carry or you could believe: there were red rubies, turquoises, silver and gold; yellow rubies, Arabian shells, pearls and jewels; a golden crown and a turquoise throne, worthy of that noble man of good fortune; both necklaces and bracelets and earrings, as well as tiaras and cups inlaid with jewels; swords, coats of mail, harnesses and helmets; horse-armour of a kind that was appropriate; fairy-faced servant-girls with glory and modesty and beautiful slaves with soft voices, all chaste and with robes decorated with gold and golden belts set with emeralds; panthers, all kinds of white, brown and black falcons and noble sparrow-hawks. The alert king of kings of enlightened mind sent them to the warrior of the world and he arranged for a robe of honour for Sīyah-dīw, whilst he gave the proud mounted heroes helmets and cuirasses, horses and belts, and money, gold and jewels of every kind. He bade them farewell with a happy heart and they left, their tongues full of praises.

When they had departed, Farṭūrtūsh, the army leader with knowledge, counsel and insight ordered the knowledgeable and brave leaders of the demons and sorcerers to go and with sorcery and by trickery and deceit fill the whole route of that ambitious champion with a demon, a wolf and a lion, and with a sorcerer and a bold dragon. In this manner, they accomplished their tasks with trickery and then cleared their hearts of the things they had done.

Sīyah-dīw returns to Farāmarz with Farṭūrtūsh's letter and a robe of honour; Farāmarz speaks with him, Sīyah-dīw's answer and the story of the seven trials

Meanwhile, Sīyah-dīw with intellect and justice was riding onwards with the commanders like the wind. When they reached the heroic army leader, Sīyah-dīw presented those presents: Farāmarz stood in amazement at those gifts and distributed them in their entirety to the Iranians. After that, Sīyah-dīw gave him the letter and recited the monarch's words to him.

When the young brave man had read the letter, he girded his loins and had his army mount. As the eminent man left his stopping place, Sīyah-dīw said, 'O battle-ready hero! On the road along which we arrived today we experienced many troubles as we travelled. For the way back, you should not travel on it now, because all the mountains and plains are full of snow. You must go via a roundabout way, as it is not safe to be on this road. But on the roundabout road, O exalted man, you will be confronted with much trouble and pain from demons, wolves and a fierce dragon, and from sorcerous lions on the day of calamity, as well as from a ghoul, a fierce-natured beast, and further a rhinoceros, which will be fear-inspiring. I do not know how you can travel along that route, what magic you can perform against these creatures.'

Farāmarz replied, 'With the strength of God, Who is my guide in my valour, I will remove their heads from their foundations with my sword, and fear will find no place in my heart. You, pugnacious lion, strong Sīyah-dīw, you must not display any sluggishness as we go along that road! You now will be my guide with insight and a pure mind on that route, and at every stage along which we pass, whether there is a demon, a lion or a fierce dragon, when I come close to one of them, you must give me some notice of them, so that one of them does not suddenly and secretly without warning pounce upon me and I will not be unprepared for the fight and my heart is not finished off by their business. If anyone from the army is attainted by any harm, my heart will be afresh constricted by grief.'

Sīyah-dīw spurred on his horse and rode in the manner of Āżargoshasp. They rode on joyfully and ready for war, all the way hunting with panthers and falcons, and when the army had marched in this manner for two days, the root of happiness had settled in the hearts of them all. When they had arrived near the dwellings of the wild animals, night fell and they pitched their tents on that plain.

The first trial: Farāmarz kills the lions and an account thereof

As the night pulled a veil woven with golden thread over her chest, the army rested; and when the sun breathed again, the army and the army leader rose and made preparations to take to the road. All day long, they were occupied by panthers and falcons and hunting, without any thought about the fight on the battlefield.

When the black demon arrived in the desert, he saw that pawmarks of large lions were to be seen and he spoke to the famous champion as follows: 'O magnanimous warrior of enlightened mind! Right now, as you are dismounting in this stopping-place, you will be greeted by lions. They are like two mountains with roars that make the ground tremble at a time of dispute and animosity. They are two huge lions, O famous man, in height larger than a mounted man. In a fight, when they display the force of their anger, they bring bloodied tears of jealousy to one's eyes. The world trembles under their assaults, whilst the sun becomes hidden within the dust.'

After the army leader had listened to this account, he put on his coat of mail and his battle-dress, mounted onto the back of his grey steed and at a gallop rode towards the fight against those two ferocious lions. When he had come closer, one lion roared and came forward to fight the brave warrior. It was a lion like a huge mountain; you would say it burned the earth with its breath. The world conqueror had his bow and arrows and, whilst he went up to the huge, raging lion, having knotted his eyebrows in a frown, he put a string upon his royal bow and on it laid an arrow, which had a tip of iron before which bedrock would be like loam, then opened his chest and shot at the waist and breast of the huge lion. The arrow pierced through to its heart, and as its blood filled the soil, it turned into dark mud. When the lion had been felled by the famous hero, the other huge lion came to fight. With force it ran towards the champion, raging like a boiling sea as it came running. The battle-eager champion shot another arrow at the chest of this proud lion, and it passed through its chest to its back. In this manner he killed both those lions. After that, he drew his sharp scimitar and with this sword cut them into small pieces.

When he had finished with them, he went running in a hurry towards a stream of water. He washed his head and body in that clear water and then went to prostrate himself on the dark earth. For a long time he rubbed his face on the ground before God, the Creator of life. When the soldiers came to that proud man and saw him in his place of prayer, as well as that place of the fight where the two lions had been felled in that manner by the pugnacious brave warrior, the warriors of the army all together started praising the famous champion. They put up the pavilion besides the stream and also pitched their tents on the meadow. The army leader came to his pavilion and that man of pure intellect arranged for some relaxation. The great men took some wine together with him and everyone spoke about hidden secrets.

The lion-like hero said to Sīyah-dīw, 'The matters of the road should not be hidden from me. What will I see next on this journey,' he asked, 'when I gird my loins tomorrow to move on?' Sīyah-dīw answered, 'O strong lord, may the heart and eyes of your enemy be blinded. When we have completed our journey tomorrow, two fierce wolves will cross our path, creatures of such a kind that no one has seen or the world conqueror will have heard of from experienced men. No animal has their height, their bodies are dark and their eyes pools of blood. Each one has a horn on its head,[60] O man of good fortune, which appears like a tree of ebony. Their teeth are longer than boars' tusks, and in the fight, O exalted nobleman, they will not turn away their faces from a raging elephant. There is no one who will seek a fight against them.' Farāmarz replied, 'With the glory of God, I will bring them down with my sword in the same manner as a raging lion on the day of the hunt causes distress to the body of a male onager with its blows.' In this way, talk went between Sīyah-dīw and the warriors of Iran, who drank some wine and became intoxicated, as they told stories in commemoration of the army leader. After that, they retired to their sleeping quarters and rested from the feast and from the fight.

The second trial: Farāmarz kills the wolves and an account thereof

When the sun started shining over the camp and the firmament became like a gilded tent, the army leader had all his soldiers mount and led them at the command of the Ruler of the universe. He had put on his armour and the horse-armour, arranged himself with his bow and arrows and rode with his army in his wake and Sīyah-dīw going ahead on the road as his guide. At the time when the sun went down in the west, the army leader reached the neighbourhood of the wolves.

When the wolves saw the horseman from afar, they rushed roaring and raging like lions at the hunt towards the champion of the army and razed the ground with their teeth. The proud archer with his strength and glory had stuck two or three arrows in his waistband, and when the wolves arrived near him in a rage, he put the string on his royal bow, laid an arrow with four feathers upon it, drew it to his thumb-stall and opened his chest. As his thumb came next to his ear, he increased the bow's arch with his hand. When he had brought his thumb right next to his ear, the arrow jumped off from the Chāchi bow: the wooden arrow hit the cavity behind the ear of the brave wolf and passed through its neck. The body of the male wolf fell to the ground and Farāmarz placed another arrow on his thumb-stall, which he shot just below the ribs of the female wolf, so that the huge animal fell to the ground. Next, he cut their bodies all to pieces and in such a manner brought the wolves to destruction.

He went towards the water with an enlightened mind and happy at heart about the turnings of heaven. That famous hero washed his head and body, and prayed, 'O pure Omnipotent! You have given me great power against these fierce lions and huge wolves. He whom You have chosen is not lowly; there is no occasion to dispute this justice. And no one on earth will be lowlier and more lamentable than he whom You made lowly. Because of Your glory, one particle of the moon exists, and because of Your power, a mountain can weigh as light as straw. We all see Your justice, and this is not injustice; it is not appropriate to complain about this justice.'

When he had completed his praise of God, his soldiers all together arrived at that place. When they saw the two huge wolves ruined in such a manner by the arrows of the young man, the entire army sang the praises of that lion-hearted select champion. They pitched the pavilion behind the green field, and that hero of pure intellect sat down to relax. The warriors took wine as they sat happily and, having become merry from it, played games.

When the face of the heaven turned dark and the lamp of the king of the stars became hidden, amongst that darkness just like charcoal in a sea of tar the lights of a thousand stars set themselves upon the ebony throne in such a manner that you would say it might be raining sandarac. They slept until the colour of the night changed and the songs of the larks rose up from the plain. As the monarch of the stars spread a yellow flame across the azure blue cupola, they loaded up their baggage and tied down the loads, then set off with in their lead the famous man, whilst Sīyah-dīw went with him as his companion, so that he could inform him about the road.

The brave champion questioned him, 'What will there be on the road in the form of elephants or lions? Sīyah-dīw gave him this answer in return: 'O battle-seeking proud noble! You will come up against a terrifying demon; wise men call that demon a ghoul. The head of this ugly, horrible creature reaches the sky, whilst both his feet are on the ground of this plain. His teeth are like those of an elephant and his body is just like a mountain. A bedrock mountain is distressed by fear of him. Both his eyes are like two pools filled with blood and his lips are hanging down like a camel's cheeks. His head is as broad as a huge tree and he has a black face, yellow cheeks and a dark body. He could pull a water-monster from the Red Sea and he could even grab birds from the sky with his claws. In these lands no lions or brave elephants dare pass by him in the heights or the lowlands.'

The third trial: Farāmarz kills the demon-ghoul and an account thereof

Whilst he was still speaking, suddenly the fierce, wretched demon roared. Raging, he turned his face towards the champion, full of violence, anger and fighting spirit. The army leader had his weapons of war, since for him fighting was more pleasing than feasting, so he put a string upon Narīmān's bow and fast as the wind went towards his opponent, whilst his bow rained a shower of death just like hail onto that cursed demon. The demon of a ghoulish stock came rushing and tore out a huge tree that stood by the road. When he arrived near the brave warrior, he emitted a roar resembling that of a lion and hit the horse of that lion-like man on the head, so that the steed fell down into the dust in pain. The brave man dismounted from his horse and roared at the demon like a fierce lion. He drew his sharp shimmering sword from his waistband and brought the day of resurrection to that battlefield. No fear or terror entered his heart as he slashed his sword at the feet of the demon-ghoul: by means of his strength and his height, the army leader with his sword hacked off one of the feet. Contumacious and blustering, the raging demon on one leg contended with the champion: he grabbed the chest and shoulders of the brave warrior, so that the pugnacious demon was on top with the army leader beneath him. The brave man thrust out his hand like a male lion and with the strength of the victorious God lifted him from his place and threw him onto the ground, so that the battleground trembled from the impact. Farāmarz hit him on the middle of his head with his sword and separated half his shoulders and chest.

When Sīyah-dīw saw his superiority, he praised the warrior at length. The army leader once more rubbed his cheeks on the dark earth before the pure God, because he owed his nobility and his victory to Him, as well as his designs, his fame and his passionate heart. The soldiers arrived all at once from the road, and every person looked at that battlefield: they saw an ugly creature laid low, fallen in destitution on that plain. Each one of the lion-like man's warriors who was present gave that exalted man much praise. Everyone was saying, 'Through this trial of strength and this deed, this lion of a man has surpassed Rostam in valour, who has achieved so many skills in the world. The World-ruler knows that not many horsemen with this kind of valour will appear in a lifetime. The world became refreshed because of this ambitious man. May the eyes of evil people be far from him.' They dismounted in that place, set up the tents, drew up the court and then arranged a feast, having cleared their enlightened hearts from sorrow.

Farāmarz questions Sīyah-dīw, who answers him about the trial of the cold and the heat; the Iranians speak with Farāmarz and Farāmarz gives them an answer

The next day, when the turquoise heavenly wheel pulled the pegs of the rust-coloured pavilion from their places and the ground became entirely filled with pure gold, as if the sun had spread gold over it, the young man made preparations to leave and set off with his renowned warriors. He said to Sīyah-dīw, 'Tell me once more what I will come to face next.' He answered, 'O champion of the army, from here where we are there is a three-day march, for which we must pass over moving sands, which cause pain to the soul and trouble to the spirit. The bones in your body will burn from the heat; I do not know how we can manage on that road. A dryness will appear without any escape. No one dares pass by this route. You will not find one drop of water along the way; you will get a share of sand and a portion of mirages. Perhaps the pure God will be your friend and lift your head from lowliness to the sky. When you have passed through there with your troops, a bedrock mountain-range will rise up before you. You will see that there is a passage, with mountains to the left and the right, and you in the middle. For three days you will have to travel in this manner and everyone will lose their strength because of the cold. So much snow will fall from a dark cloud that the world will become like the jaws of a lion: its height will reach higher than a lance, your body, skin and blood will freeze from the cold, and your mounts surely will not find any grass. It is in this manner as I have told you as your guide.'

The heart of every person who heard this speech became dejected and his cheeks turned the colour of fenugreek. Everyone said to that famous man, 'O pugnacious lion at a time of battle! You are wise and a warrior who obtains fame; you are the leader of this huge army. Do not lead the lives of your soldiers so rashly to ruin; may you not have to remember these words. With his foot in the traps of death, O lion, no one can make preparations or provisions. This is no lion, wolf or dragon from which one should find an escape through manliness, nor a battle with arrows or swords that will now come up before us, nor will there be any manliness, strength or a place to flee. Think about this dark day full of calamity and do not burn the hearts of the innocent Iranians!'

When the raging lion heard this speech and the state of the hearts and minds of the Iranians, his heart became enraged, and he said, 'The heart of a man of good disposition does not twist away from his wish. Anyone for whom wisdom is a guide in the world cannot be pleased with such words. Every person who does not have wisdom in his foundation will agree to a speech of this essence. But someone with knowledge will know, as is appropriate, that God is the ruler over our lives. In everything that He has written upon our heads, about good or bad behaviour or beautiful or ugly things, lies everything, great or small, that will have to happen to our souls, whether it is happiness or grief and sorrow. Someone whose death will occur in the water of the sea and who fears fire is not respectable. Or if his life comes to an end because of snow and cold, how can he avert this from himself? We all inevitably must depart: for one it will be in the claws of a fierce lion, for another by a demon and for yet another by a wolf; for one it will be by the sword and for another by an arrow. One will end his life in his bed; another will suddenly fall into a well. Indeed, since no one has access to this thing, no wise man is informed of this knowledge. The World-ruler, the Creator of life, is our king; it is suitable for Him to know bad and good. In everything His decree shall be executed; a wise man is helpless before such matters. All that is to be, must be. We must not prick our soul with worries. Since you know you will not be informed of this secret and you will not share the secret of the Lord, why do you want to rule over the course of your life? In your ignorance you will deviate from the path of rectitude.'

When the Iranians considered his mind and insight, as well as that stature and height of his, they all together opened their mouths in apology and said, 'O warrior of enlightened mind! Listen to these friendly words of ours and also to these utterances of thanks to you, which we are speaking to you with burning hearts. As one man, we bow our heads to your counsel, because you will not withhold your own life from the snow or the heat or from the mace or the sword. Our bodies are not dearer to us than you, nor is there any person who is more illustrious than you. As long as we shall live, we offer our heads in fidelity to you; we will accompany you on every road upon which you gallop.' The heart of the champion became happy with them and his soul got some rest on the wide plain.

The fourth and fifth trials in the heat of the desert and in the cold of the snow; Farāmarz and the Iranians pray to God and they escape from calamity

They arrived at the moving sands, and Farāmarz ordered camel drivers to come to him and bring a hundred caravans of camels and fully load them all with water or grass. He set off in the lead and rode at a gallop, going across that dark flowing sand. Their bodies were burning in their armours from the heat, and there was no day of battle and no time for fun. Their tongues had dropped out of their mouths and everyone was homesick for their families and homes. The bodies of their mounts had become soaked with sweat and on that waterless plain their hearts were filled with haste. Everyone lamented to God in pain about that dark road full of wind and dust. In this manner, they traversed three day-marches, until the army arrived between two mountain ranges. When he had led the army, himself with his renowned men in the troops in his wake, between the two mountain-chains, he set up his pavilion on the edge of a stream, with his famous army behind him. Night fell and they slept, rested and wetted their dry lips a bit. That battle-ready army rested from the troubles and sorrows of the difficult and long road.

When one part of that dark night had gone by, the sky was darkened by a black cloud: a cloud like tar arrived and entirely covered the mountains, and that dark cloud and the raging wind turned the world completely into a trap of Ahrīman. Snow fell in the amount of a mountain, so that the hearts of the famous men became distressed. As the snow reached the height of a lance, the magnificent mountain range became filled with snow. The pavilion and the tents were full of ice and a carpet of snow was laid out over the plain; no one could use their hands or arms, whilst that mountain was full of snow and coldness. When the soldiers had become wholly helpless from the snow and the cold, the army leader spoke to his wise men as follows: 'O illustrious men with noble spirits! Let us raise our hands in prayer to God against this evil and let us clear our hearts from presumption and pride. In this trouble, we must turn our faces towards Him and bring tears of grief from our eyes to our cheeks. Perhaps He will deliver us from this difficult place, for He is a guide for helpless people.' All the great men and warriors of the army, every soldier who was present, all together raised up their hands in supplication, as their cries went beyond measure: 'O, You are the Creator of mankind and life, higher than knowledge, intellect and the soul, take our hands in this place without any recourse, take pity on the need of all these exhausted people.'

When they had prayed a lot in this manner, no one had to accommodate himself to the cold, because the Distributor of justice and love delivered them: that very moment the appearance of the heavens was refreshed and immediately a strong wind arose and carried off the large clouds from the face of the sky. Because it was the favour and justice of God, spring, winter and summer occurred at once. The hearts of the great men returned to their places, as they stood giving praise to God. Then they spread out the pavilion and the tents, which had been cleared from snow and ice, upon the mountain and its skirts, and when the tents and the pavilion were dry, the nobles as one body departed from that place. They hastily did the things that had to be done and disappeared from there like smoke. For three days, their journey went across the snow, the ground being full of snow and the sky full of beauty. On the fourth, when they exited from between those two mountain-ranges, the soldiers were entirely exhausted. They saw the world full of greenery, water and flowers, which was rightly a place for pleasure and for harps and wine. They started to praise God, the victorious Lord, the Creator of life. Although they had seen much trouble, everyone had his share in treasures from that delightful place. When no sorrow, suffering or pain remains for the people, nor goodness, rest, heat and cold, profit and gain or good and evil, why should a wise man suffer sorrow?! Having dismounted on that plain full of flowers, they busied themselves with entertainment, flutes and harps. They arranged a pleasant feast and occupied themselves with wine in golden cups.

When they had drunk in happiness for three days, on the fourth, when the world-illuminator raised up his shimmering golden banner from heaven and the night tore her purple silk, the brave men lifted up their heads in order to leave and cleared their hearts from trouble and hardship. The champion was riding in the vanguard with Sīyah-dīw briskly accompanying him. Once more, that great champion asked of the robust, feisty demon: 'What other amazing thing will I see upon the road? Tell it all, O well-willing hero!' He told him, 'Right now a noise will reach your ears from a violent, demonic rhinoceros, an animal full of rage of such a kind that no one has ever seen in the world. He tears mountains and rocks with his roars, and a fierce lion bites its claws out of fear for him. He has the body of an elephant, the head of a rhinoceros and a horn on his head like a huge tree. When he runs, he tramples the wind underfoot and he hunts with his teeth like those of a fierce lion. He will thrust his horn underneath a huge elephant and as fast as the wind uproot it from the ground, and it won't have the weight of one gnat for him. On the day of battle a mountain becomes contorted by him.' Whilst they were still feasting, Farāmarz ordered his apparel of battle to be brought to him, everything that was indispensable for a fight, such as his sword, his mace and his bow and arrows. He covered himself completely with those arms of war and rushed outside like a lion or a leopard. The army also left, whilst he himself remained up in front, as if Mount Bīstūn had set off in a run.

The sixth trial: Farāmarz kills the rhinoceros and an account thereof

As the sun turned his face towards the west, that pugnacious hero reached his destination, in his hand an animal-killing sword. When he had found out the dwelling of that rhinoceros, the brave champion emitted a shout, which shout of his would make a lion tremble, and as soon as that creature heard that yell from the warrior with grace and fortune, it dashed up vehemently. The rhinoceros like a violent demon came towards him, let out a roar towards the wheel of heaven and in a rage raised its head up to the clouds, so that the mountain turned upside-down out of fear for it. When the horseman of battle saw it from afar, he roared like a lion at the hunt and rained down poplar-wood arrows onto it, making the world constricted for it with the arrowheads. The sharp-toothed beast came like the wind and fell upon the feet of the young man's steed, then thrust its horn into the horse's underbelly and with one thrust threw him onto the dark earth. The army leader jumped off the back of his fast steed and moved from his place like a raging elephant. On foot, that elephant-bodied man started to fight the rhinoceros with a sword in his fist: he stabbed his sharp sword at the middle of its head and with his valour brought down the day of resurrection upon it. Its elephant-like body was split in two halves and its shoulders and chest fell down onto the ground.

Farāmarz went off, praying to God, the strength-giving and guiding Lord. He prayed at length and gave thanks, rubbing his cheeks on the ground. At that moment, Sīyah-dīw arrived and saw him in his place of worship, with the rhinoceros fallen close to him, its body hacked into two halves with his sword. The brave demon praised the famous male lion abundantly for his strength. His soldiers also had come along the long road, and they each in turn showed their respects to him. Everyone gave him much praise, saying, 'May the ambitious hero live forever!' On that very place they pitched the tents on the green fields and set up the pavilion close to the road. They sat down to entertainment, asked for wine and adorned their hearts with pleasure. When everyone was drunk, they went to their sleeping quarters, and the entire army rested.

The next day, when the sun turned yellow and spread his golden drops over the azure sky, that heroic champion and all his famous men of enlightened mind made preparations to travel. Once more he spoke with that black demon, saying, 'Do not keep your knowledge hidden about this business: what will I see next time, in the form of demons or animals? What will I encounter on this road, good or bad?' In reply the warrior Sīyah-dīw said to him, 'O man with knowledge and superiority! One more task remains for you and that is all, but no one has seen anything more terrifying than that. When you have finished with this, no more troubles will be left for you and nothing but a country, a crown and a treasure will remain for you. There is a dragon on the way, which the turning wheel of heaven seeks to avoid. It has a body like a mountain, and vapours and heat from which the sun in the sky flees. Its eyes are like two dishes full of blood, and fire comes out of its throat and mouth: its breath is just like the burning Āżargoshasp and it can draw elephants and horses into its mouth from a mile away. On its head there are two extremely sharp horns, their thickness greater than branches on a tree. It has strong feet and a massive chest, and its claws resemble those of a fierce lion. If you exert yourself in a fight against it and with your courage lay its body low, you must know that he who knows beauty and ugliness will write a mandate of valour in your name.'

The raging lion said to Sīyah-dīw, 'O sweet-tongued knowledgeable man! I have seen many dragons of this kind and more difficult places of battle and calamity than this one, and I have never turned my head away from a battle or displayed any delay in seeking a fight. With the strength of the World-ruler I will bring this dragon to destruction and he will not find any deliverance.' Having said this, he laid the black horse-armour on a battle-seeking Arabian steed, put on a coat of mail over his tunic and mounted his swift horse like a lion.

The seventh trial: Farāmarz kills the dragon and an account thereof

A stream of brackish water lay before him, but there were no plants around its source, and for at least ten parasangs around it there was no tree or anything else growing besides it. As the brave man approached it, the young man roared just like a lion, and when the dragon heard his voice, roaring in the manner of the wind from the sky, it came to fight the young warrior, poison pouring from its mouth like smoke. The brave man was not afraid of that smoke or poison, nor of its thundering noise that deafened the world. The height of the dragon was eighty cubits, and in its avidity it could draw in an elephant from one mile distance. As it came closer, the champion directed his supplications about it at the Creator of the world. Then, he brought his fist to his quiver and took out his bow and arrows of poplar wood. On the arch he placed an arrow on which the feathers of an eagle had been tied to the poplar wood. When he had brought the arrow-point next to his hand, he released the orifice of the arrow from his thumb-stall and shot the arrow at the dragon's mouth, so that poison was strewn about by the fierce creature. He shot another arrow at its head, which went straight into its brain. It seized the bow from the heroic army leader,[61] but the commander stepped forward with superiority, bravely went up to the dragon and, as soon as that lion had come close, grabbed his sword. The terrible dragon had its mouth open, so that the face of the sky was burning with its breath, and it also seized the sword from the famous pugnacious man. His grey horse was afraid of that vile creature, so the man dismounted and tucked his hem in his belt.[62] Pugnaciously he grabbed a lance and cast that ten cubit-long iron spear into the middle of its mouth with a vengeance. The point of the lance exited through its neck, and the whole mountain and plain became filled with poison and blood. He drew his shimmering scimitar from his waistband, thrust this sword and threw it upside-down.

He addressed himself to God the Creator and laid both his cheeks on the ground in humbleness, as he said, 'O Ruler of heaven, You are higher than knowledge or imagination. You have given me knowledge, glory and strength, so that I could bring down turmoil and destruction upon the dragon. I am your modest, lowly servant. What is produced by me that can be counted?! Who am I to seek greatness from You? How could such a thought be on my mind?!' When he had prayed in this manner for a long time, the alert man rose up from the ground. At that moment, the warriors reached him and saw that feat and his good fortune, and every person recited his praise of that honourable warrior of noble birth. They set up the pavilions on the plain and the prairie, and the brave men went out to hunt. Not one beast was left on that plain now the lands had been emptied of that dragon.

Farṭūrtūsh rides out to receive Farāmarz and brings him to his own home; a description of his hospitality

For one week he rested there beside the brackish water, exhausted from the depravities and the exertions. At the end of the week, he departed from that place with his army, his elephants, his drums and his soldiers. As he came closer to the king of the fairies, he sent someone from the army to give news to the powerful monarch and inform him about the famous champion. When the message reached Farṭūrtūsh that the eminent warrior with intellect and understanding, together with his elephants and soldiers, had completed the roundabout way on his horse like Āżargoshasp, the monarch stood very amazed at that, and everyone was saying, 'This champion surely is Sorūsh in terms of intellect and glory, that he could pass along this route in this manner. If he did not possess the glory of God, the face of fortune would not be smiling upon him. Since the brave man went with God's glory, it was easy for him to travel along this road. Surely, even if he were an iron mountain or if the heavenly wheel were the coat of mail on his body, he could not pass over his road on valour alone, nor could a demon, a lion or a fierce wolf. The pretext of valour would not remain valid for him when he drove his horse over Jupiter's crown.'

When he arrived in the neighbourhood of the king's city, the king of kings came to meet him with his army and with elephants, cymbals, trumpets and drums, so that the world became completely ebony-coloured from the dust. When they came close to one another, the young man without delay dismounted from his horse, and the king also came down and took him in an embrace. Farṭūrtūsh looked at that strong body, at that stature and height and that glory and intellect, and the monarch was taken aback with amazement. They took a long time to ask each other about their well-being, and after that the king of kings and the brave warrior briskly mounted their swift steeds and went riding with all their men in front of and behind them.

He had a city by the name of Shahābād,[63] a place entirely endowed with goodness, tranquillity and pleasure, filled with gardens, flowers and trees and completely full of people of good fortune. In it was a royal castle of a paradisiacal kind, full of colours and scents. Its doors, roof and walls were made of crystal, displaying a shimmering like the sun from afar. He brought him into that castle of his and had Chinese brocade carpets spread out all over. Next, the king sent the young man so many servants, fairy-faced and moon-cheeked slaves and jasmine-scented idols of houri descent with cypress-like statures and jasmine-coloured chests and of spirit origin, that Paradise lost its beauty without its houris – together with everything that would be of use and was worthy of that lion-hearted man for his food, sleep and rest, and also to fulfil his happiness and his desires.

After that, he came to the champion with his famous men, young and old, and arranged such a feast that the moon from its sphere would be humbled at this banquet, where there were ass-loads of narcissi and jonquils, as well as lilies, tulips and jasmine. They sat down, placed cups on their palms and toasted to their just kings. Fairy-faced slaves drew up ranks, all with cups of happiness placed in their hands, with smiling lips, smooth-speaking tongues and liver-piercing and honour-seeking winks. Just like dew that sits on the leaves of a flower at dawn, the blood-coloured drops of wine had made their lovely cheeks blush, as the juices of their beauty were flowing in streams. The face of the cup-bearer cast its splendour onto the wine, turning the reflection of the shining sun into a delusion. The reflections of the cup-bearers' faces in the drinks filled the entire castle with moons and suns, and as beautiful as they were in the crystal cups, they appeared to the eyes of the nobles as if fire had been poured into water or as if milk had been mixed with wine. The minstrels sat in a row, having lined up with their harps and lutes, and when they combined the high notes with the low ones, they caused the heart of loveliness to leave its body. The notes played by the beautiful women on the lutes and the sounds of the strings, the harps and the flutes would make one believe that the sky was making music or that the heavenly wheel was playing the lute. Manifold roses, hyacinths, narcissi and jonquils that had been brought, along with tulips and jasmine, which were mixed with jewels and over which much musk and amber was poured, were strewn from the roof of the king's precious palace onto that feast. The heaven was dazzled by that feast and scattered every means it had at its disposal over it. In this manner, they all together rested for one month in happiness and glory in comfortable entertainment.

Farāmarz plays polo with Farṭūrtūsh, the king of the fairies, and they both go hunting; a description of Farāmarz's valour

At the end of the month, they went to the king's playing-field and challenged each other to a game of polo and some sport. The soldiers set themselves in order on both sides and arranged their ranks for the ball and stick. On one side stood the eminent raging lion with ten brave Iranians and on the other side, king Farṭūrtūsh with ten young men of intellect and understanding. Whilst the dust of the contest was stirred up from the field, the roar of the strife swelled. Horsemen rode up in front of other horsemen and the steam from the polo game rose up to Saturn. Sometimes this one let out a sigh and then again that one drove off the ball, their cheeks distressed by the interaction, as the knights of Iran and the brave warrior went at the ball like lions. The tall champion gave the ball such a whack that you would think he launched it to the top of the moon. Every time he hit the ball with his stick, he caused the turning ball to make heads turn: it became invisible in the sky in such a manner that you would say heaven pulled it towards itself. It had not yet come down from the sky onto the ground, or that lion-hearted select champion sent it off again with such a sharp stroke that everyone who saw this believed that, after it had jumped off the curve of the new moon, it had gone straight back up to sit on the moon's lap. If the sun had hit the ball out of Scorpio's tail, the turning heaven had taken it back into its bosom. On the playing-field no one dared to go towards the ball because of the blows of his polo stick. The knights who were with him on the field were all celebrated men and warriors, but they were powerless against those blows of his stick, and they praised him abundantly.

After the game had gone on in this manner for a while, the famous leader rested from playing ball and they went from the playing-field to the castle and the palace and happily set themselves to entertainment and a feast. They placed tulip-coloured wine in their palms, whilst on every side fairy-faced girls were playing harps. In his intoxication Farṭūrtūsh spoke as follows to that man full of wisdom and with intellect and understanding: 'Close to the city at one day's distance there is a prairie and a hunting-ground. It would be convenient if we went over there and spent a week there at the hunt.' Farāmarz replied to him, 'As you command. You are the leader and you have insight and a covenant.'

When the dawn showed its crown from the mountain, like ivory above a heart full of musk and above verdigris, the king's warriors mounted their horses with the lion-hearted champion of the army. They headed for the hunting grounds, all the way happy and seeking prey. The elect world-ruler Farṭūrtūsh with his guiding priest of pure religion did not separate from the champion, and in every place where he pulled on his reins, they together rode side by side with him, so that they could see the greater and smaller skills of that valiant lion of a man vis-à-vis the gazelles, the mountain sheep and the brave onagers.

As the onagers appeared on the hunting ground, excitement fell upon the hearts of the warriors, and the world champion spurred on his steed to bring the gazelles and onagers to ruin. The brave warrior saw a male onager that was coming down from the top of a height with a rugged lion running after it, swiftly and powerful, and all the while roaring. He shot a poplar arrow at the onager's breast and with its sharpness brought the male in distress: the arrow passed through the onager's breast and entered the forehead of the rugged lion, and as the poplar-wood arrow entered its brain, it fell onto the field of strife without delay. In this manner he destroyed both the onager and its predator on the hunting ground.

On another occasion, a male lion came up and roared at the famous champion. The young man opened the thumb-stall on his bow and hit the predator's breast, which he pierced with his arrow, so that the sharp-clawed animal came up to fight and moved in close behind that lion-like man's back. It lifted up both its claws and struck down, how amazing! As it grabbed the buttocks of the army leader's steed, the brave man twisted on the back of his saddle, drew his shimmering battle-sword from his waistband, thrust his sword at the middle of its mouth and separated its two ears and its head from its body. The raging lion fell down on the spot and its soul swiftly started to lament.

Another lion was sitting on an onager's hindquarters, having inflicted terror upon the onager. The famous champion rode up behind it, so that he could display his skills of valour. When he came closer to the onager and the lion, with the lion being on top and the onager below, the lion-like man wielded his glittering sword and in one blow dispensed with them both. The brave man had aimed his sword so precisely that if anyone weighed one half of the onager and one half of the lion against the other halves, one would not be much greater than the other. With one poplar arrow full of heat the young man shot at two mountain sheep that were running after one another, with which arrow he hit the side of one dark-souled mountain sheep, so that it exited the breast of the sheep in front, without any blood showing on the arrow's feathers or tip. A mountain-ox like a huge mountain came running down to the plain from the mountain. Farāmarz spurred on his steed with passion and fire, and when he reached the ox, from the back of his horse he stretched out his fists and roared in the manner of Āżargoshasp, then grabbed both its neck and shoulders and its feet, twisted and laid it low upon the ground. A leopard had brought down an onager, but the onager was still alive in its claws. That quick-fisted hero galloped his horse in such a way that he seized the onager from the grip of that leopard. After he had taken that onager from its claws, he came forward once more as fast as smoke, stretched out his fists, grabbed the leopard by his shoulders, turned it and without delay threw it onto the onager. He hit it on the head with a heavy stone in such a way that its shoulders, back and chest were smashed to pieces.

When Farṭūrtūsh saw such superiority from the young exalted warrior, his face was refreshed at the sight of him and he called down many praises from the face of the sun. He thought to himself, 'No one will see anyone of such a kind, even if he remains a long time in this world. Such athleticism and such strength and glory, such exaltedness and such skills neither Saturn nor the sun has ever seen or will ever see. May the evil eye forever be far from him. Any person, demon, lion or leopard has in his eyes as little weight or power as a gazelle. O, God, be the protector of this heroic lion! May he forever remain happy and courageous.'

When they had spent some time on the hunting grounds enjoying entertainment with the army, they returned from there to the city, riding adorned at heart by their success and glory. They sat down to a feast for another month and they all rested their heads from fighting.

Farṭūrtūsh gives his daughter to Farāmarz, accepts him as his son-in-law and gives presents of every kind; a description thereof

At the end of the month, the vizier of Farṭūrtūsh spoke as follows with the king of pure intellect: 'Although the entertainment is pleasant and cheerful, the thoughts in my heart full of wisdom are sorrowed. It would be proper now for Your Majesty of enlightened mind to examine the circumstances of this champion for a while.' The heart of the king was refreshed by his speech and the happiness inside him became boundless. When the renowned gathering had ended and the leaders had dispersed one by one, he said to the vizier, 'Because of his deeds, this male lion as a young man has the likes of an old man. In manliness and knowledge, in intellect and wisdom he even surpasses the elevated heavens.' The vizier replied to him, 'O Your Majesty, wise and worthy to be remembered in the world! No pretext of any kind remains for this famous young lion of a man, eminent, just and of an enlightened mind. You must now investigate his insight and thoughts.'

He ordered the astrologers to come quietly to the king's court and examine the horoscope of his daughter, whether her head and crown would be refreshed and how she would be with the world champion: would the stars of those two match? The astrologer went off to look at the horoscopes and bit his lip between his teeth about their auspiciousness. He returned before the king and said, 'Your daughter is joined with good fortune. From this king's daughter and that champion a warrior will appear in the world, brave, exalted, famous, wise and with honour, understanding and glory. The name of Sām the knight will be alive through him; his tree of greatness will come to fruit. He will be king of the land of Nīmrūz, he will be a leader and a warrior and he will set the world alight. He will be successful in all his wishes, so you need not harbour any grief, Your Majesty.'

When Farṭūrtūsh heard these words, he blossomed like narcissus and jasmine and he opened the doors to his two precious treasuries, which he had inherited through five generations. They were completely filled with rubies, turquoises, sapphires, uncut gems, carnelians and emeralds, more than could be counted, which he ordered in their entirety to be loaded up. A hundred camels were loaded with them, as were a hundred caravans with carpets and bedding. In a similar manner, the king of the world gave orders for accoutrements for feasts and apparel for banquets; two hundred of his sun-faced Turkish servant-boys and also two hundred slave-girls with colours and scents, all youths with crowns and belts, obedient in their tiaras and golden necklaces; further, coats of mail, helmets, horse-armour, tunics, corselets and bows and arrows; also, twice five hundred horses of Arabian stock, around which the wind could not settle the dust. All these things were sent by that king of enlightened mind as gifts for the young warrior. To his soldiers, the nobles and the lowly men, both subjects and free warriors, he sent a great quantity of robes of honour and he gave them many beautiful and nice things.

After that, his knowledgeable men, wise priests of auspicious trace, went and sat down in the king's castle according to tradition. All the priests and the king of good intentions called the young exalted man before them and, as was the custom of their pure religion, concluded a covenant with justice and insight and to the contentment of the pure God of the universe. Next, the mother of the moon-faced girl attended to the adornment of the face of Ārezū. She adorned that rose-scented, heart-pleasing, life-granting, moon-faced cypress in the manner of the sun at dawn, which cleanses sorrow from a troubled soul. They dressed her according to tradition and asked for all the best things for her. Venus attested to her beauty and bestowed the grace of her own nature upon her. If she had been Sirius in action on the heavenly wheel, the sun would have showered coins all over her and old Mars would have given his bow as well as his darts, sword and arrows for her eyelashes and eyebrows. That idol was adorned in such a manner that the moon proposed to her from the sky.

When her adornments had been completed and all her affairs been arranged in goodness, a hundred pure-minded servants, wise, knowledgeable and guiding, went with a hundred slave-girls from the king's palace, adorned like the sun and the moon, carrying a hundred golden litters in such a manner as a wise man considered proper. Countless musicians went with them and the world was full of singing and wine-drinking. The musicians were one by one covered in rubies and jewels and in silver and gold from head to toe. One danced and another sounded the harp, a third one played the lute and yet another sang. One spread amber, another carried musk, yet another drank wine and another one again threw seductive glances. From end to end the earth was filled with scattered coins and resonant with the chords of the musicians' instruments. In this manner, they brought the moon-faced girl, that rose-scented sun with her cypress stature, to that famous champion, the world conqueror and descendant of the white-haired Zāl. When Farāmarz saw that idol, his heart palpitated with happiness in his chest. That champion of Nīmrūz stood victorious opposed to that heart-kindling face and, having become happy of heart now he had obtained his desire and fame, he lifted his cup to his heart's desire.

Farāmarz thinks about returning to his own country from there

For one year he stayed there in happiness and fulfilled his wishes in every manner. At the end of that year, a wish entered his heart to return to the road with his army. He conceived a strong longing to see his father, as well as his victorious king of noble fortune. His father was also wishing day and night and opening his lips in memory of Farāmarz, and also the white-haired Zāl and his relatives were equally filled with pain and their faces full of tears. What did that wise man with fame and status say when he had come to be far from home for some time? 'Even if I carry out a kingship when I am abroad and am successful in every wish, when I remember my own place of rest, my homelands and my family with their own pursuits, my heart turns bitter about this kingship, glory and pursuit and my cup becomes filled with poison.'

Farāmarz asks Farṭūrtūsh for permission to return and a description of Farāmarz setting off for the land of Iran

One day, the celebrated champion came before the just, crown-bearing king and said to him, 'Your Majesty with justice and guidance, many years have passed since I with my guide left the presence of my father, as well as of that famous king Keykhosrow. No night goes by for me slowly that I do not dream of my father and my king. Even though the king of kings with insight and glory, the exalted and renowned world-ruler, is very happy that I am staying happily in this region with entertainment and wine-drinking, I nevertheless, after a long time, must return to my tranquillity. The occasion has arisen for the king to grant me permission to take my army back to Iran.'

When Farṭūrtūsh heard this speech, his heart started to boil with grief for his daughter. Against his will he had to give permission, so he arranged for many provisions and accoutrements, and he gave orders for more horses and camels than could be counted all together to be loaded up with all kinds of equipment as was to his taste, for the noble man and his army. The king of good fortune commanded so many treasures, money, crowns and thrones that an engineer would not know how to count them and that none of the famous men of old had heard of.

When the raven fluffed up the feathers of his crop and Saturn lit his lamp in the dark-blue sky, the army leader Farāmarz of enlightened mind rode out with his renowned commanders. The whole city became filled with lament and pain, and the faces of the benevolent people turned yellow with grief. They all together, great and small, went to accompany that great lion of a man, wailing for twenty parasangs as they said goodbye, whilst every person was crying bloody tears for him. After that, they turned back from him in pain, all with grief and laments and cold sighs. When Farṭūrtūsh had departed from him, the young proud man with intellect and insight headed down the road at a gallop, like a raging lion on the trail of a male onager. He did not delay much on the road, as he approached the marches of China – for China was a neighbour of the Indians, and that land was close to Qannowj – since the young man quickly wanted to turn via that road to India, now that fifteen years had passed since the army leader had left Iran.

Every year, someone who travelled with the select warrior went as a messenger to the land of Iran to report to his father and the just king about everything good and bad that had happened to him. This year, the king of the world, the master of his country, had sent back the messenger of the warrior of pure intellect, whose name was Karzasp the lion and who also was of the lineage of Keshwād the brave warrior, with a hundred horsemen from amongst his heroes, brave men and warriors of enlightened mind, to tell the son of the champion, the noble-born army leader Farāmarz, to come to the king's court and make the army happy to see him.

King Keykhosrow writes a letter to Farāmarz to call him back to him and he has it delivered by Karzasp, who reaches Farāmarz son of Rostam

He dictated a letter with insight and counsel to the army leader, the strong hero, and in the letter he recollected the following matters: 'O son of a champion of a great lineage, you are a branch from the very seed of Pīltan and you are equally exalted in every gathering. You have travelled a lot around the world and did not rest for one day in one place. Deserts, plains, seas and mountains: you surely must have become tired of them. Whether you sought a fight against demons or against lions, you did not rest night or day from your undertakings. Whether you walk or run around the world, the universe will not reveal its hidden things; even if you strive a lot and put yourself through trouble, you still will not count one of its thousand things. It is better that you turn your head towards Iran and that you, with your noble fate and your good fortune, come here in person with your bellicose army, because we have conceived a need to see you. It is not such a need for the sake of justice that can be recollected in a letter. As soon as you have read this letter, you must hurry; if you are thirsty, do not even think about drinking water. Lead your army like the wind from its place and come to this court without stopping in any place. For it is the time of battle and demanding vengeance, and of raising our heads in the direction of the lands of Tūrān.'

The messenger of the king of Iran leapt into his saddle like the raging wind and rode onwards with a hundred illustrious horsemen on the order of the victorious monarch. When he arrived in the area of the borderlands of China, he saw a verdant plain where the land was pleasant. There was a spring in that wide plain, the delight of which dazzled the eyes: all its rocks were made of ruby and water like pearls filled that spring the whole year round. They dismounted next to that spring and rested a while in that pleasant place. The exalted Farāmarz was travelling on that long and distant, endless road at ten days' distance from that spring, unaware of Karzasp and his company, whilst Karzasp all the while stayed in his spot by that stream, so that he could rest from his exertions.

When he had spent one week in that place, Farāmarz arrived with his army, and Karzasp the lion became happy at heart and praised God for a long time. The bold Farāmarz, the proud horseman with worth and justice, dismounted from his horse and embraced the heroes one by one. He started to ask about the affairs of the nobles, as well as about his father, about the monarch of the world and about the warriors of Iran great and small. About each one he asked of that famous man, 'Are they happy and cheerful?', and Karzasp told him, 'O champion, they are healthy and they are happy and of enlightened mind.' Then he gave that letter from the king of Iran to Farāmarz and praised him.

When Farāmarz had read the king's letter, he immediately rode towards Iran. He made two stages into one, as he went galloping with the famous men and noble heroes. In this manner, the warriors travelled night and day along the road towards the king of Qannowj. Then the lion instructed Karzasp: 'O famous brave champion! You must go to our king to inform him about his well-willing servant and say, "That traveller, who has seen much trouble and has remained separated from the throne of greatness, has been afflicted by the long and distant road and will remain for a week in Qannowj. When the moon has turned at ease towards the sun, he will come striding towards the king."' After that, he gave many horses, silver coins, gold pieces, silks and other things great and small to Karzasp and to the Iranians, who all became happy with him.

Whilst Karzasp went in one direction to the king, the battle-ready warrior rode in the other direction towards the monarch of the Indians. When the Raja of enlightened mind was informed of this, the nobles of India and the brave men of Sind rode out to meet him in accordance with Indian custom. When the champion came into the Raja's view, he dismounted from his horse with a happy heart. The eminent Raja at length asked about his well-being, saying, 'O lion-hearted select champion, you went and left us behind in sorrow, our hearts every day distressed in their longing.' They happily went to the city of Qannowj, their souls all full of affection and their hearts full of justice. For one month he rested with ease at feasts and banquets and was cleared of the sufferings of the long voyage. At the end of the month, the honourable hero made preparations and set off towards Zābolestān.

Farāmarz arrives in Zābol and a description of his conversation with Zāl-Dastān

When news of him reached Dastān, you could say that Zāl's heart palpitated in his chest. He came out from Zābolestān onto the road with many soldiers to meet his grandson, and they halted at three days' march from his city, arriving with a need to see him. When Dastān son of Sām saw the face of his grandson, he dismounted from his fast-paced grey horse. His grandson also dismounted quickly from his horse and gave his grandfather many blessings. The world-wise Zāl took him in his arms and said to him, 'O champion without equal! Whilst your mother, your grandfather and your father were waiting for you, how did you fare, warrior with sun-like glory? For we, because of our longing, night nor day had no appetite for hunting or polo.' He kissed his head, face, eyes and chest, and then they went to his castle, victorious and happy.

Farāmarz kissed the ground before Zāl and said to him, 'O grandfather of noble stock, by the life and head of the king of Iran and by the grave of the praiseworthy Sīyāwakhsh, day and night I have been kissing the ground whilst praying to the pure God that I would again see the face of the white-haired Zāl, as well as of the king and also of the illustrious Rostam.' Zāl asked of him, 'O praiseworthy hero, what have you done in India and China?' Until the sky turned dark, Farāmarz told of his adventures of every kind, of the actions of Sīmorgh and the land of Maranj, about the deep sea and of every kind of trouble, as well as of the dragons, the wolves and the raging lions, of the beasts and demons and of the sorcerers and of everything that had come across his path, including the actions and the speeches of that army of his. Whilst he was speaking, Dastān paid attention to him, and he praised that powerful lion abundantly. Zāl said to him, 'O horseman of battle, since the times of Garshāsp and Sām the knight, no one in the world has ever seen, nor has any of the experienced great men ever heard about, such troubles as you experienced, O warrior of good fortune. May the crown and the throne be worthy of you!'

Farāmarz goes to King Keykhosrow and his conversation with Rostam and King Keykhosrow; the questioning by the king and Farāmarz's answers to him

When he had rested for a while at his grandfather's, the young exalted man full of passion made preparations to travel towards the land of Iran with his treasures and with his elephants, drums and soldiers. Everything he had obtained from every direction during those days, countless treasures, accoutrements, crowns and thrones, he carried to the king of good fortune. When he had come close to the land of Iran, the select king received news of him, and someone went to tell Pīltan that Farāmarz and his troops were coming. The heart of the champion beat with joy and he immediately rushed towards the king of Iran. The king of kings ordered his commanders, the nobles and brave men of Iran, such as Gūdarz son of Keshwād, the brave Gīw, Ṭūs, Gostaham and Gorgīn the lion, to ride out along a three days' march to meet him, with elephants and drums and the purple banner, as well as with flutes, trumpets and their golden shoes, and with Pīltan and his army in the vanguard.

When the lion of a man got his father in his sight and saw his father's banner sticking out of the dark dust-cloud, he dismounted and walked half a parasang along the road with his well-wishing soldiers. When he arrived at Pīltan the champion, he blessed his father with his enlightened mind. And Tahamtan, as soon as he saw Farāmarz's face and at the same time saw those famous men of worth, dismounted from the peerless Rakhsh, and Zawāre with his company did the same. He took his dear son in an embrace and started to wail with happiness. He kissed the cheeks of his young son and became enlightened of mind at the sight of him. He also embraced the nobles that accompanied him, who were brave and endowed with affection and strength, and he kissed them on their precious faces as suited them. The great men of Iran all, one by one, came before Pīltan's child and they embraced the young man and then each one of his nobles, his proud men, warriors and lions, having become happy with the turnings of fate.

From there, they went towards the king, and when Farāmarz entered the court, the king of kings rose up from his golden throne and came striding to his side. He held Farāmarz tightly in an embrace, and when he had sat down, he started to ask questions. He asked him before the gathering, 'O son of the elephant-bodied champion! Why did you choose to be so far from us and cut your heart from the sight of us?' The celebrated man kissed the surface of the ground and praised the monarch at length, then said to him, 'O monarch of the country, in every place where I was, whether in India or in China, night and day I requested from the court of God an augmentation of the monarch's power. By the fortune of the king of kings with good intentions I took whole the kingdom of India. If I speak about my deeds and actions, about everything good and bad that happened to me, Your Majesty will sit in amazement about that, as will this famous assembly of illustrious men.' Next, he brought the things he had taken with him, whether they were treasures, crowns or seats. Of rubies, carnelians, silver and gold, turquoise and various jewels; of horses, swords, horse-armour, helmets, coats of mail and heavy maces; of camphor, amber, aloe and musk; of all kinds of spices both fresh and dried; of servant girls from Tatary and Kashmir and Chinese as well as Berber slaves; of furs of squirrels, ermines and martens, such as he had gathered during his distant travels, he brought so many that the king of the world and his nobles all together were taken aback in their amazement at him. That battle-ready man gave gifts to the great men of the Iranian army according to their measure.

After that, the king of kings sat down to entertainment with his famous, monarch-obeying men. The king let Farāmarz sit down beside him and posed all kinds of questions. The brave young man loosened his tongue and recounted his actions of every kind. About everything that had happened to him, whether in the mountains, at sea, or on the plains and prairies, the brave man kept on speaking, whilst the king of the world and the great men and exalted nobles of Iran were stupefied with amazement about his deeds, as well as his manliness, insight and behaviour, that in these times a young man of such a kind, whose life had not surpassed forty years, had in such a manner traversed the face of the earth, sometimes seeking a feast and sometimes battle and vengeance. With his valour he had subjugated the world and established the royal name. A story about him remained in the world, so that in every place where there was an ambitious man, when they mentioned the name of Farāmarz son of Rostam, they would all drink wine to his happiness, saying, 'May the evil eye remain far from this famous man and may his ending and his beginning be a feast. The name of Sām the knight is alive through him. May the times be glittering for him.'

Farāmarz returns to India and Keykhosrow concludes a pact and entrusts the kingship of India to Farāmarz; King Keykhosrow gives Farāmarz counsel

When that exalted man of enlightened mind had spent some time in the presence of the king of the world, he started talking to the king about returning to India. The king wrote a new mandate on behalf of Farāmarz, the protector of the country: the whole country of India and of Zābolestān, as well as the lands of Ghaznīn and Kābolestān and also the region of Marw as far as the borderlands of China, the king of the world gave to him as a continuous domain. The king also gave Farāmarz a crown, together with a necklace and earrings, as well as a fully decorated turquoise throne, and he said to him, 'O warrior of enlightened mind! See that you do not use your hand for injustice, for the world is not a permanent place. Bring to destruction the lands and army of every person who makes war upon you, but never torture the hearts of your subjects, so that you will not experience much pain and torture in the hereafter. In every place, be a friend to the poor and be like family to landlords and poor people. Act in such a manner that your name will be mentioned in every place and praises of you will be spread with goodness.' Farāmarz kissed the ground of the court and replied to him, 'Your illustrious Majesty! I will not deviate from my covenant with the king of the world. In every place where I will be, I will be your lesser servant.' The king selected twelve thousand brave warriors and entrusted them to him.

At dawn, the trumpets were sounded and the brave man mounted his swift steed. He quickly led his army towards the Indians and came to Zābol, where he remained two weeks. Pīltan the warrior was with him all the time and gave him much counsel before the assembly, saying, 'You must be vigilant in your actions, for your enemy must not make an attack.' The famous Zāl, son of Sām the knight, also spoke with him: 'O famous champion! Confer with the priests on every matter, and after that reconcile yourself with their counsel. It must not be that you receive trouble from fate; may fortune also grant you a share in pleasantness. And further, you must send news to us about every good and bad thing that happens to you.' He accepted the speeches of his grandfather and his father, kissed the ground and went on his way. From there, he went to Qannowj with his army, and the world became affectionate at heart towards him. When he had arrived there, he rested and lived pleasantly, spending his life at the hunt and at entertainment.

Sām is born of the daughter of Farṭūrtūsh and Ādar-borzīn is born of the daughter of King Kahīlā; a description of them

When one year had passed since those days, God the Creator of life granted him that from the daughter of King Farṭūrtūsh a son was born to him like the noble Sorūsh. He was given the name Sām the brave and he was exalted, auspicious and heart-pleasing. You might think that perhaps Sām the warrior was alive or that he had entrusted him with his greatness and warriorship. After another year, the pure God, the Creator of life, made it happen for him in a similar manner, as a sweet-cheeked child was born of the daughter of King Kahīlā. You might say that the hero Garshāsp was alive and that heaven was a servant to that famous man, or that Rostam son of Zāl had bestowed his manliness and strength upon the son of that celebrated warrior. He called him Borzīn-ādar by name, because he obtained his power and intentions from his glory.[64]

When Farāmarz had named him, he quickly dispatched a messenger as fast as smoke to Zāl the world champion, with enlightened mind having written a letter, which read: 'The Ruler of life and Creator of the world has augmented the pure religion with two servants on your behalf. One has been named Borzīn and the other, Sām the warrior. I know that they will be powerful. By the Ruler of the day of reckoning, I hope that they will be an adornment to the service of the king.' When the letter reached the famous men, their spirits rested in happiness in their souls. With their faces to the ground they directed many benedictions at the court of the Creator of life, because two sons with the likes of robust warriors had been born to the great champion. When they had completed their praises, they sat down satisfied to music and wine. The army leader and famous hero Pīltan, protector of the world and leader of the people, wrote a covenant with intellect and justice to the name of the two boys of noble descent. The whole section of Zābolestān that was his, with its castles, palaces and rose-gardens, he gave to his two precious grandsons, and he said, 'They should always be joined to their intentions.' He bestowed a robe of honour upon the messenger, who left and hurried towards the army leader Farāmarz, who kissed that letter, touched it to his forehead and praised that famous man at length.

Farāmarz remained in India, spending every day in entertainment and joy. At the sight of those two young sons he was always happy and of enlightened mind. He was king of the Indians for sixty years and no one in the world was his equal.

Notes to the Translation

1 'Bull's head' refers to the mythological bull that stands on a giant fish (*gāwmāhi*, 'bull-fish') and supports the earth.

2 The translation is based on an alteration to the text of the Persian edition from its original reading, *najonbad be dīn* ('won't be stirred by religion'), to *nakhandad bedīn* ('won't laugh at this'). On the alterations to the Persian text which have influenced the translation see the Preface and note 2 to the Introduction.

3 'Earth-bearing bull' is a translation of *gāwmāhi* ('bull-fish'); see note 1.

4 Shīr-mard literally translates as 'Lion-man'. The term 'lion' is often used in Persian epic poetry as a metaphor for a brave warrior.

5 The reference is to the practice of scattering dust over one's head as a display of mourning.

6 Jādūstān means 'Country of sorcerers (*jādūān*)': both terms are often used in combination with India/Indians (*hendūstān/hendūān*) because of the rhyme, and probably also in a reference to the 'otherness' of the Indians, who adhere to a non-monotheistic religion.

7 This is a reference to a beheading by the sword over a basin to catch the victim's blood.

8 The translation is based on an alteration to the Persian text from *wālī-ye chīn* ('governor of China') to *rāy-barīn*, which should be a place in India.

9 The Persian text has been altered from *be hengām-e gorg-o hezhabr* ('at a time of wolves and lions') to *be kām-e nahang-o hezabr*, meaning that the dust turned the world as black as the inside of the mouth of a crocodile or a lion.

10 With Rūm being the Persian name for the lands encompassed by the Roman empire, or Byzantium, a Rūmi coat of mail should derive from that region, although what it should look like is unclear. The famous tiger-skin cuirass (*babr-e bayān*) of Rostam (or Tahamtan) is impenetrable by fire, water or arms.

11 The text actually reads *jādūān*, 'sorcerers', which term is generally used as a

synonym for Indians; it is clear that the Raja is addressing his warriors here and not a specific group of magicians. See also note 6.

12 The Persian text has been altered from *bebāyad* ('he must' [relinquish]) to *beyāyad* ('he will come').

13 Khallokh is a place in eastern Turkestan, or western China, famed for its beautiful women.

14 The Iranian new year (*nowrūz*) begins on the first day of spring, 20 or 21 March.

15 Qandahar (Kandahar) is a city in Afghanistan, but the name might be an adulteration of Gandhara in north-west India, which place seems more likely to be associated with idols.

16 Gīlaki is the attributive form of Gīlān, a province in northern Iran. It is unclear what a Gīlaki shield should look like, but it was apparently known for its large size.

17 The reference is to the Persian expression that one cries blood, rather than tears.

18 The Persian text has been altered from *be del* ('in [my] heart') to *badal* ('change').

19 Qomār (or Kumar) supposedly is a place in India famed for its aloe wood. Since a number of places in modern-day India are called Kumar, it is difficult to know where this Qomār should be located.

20 The term *pā-dawāl*, or *dawāl-pā* (pl. *dawāl-pāyān*), means 'strap-legged': the fact that these people have limber legs is implied in the text by them jumping up and being pushed forward by the wind.

21 This explains the name of these people, *pīl-gūshān* meaning 'elephant-ears'.

22 The famous story of Rostam defeating this formidable white demon in Māzandarān is told in Ferdowsī's *Shāhnāme*.

23 The Persian text has been altered from *wīzhe'ī* ('special [horse]') to *dīze'ī* ('black horse').

24 The word 'ungratefulness' seems to be a mistake in the text at this point, for not only does the Brahman next talk about self-willedness, but he also presents 'ingratitude' later on as the tenth demon.

25 The text has been altered from *dūsh* ('shoulder') to *gūsh* ('ear').

26 The text has been altered from *bedū mah* ('upon it the moon') to *be-dey mah* ('in the month of Dey'). Dey is the tenth month of the Persian (Zoroastrian) solar calendar and the first of winter, running from 22 December to 20 January.

27 The text has been altered from *mehr-o māh* ('the sun and the moon') to

mehr māh ('the month of Mehr'). Mehr is the seventh month of the Persian calendar and the first of autumn, running from 23 September to 22 October.

28 Ṭāqdīs (lit. 'portico', 'veranda') is known in the Persian tradition as the name of the royal throne: as described in the next sentence, Ferdowsī's *Shāhnāme* also mentions how a series of kings embellished this special throne (see Khaleghi-Motlagh, ed., vol. VII, 274–275).

29 During the rule of the second caliph 'Omar (r. 634–644 AD), the Islamic conquest of Persia took place (642–644), which led to the end of the Sasanian dynasty (r. 225–651).

30 The reference is to the famous story, as told in Ferdowsī's *Shāhnāme*, of how Kāwe the blacksmith made a makeshift banner from a spear and his leather apron when he led the Iranian people in a rebellion against Ẓaḥḥāk, thus paving the way for the Iranian prince Fereydūn to overthrow this tyrant. This banner of Kāwe (*derafsh-e kāwīyān*), grandly embellished, became the official banner of the Iranian kings, but was captured and destroyed during the Muslim conquest.

31 *Zangī* translates as 'Ethiopian, African', or more generically, 'Black'.

32 Abolfazl Khatibi maintains that, although this eulogy is addressed to both a sultan and a vizier, the part dedicated to the sultan itself has been lost from the text and the remaining section pertains to the vizier only, who might be the Neẕām al-Dowle ('Administrator of the state') of the rubric and whom Khatibi tentatively identifies as a son of the famous Seljuk vizier Neẕām al-Molk, Abū Bakr (444/1052–494/1101), one of whose often used epithets was Neẕām al-Dowle or Neẕām al-Dowal. See also the Introduction: Farāmarz and the *Farāmarznāmes*.

33 The reference is to Jesus ('Isā) having the God-given power to restore the dead to life (Quran 5:110).

34 The text reads *neẕām al-dowal*, the plural of *dowle* and an alternative form of the name mentioned in the rubric; see also note 32.

35 The references are to Jesus as giver of life (see note 33) and to Moses (Mūsā) proving the truth of his religion by showing the Pharaoh his hand which has turned white (Quran 7:108). For the name Abū Bakr see above at note 32.

36 Qīrwān equals the end of the world, or the horizon, lying either in the west or the east. From the context of the story one may conclude that the Qīrwān Farāmarz visits lies in the far West.

37 Garshāsp's conquest of Qīrwān is recounted in Asadī Ṭūsī's *Garshāspnāme*; see the Introduction.

38 Ormozd, or Hormozd, is another name for Ahora Mazda, the God of the Zoroastrian religion.

39 Two minor alterations have been made to the Persian text: *jāy* has been replaced by *jā'ī* and the question mark at the end of the verse by a comma, which connects this verse to the following one, so that the internal order of this sentence has changed, rather than its meaning.

40 Although this mountain-range is not mentioned by name, the implication is that it is Mount Qāf, the mythological mountain or mountain-range lying on the edge of the world.

41 A *setīr* is a weight of 6.5 drachms, which should be the equivalent of c. 23 grams (one drachm being 1/8 of an ounce) – so each arrow-point should weigh c. 230 grams or about half a British pound.

42 This saying means that one should do good, even if one may not receive a reward.

43 In pre-modern geocentric cosmology, the first three spheres surrounding Earth are occupied by the moon, Mercury and Venus, respectively, and the fourth by the sun, beyond which lie the spheres of Mars, Jupiter, Saturn and the stars. Including the one containing Earth itself, there thus are nine heavenly spheres.

44 Horned wolves also appear in different stories of the *Shāhnāme*, where they are slain by Goshtāsp before he becomes king, by his son Esfandīyār and by the Sasanian king Bahrām Gūr. These creatures appear to be some kind of unicorn, but sometimes are also interpreted as rhinoceroses, a confusion that derives from the uncertainty of whether one should read their generic name as *gorg*, 'wolf', or as *karg*, 'rhinoceros' – bearing in mind that in manuscripts generally no distinction is made between *kāf* ('k') and *gāf* ('g'). Most likely, originally rhinoceroses were meant, but, probably because the medieval audience was unfamiliar with these alien creatures, in addition to the confusion surrounding their name, they often came to be interpreted and described (both in word and in image) as wolves with long horns.

45 These people are called here *asp-chehrān*, 'horse-faces', whereas in the rubric they are referred to as *asp-sarān*, 'horse-heads'.

46 'Frank' (*farang*) is the name used for a European in a general sense.

47 Jeypāl (or Jaipāl), the Arabicised form of Gopāla, was an Indian raja in the Punjab who in the early eleventh century was defeated by Sultan Maḥmūd (r. 998–1030) of the eastern-Iranian Ghaznawid dynasty. The poet of the *Farāmarznāme* will not have been referring to this historical figure, but it is likely that the name Jeypāl stuck in the minds of people as that of a great and noble foreign ruler, and consequently reappeared as such in works of fiction.

48 A minor alteration has been made to the Persian text: *jāy* has been replaced by *jā'ī*, which changes the translation from 'the/his place' to 'a(ny) place'.

49 *Kalān-kūh* means 'Large mountain'.

50 The darts here are metaphors for eyelashes.

51 Her answer contains a pun, which does not become quite clear from the text at this point, but later on in the story, when Farāmarz writes a letter to her father Farṭūrtūsh, we are informed that the fairy's name is Ārezū, 'wish, desire': this word is used both at this point in the text and in Farāmarz's speech in the next paragraph.

52 *Sīyah* (or *Sīyāh*) *dīw* means 'Black demon'.

53 Her name (*ārezū*) means 'wish, desire', with which Farāmarz forms a play on words in this sentence. See also above, at note 51.

54 The Persian text has been altered from *be rūy* ('on [its] surface') to *bar ūy* ('(up)on it').

55 The text has been altered from *mehtarī* ('superior') to *behtarī* ('better').

56 For the month of Dey, the beginning of winter, see note 26.

57 The Persian text has been altered from *az* ('since') to *ar* ('if').

58 Kūrang is Garshāsp's brother, or according to some traditions his son, and Aśraṭ (or Atrat) is Garshāsp's father. Although Rostam's lineage according to the *Shāhnāme* does not go back to the Iranian kings, the later epic traditions identify King Jamshīd as Garshāsp's ancestor.

59 The stories about Garshāsp slaying a dragon – his first heroic feat, at the age of fourteen – and about his defeat of a demon called Menharās during his later peregrinations are narrated in Asadī Ṭūsī's *Garshāspnāme* (see the Introduction).

60 On the horned wolves see above, at note 44.

61 The Persian text seems to be missing at least one verse just before this sentence, as it is not made clear how Farāmarz's bow comes to be seized from him. One imagines it is either swallowed by the dragon or dissolves in its poisonous fumes. A few verses later, Farāmarz also loses his sword to the dragon, when it breathes at him.

62 The text literally reads, 'made a tear in his belt' (*chāk zad bar kamar*), but the meaning of this is unclear.

63 This name, *Shahābād*, means 'Dwelling of the king'.

64 Both *ādar* (often also rendered as *āżar*) and *borzīn* mean 'fire'. Ādar-borzīn (or Āżar-borzīn) was the name of an important Iranian fire-temple of the Zoroastrian religion.

List of Names and Places Appearing in *The Large Farāmarznāme*

This list includes all the names of people that appear in the poem as taking active part in the story, as well as of places which are stations on Farāmarz's peregrinations or belong to his domains. In addition, it includes the names of places or figures who do not play an actual role in the story, but to which reference is made more than once in the text. Similar kinds of names which are mentioned only once are explained in footnotes.

Ādar-borzīn – name of the son of Farāmarz and the daughter of the king of Kahīlā; also referred to as Borzīn or Borzīn-ādar

Afrāsīyāb – king of Tūrān

Āfrīdūn – *see* Fereydūn

Ahrīman – divine personification of evil

Ālāns – a tribe of Iranian peoples, of which in the course of history different groups migrated to different regions, one of which was the Caucasus

Ārezū – name of the fairy princess, Farṭūrtūsh's daughter, with whom Farāmarz falls in love

Ashkash – Iranian warrior of the *Shāhnāme*, one of the commanders in Keykhosrow's war of vengeance against Tūrān. Also the name of a commander in Farāmarz's army.

Asp-sarān – name of a people on one of the islands in the East, where Farāmarz is shipwrecked; the name translates as 'Horse-heads'

Aśraṭ (or Atrat) – name of Garshāsp's father

Āżargoshasp – name of the founder of one of the most sacred Zoroastrian fire-temples and consequently also of that fire-temple; the name is also used as a metaphor for speed, as it literally means 'fire-stallion'

Bīstūn – high mountain in south-west Iran; mentioned in the story as a commonplace reference to a very large mountain

Bīzhan – Iranian warrior of the *Shāhnāme*, son of Gīw

Borzīn(-ādar) – *see* Ādar-borzīn

Brahman – member of a group of ascetics living on one of the islands of the

West; Farāmarz questions one of these men on matters of a philosophical nature

Chāchi – adjective of Chāch (present-day Tashkent in Uzbekistan), a place famed for the bows made there

Changū – warrior in service of Farṭūrtūsh

China – translation of *chīn*; generally the western part of the modern-day country of China is meant

Dastān – alternative name of Zāl

Dawāl-pāyān – pugnacious people on one of the islands of the West, defeated by Farāmarz; also referred to as Pā-dawāl; their name translates as 'strap-legged', 'limber-legged'

Farāmarz – Iranian warrior and hero of the poem, son of Rostam

Farāsang – island in the West, where Farāmarz fights and kills the king

Farghān – name of the king of a land in the East, who is defeated by Farāmarz; his subjects are called Farghāni(s) (*farghānī*(*yān*))

Farhād – Iranian warrior of the *Shāhnāme*, son of king Nowżar

Farīborz – Iranian warrior of the *Shāhnāme*

Farṭūrtūsh – king of the fairies, father of Ārezū, whom Farāmarz marries

Ferdowsī of Ṭūs – poet of the *Shāhnāme*

Fereydūn (or Āfrīdūn) – ancient Iranian king: he divided his empire among his three sons, giving the west (Rūm) to Salm, the east (Tūrān) to Tūr and Iran to Īraj. Jealous of Īraj, Salm and Tūr killed their brother, which led to a war between Iran and Tūrān and a centuries-long feud between the two countries.

Garshāsp – ancestor of Farāmarz, father of Narīmān and grandfather of Sām; son of Aṡraṭ (or Atrat)

Garsīwaz – Tūrānian warrior of the *Shāhnāme*, who put his brother Afrāsīyāb up against Sīyāwakhsh

Ghaznīn – city in Afghanistan, part of the domains granted to Farāmarz by Keykhosrow; in historical reality the place of origin of the dynasty of the Ghaznawid sultans, who ruled from the late tenth to the mid-twelfth century in eastern Iran and northern India

Ghūr – region in central Afghanistan

Gīw – Iranian warrior of the *Shāhnāme*, son of Gūdarz and father of Bīzhan

Gorgsārān – fictional country, known from the *Shāhnāme* as inhabited by otherworldly and often hostile creatures and conquered by Sām; in the *Farāmarznāme*, this country, together with Māzandarān, is said to be ruled by the king of the fairies, Farṭūrtūsh

Gorgīn – Iranian warrior of the *Shāhnāme*

Gostaham – Iranian warrior of the *Shāhnāme*

Gūdarz – Iranian warrior of the *Shāhnāme*, father of Gīw and son of Keshwād; one of the commanders in Keykhosrow's war of vengeance against Tūrān

Homāyūn – Iranian army leader in the service of Farāmarz and his cousin; son of Zawāre

Hūshang – ancient Iranian king, father of Ṭahmūraṡ

India – translation of *hendūstān*; generally indicates the northern, or north-western, part of modern-day India

Jādūstān – literally means 'country of sorcerers', supposedly a region that is part of or borders on – or is synonymous with – India (Hendūstān) and is inhabited by *jādūān* ('sorcerers')

Jamshīd – ancient Iranian king, son of Ṭahmūraṡ; was overthrown by Ẓaḥḥāk; in the later epic traditions identified as the ancestor of Garshāsp

Jeyḥūn – river that marks the border between Iran and Tūrān; Persian name for the Amu Darya (the Oxus)

Jeypāl – name of the king installed by Farāmarz to replace King Farghān

Kābol, Kābolestān – region in Afghanistan, tributary to the rulers of Zābolestān

Kahīlā – name of an island in the West and of its king, whose daughter Farāmarz marries

Kāhū – Iranian warrior, member of Farāmarz's army

Kalān-kūh – large mountain in the East, near China, inhabited by demon-sorcerers who are defeated by Farāmarz; the name literally means 'Large Mountain'

Karzasp – Iranian warrior in the service of Farāmarz, delivers a message from Keykhosrow

Kashmir – province to the north-west of India, is conquered by Farāmarz

Kāwos – *see* Keykāwos

Keshwād – Iranian warrior of the *Shāhnāme*, father of Gūdarz; ancestor of Karzasp

Keyānid – term to indicate a dynasty of ancient Iranian kings, including Keyqobād, Keykāwos and Keykhosrow

Keyānūsh – Iranian army leader in the service of Farāmarz

Keykāwos – Iranian king, father of Sīyāwakhsh and grandfather of Keykhosrow

Keykhosrow – Iranian king who sends Farāmarz on his expedition to Khargāh and India

Keyqobād – Iranian king, father of Keykāwos and first of the Keyānid line; his lineage goes back to Fereydūn

Khargāh – fictional country bordering to the west on India, conquered by Farāmarz

Khotan – region in western China

Khwārazm – country to the north of Iran and to the south of Lake Aral, can be located in present-day Uzbekistan and northern Turkmenistan

Lohrāsp – Iranian warrior, one of the commanders in Keykhosrow's war of vengeance against Tūrān; in the *Shāhnāme* he succeeds Keykhosrow to the throne

Māchīn – undefined region that is usually mentioned together with Chīn (China) and therefore designated as a part of, or a neighbour of, China; often thought to be southern China

Mahārak – king of Kashmir, usurps the throne of the Raja; is defeated and killed by Farāmarz

Mahāwar – warrior in the service of Ṭoworg

Manūchehr – ancient Iranian king, great-grandson of Fereydūn; defeated the Tūrānians and killed Salm and Tūr, the murderers of his grandfather Īraj (see under Fereydūn)

Maranj – island where Sīmorgh takes Farāmarz after his shipwreck; according to the *Large Farāmarznāme*, Zāl was raised by Sīmorgh in a castle here, which tradition differs from the one told in the *Shāhnāme*, which says Zāl grows up in Sīmorgh's nest on top of a mountain

Marw – modern-day city of Mary in Turkmenistan; part of the domains granted to Farāmarz by Keykhosrow

Māzandarān – in reality a province in northern Iran, but in the *Shāhnāme* a fictional land inhabited by demons and other creatures with non-human features; in the *Large Farāmarznāme* the land is said to be ruled, together with Gorgsārān, by the king of the fairies, Farṭūrtūsh

Narīmān – ancestor of Farāmarz, father of Sām

Nastūr – Iranian warrior, a commander in Farāmarz's army

Neẕām al-Dowle – vizier, in praise of whom the *Farāmarznāme* dedicates a number of verses; possibly the historical Seljuk vizier Abū Bakr Neẕām al-Dowal (1052–1100)

Nīmrūz – province ruled by Farāmarz's family; practically synonymous with Sīstān

Nowżar – ancient Iranian king, son of Manūchehr; was defeated and executed by Afrāsīyāb

Pā-dawāl – see Dawāl-pāyān

Pīl-gūshān – pugnacious people on one of the islands of the West, defeated by Farāmarz; their name translates as 'elephant-ears'

Pīltan – epithet of Rostam, meaning 'elephant-body'
Qāf – mythological mountain on the edge of the world or the mountain-range surrounding the world
Qannowj – city in northern India; seat of the Raja; conquered by Farāmarz
Qīrwān – country at the western end of the world, visited by Farāmarz during his journeys; was previously conquered by Garshāsp; its name means 'horizon' or 'end of the earth'
Qolūn – warrior in the service of Ṭoworg
Raja – ruler of India, is defeated by Farāmarz and submits himself to the Iranian king
Rakhsh – Rostam's horse
Rāy-barīn – a place in India, mentioned as one of the places under the Raja's command
Rostam – Iranian warrior, famous *Shāhnāme* hero and father of Farāmarz; is also called Tahamtan or Pīltan ('Elephant-bodied')
Sām – great-grandfather of Farāmarz, father of Zāl. Also the name of the son of Farāmarz and Farṭūrtūsh's daughter Ārezū.
Shahābād – capital city and residence of king Farṭūrtūsh; its name means 'dwelling of the king'
Shīde – Tūrānian prince, son of Afrāsīyāb
Shīrmard – Tūrānian warrior dispatched by Afrāsīyāb to assist Ṭoworg; is defeated by Farāmarz
Shīrū(y) – Iranian army leader in the service of Farāmarz, fights Mahārak. The same name also appears once in the text as that of an ancestor of Shīrmard.
Sīmorgh – huge mythical bird (whose name literally means 'thirty-birds'); known from the *Shāhnāme* as having raised Zāl (after he had been rejected as a baby by his father Sām because of his white hair) and thereafter a couple of times coming to his assistance in times of trouble
Sind – province in western India
Sīstān – province in south-east Iran, homelands of the family of Rostam, who are the noble rulers of this domain; more or less used synonymously with Zābolestān or Nīmrūz
Sīyah-dīw (or Sīyāh-dīw) – 'Black Demon', whom Farāmarz defeats in the lands of the East and who guides him through his seven trials to the court of the fairy king Farṭūrtūsh
Sīyāwakhsh – son of Keykāwos; was killed whilst living at the Tūrānian court
Sorūsh – an angel from Persian folklore, with Zoroastrian origins, who

often appears as a messenger from God; will also announce the Day of Resurrection

Tahamtan – alternative name of Rostam

Ṭahmūraṡ – ancient Iranian king, father of Jamshīd

Tajānū – army leader in service of the Raja; is defeated by Farāmarz

Tohūn – Indian noble, is appointed king of Kashmir by Farāmarz after Mahārak's death

Tokhwār – Iranian army leader in the service of Farāmarz

Ṭoworg – commander of Khargāh, a kinsman and ally of Afrāsīyāb; is killed by Farāmarz

Tūrān – country to the north-east of Iran and its centuries-long arch-enemy

Ṭūs – Iranian warrior of the *Shāhnāme*, son of king Nowżar. Also the name of a town in Iran (near modern-day Mashhad) and the place of origin of the poet Ferdowsī.

Zābol, Zābolestān – province in south-east Iran, ruled by the noble family of Rostam; used more or less synonymously with Sīstān

Ẓaḥḥāk – tyrant Arabian king who usurped the Iranian throne and ruled for a thousand years, until he was overthrown by Fereydūn

Zāl – father of Rostam and grandfather of Farāmarz; also referred to as Dastān; known for his white hair, with which he was born

Zange-Shāwrān – Iranian warrior of the *Shāhnāme*

Zangīs (sg. Zangī) – name of a people of black savages in an undefined country in the West

Zawāre – brother of Rostam and father of Homāyūn

Index